More love to Thee, O Christ, more love to Thee!
Hear Thou the prayer I make on bended knee;
This is my earnest plea,
More love, O Christ, to Thee,
More love to Thee, more love to Thee!

Once earthly joy I craved, sought peace and rest;
Now Thee alone I seek; give what is best:
This all my prayer shall be,
More love, O Christ, to Thee,
More love to Thee, more love to Thee!

Let sorrow do its work, send grief or pain;
Sweet are Thy messengers, sweet their refrain,
When they can sing with me,
More love, O Christ, to Thee,
More love to Thee, more love to Thee!

Then shall my latest breath whisper Thy praise;
This be the parting cry my heart shall raise,
This still its prayer shall be,
More love, O Christ to Thee,
More love to Thee, more love to Thee!

ELIZABETH
PRENTISS

ELIZABETH PRENTISS

'More Love to Thee'

Sharon James

THE BANNER OF TRUTH TRUST

THE BANNER OF TRUTH TRUST
3 Murrayfield Road, Edinburgh EH12 6EL, UK
P O Box 621, Carlisle, PA 17013, USA

★

ISBN-10: 0 85151 926 1
ISBN-13: 978 0 85151 926 5

★

Typeset in 12/14 pt Bembo at
the Banner of Truth Trust
Printed in the U.S.A. by
Versa Press, Inc.,
East Peoria, IL

TO ANDREW AND MICHELLE
AND IN LOVING MEMORY
OF SARAH

CONTENTS

FOREWORD

I FIRST HEARD the name of Elizabeth Prentiss when my married daughter enthusiastically recommended her book, *Stepping Heavenward*. This book, though written in 1869, was obviously ministering to the needs of a contemporary young woman. This impressed me, but I disregarded my daughter's recommendation because I thought that *Stepping Heavenward*, written in the form of a novel and coming from such a historical context, would undoubtedly be too sentimental for my liking. How wrong I was!

Now, thirteen years later, given the opportunity to write this Foreword, I have happily read and re-read the timeless words of this truly godly woman. Sharon James' gripping biography draws us into an age when Christian women freely embraced their God-given roles of submission and maternity. Drawing on original letters and journals, the author has given us insight into Prentiss' innermost thoughts. In particular, we witness her struggle to bring faith and practice together and her longing for a greater love for Christ.

'Elizabeth's letters', writes Mrs James, 'did not merely convey information; they described life, atmospheres, feelings, emotions, the minutiae of household doings.' The authentic, 'flesh and blood' character of her writings helps to convey truth to the soul of the reader in a way that the mere statement of principles could not. In a day of 'literary realism', which often merely celebrates the ugly, Elizabeth Prentiss' eye for beauty in the midst of the harsh realities of life is truly elevating.

Elizabeth used her intellectual and poetic gifts to write on a variety of themes, especially that of suffering. She also touched on the theological controversies of the day and, though her conclusions were not always right, as Sharon James shows, she did give effective critiques of some of the errors of Victorian evangelicalism, especially perfectionism.

As I read this marvellous biography, I was constantly reminded of Edith Schaeffer whose commitment to theology, culture, beauty, art, and poetry, as lived out in the home, were very similar. Elizabeth Prentiss practised Schaeffer's *Hidden Art,* using the simple things of God's creation to adorn the family's summer cabin in Dorset, Vermont, as well as their home in New York. She believed that since God had created a beautiful world, human creativity glorified him, especially when used to make drab surroundings attractive and pleasant. As a warm and generous hostess, she took the biblical injunction to practise hospitality to what the author calls 'a legendary level'.

The account of Elizabeth's childhood in Maine under the wise and loving eye of her parents, Edward and Louisa Payson, is particularly moving. George and Elizabeth Prentiss sought to follow that example in their own marriage. In doing this they show that the benefits of living out the Bible's timeless wisdom can pass down the generations. Their example here challenged me to pray that the Spirit's filling would make me, as a mother and grandmother, more like Christ.

I found solace in the fact that the subject of this biography was far from perfect. Elizabeth was by nature (like the present writer) volatile, passionate and energetic. 'She would throw herself furiously into whatever project was occupying her at the time. This would be followed by total exhaustion and corresponding depression.' Like me, too, she had to acknowledge her spiritual shortcomings. 'I find it hard to be patient with myself when I see how far I am from reaching even my own poor standard, but if I do not love Christ and long to please him, I do not love anybody or anything.'

Sharon James points out that suffering was often the means God used to deepen Elizabeth Prentiss's love of Christ. Surely there is no greater sorrow for a woman than the loss of a child. Elizabeth was six months pregnant with her second child when her young son Eddy died. Just four months later she lost her baby daughter, Bessie. Grief upon grief did not blunt her conviction that 'God never makes a mistake'. As a pastor's wife she had opportunities to sympathize with nearly one hundred other women in similar circumstances and strengthen them with the truth she had painfully learned.

If you would rather avoid a painfully sanctifying comparison of your own faith with that of this woman, perhaps you should stop reading now. But please read on!

I am grateful to Sharon James for sharing the story of this choice soul with us. The exalted words of her hymn, 'More Love to Thee', one of my own favourites, give expression, I believe, to the cry of many weary hearts in our twenty-first century:

> Let sorrow do its work, send grief or pain,
> Sweet are Thy messengers, sweet their refrain,
> When they can sing with me,
> More love, O Christ to Thee,
> More love to Thee, more love to Thee!

BARBARA HUGHES
February 2006

PREFACE

ELIZABETH PRENTISS IS BEST KNOWN as the author of the novel *Stepping Heavenward,* published in 1869. Within thirty years more than 200,000 copies were sold. A number of other novels, poems, hymns and children's books also bear her name.

The central theme of Elizabeth Prentiss's life and writings is captured in her best-known hymn, 'More Love to Thee, O Christ.' This is what she wanted for herself, her family, and her readers. She believed that the trials of this life are designed to draw Christians closer to God and thus increase their love for him. Surrender to the will of God is the path to true peace and happiness. *Stepping Heavenward* conveys these themes in the form of a story, tracing out how the day-to-day events of a woman's life can be used to prepare her for eternity.

A secondary, but pervasive theme of her life and writings is the notion of 'true womanhood'. This phrase captures the view of many in the nineteenth century that women should be characterized by piety, domesticity, modesty, and submissiveness. For this reason, her books, and others like them, fell out of favour in the twentieth century. Feminists wanted women to be liberated from such deeply unfashionable concepts as domesticity and submission.

In most Western nations equal opportunities for women had been achieved by the mid-twentieth century. A small group of radical feminists then shifted focus, and began to challenge all role distinctions between men and women. They poured scorn on those things that are of central importance in the lives of the majority of women: marriage, motherhood, and homemaking. Inevitably reaction set in. By the 1990s many women were willing to challenge the dogmas of extreme feminism. They wanted to make family and home their priority. There was something of a revival of femininity and domesticity. In this climate the writings of Elizabeth Prentiss once more found a ready audience. Since being reprinted in the 1990s, over 100,000 copies of *Stepping Heavenward* have been sold, and several of her other books have also been reprinted.

Shortly after her death in 1878, Elizabeth's husband set about the task of compiling a memoir, which appeared in 1882 under the title *The Life and Letters of Elizabeth Prentiss*. It was reprinted in 1994 under the title *More Love to Thee*. This new biography draws heavily on that work, but also includes material from the family history written by her husband and privately printed in 1901, as well as material from Elizabeth Prentiss' various writings, including those now out of print.[1]

The writing of this book was prompted by requests from a number of people who have enjoyed Prentiss' writings. They asked for a somewhat more accessible biography than the nineteenth-century memoir. This, therefore, is not an academic biography. Rather its purpose is be an introduction to Prentiss' life and to encourage readers to explore her own writings further. My thanks to all who spurred me on to write this book and my apologies that I cannot name you all.

Tricia Rubens and Faith Cook have urged me to keep going with this project; as have Hazel Moore (who gave me *Aunt Jane's Hero*); Janice van Eck (who gave me *Thoughts*

---

[1] The sources of longer quotes are given. All shorter quotes (unless otherwise noted) are from George Lewis Prentiss, *More Love to Thee: The Life and Letters of Elizabeth Prentiss,* (New York: A. D. F. Randolph & Co., 1882; repr. Amityville, New York: Calvary Press, 1993).

concerning the King) and Leo Lucas (who commented on an early draft). As always, I am grateful for the fellowship and prayers of our church family at Emmanuel: I have learned so much from you all over the past fourteen years. I could not do any writing without the consistent help of Bill, my husband (and pastor and best friend). Our children, Peter and Lydia, are ever supportive of my work.

As a young teenager, one of the key factors in my conversion was reading a Banner of Truth reprint of 'Heaven – a World of Love' by Jonathan Edwards.[2] I am thus personally thankful for the ministry of the Banner of Truth. I feel honoured that they have agreed to publish this biography. The Rev. Iain Murray graciously offered much helpful and constructive comment on the manuscript. I am also very grateful for the careful and positive editorial input of Jonathan Watson, and for his work in finding the illustrations. My warm thanks to Janice van Eck for her work in designing the cover. Each of these provided much genuine encouragement along the way: I take full responsibility for remaining errors and shortcomings. My thanks also to Lawrence Evans, a friend from Cuckfield days, who provided the map, and to Douglas Taylor for compiling the Index.

I was privileged to hear Barbara Hughes speak at a conference in Dallas, in March 2000. Her message challenged me profoundly. I am thus not only grateful to Barbara for providing the Foreword for this book, but will always be thankful for the effect her ministry has had on my life.

I am thankful for the postal service offered by the Evangelical Library, London. Steve Taylor and the staff have been, as always, unfailingly kind and efficient. I am also grateful to have been able to use the British Library, London, and the Bodleian Library, Oxford.

---

[2] This appears as the last chapter in Edwards' *Charity and Its Fruits* (1852; repr. London: Banner of Truth, 1969).

Above all, I am thankful to God for the lessons I have learned through the testimony of this remarkable woman. I have attempted to be honest, and not to gloss over some of the weaknesses found in her writings. But despite her failings, she lived out the truth that she taught – surrender to the will of God. As I have been exposed to her life and writings, I have been deeply convicted about my own need to surrender more fully to God, each day and in every detail of life. I have found her message of surrender to the will of God to be truly liberating. 'His service is perfect freedom.' My prayer is that the story of Elizabeth Prentiss will help many others to find that same liberation.

SHARON JAMES
Leamington Spa,
February 2006

Biographical Table

1858	April	Departure for Europe
1859	July	Birth of Henry in Switzerland
1860	Feb–June	Paris; George Chaplain of American Church
1860	June–Sept	London, and other travels in U.K.
1860	Sept	Return to New York
1861–5		Civil War
1862	24 Jan	Death of Louisa Hopkins (sister)
1864	Summer	Annie (17) joins the church.
1865	Spring	New building for Church of the Covenant dedicated
		Elizabeth begins 'Water Cure'.
1866	Summer	First summer at Dorset, Vermont
1867		*The Little Preacher* published
1868		*Little Threads; Little Lou's Sayings and Doings; Fred and Maria and Me; The Old Brown Pitcher* published
1869		Prentisses move into their own house in Dorset.
		Stepping Heavenward published
1870		*The Percys; The Story Lizzy Told* published
1871		*Six Little Princesses; Aunt Jane's Hero* published
1872	June	Minnie (17), George (15) and Henry (13) join the church.
1873		George accepts Chair at Union Theological Seminary
1873	July	Elizabeth critically ill
1873		*Golden Hours* published
1874	May	George (husband) critically ill
1874		*Urbane and His Friends* published
1875–6	Winter	Elizabeth helps with Moody Campaign, New York Hippodrome.

1875	August	Minnie critically ill
1876		*The Home at Greylock*; *Griselda* (translation of German poem) published
1877		*Pemaquid* published
1878	13 August	Death of Elizabeth, aged 59

ILLUSTRATIONS

I

GROWING UP IN MAINE
1818–27

'No one, indeed, could know her without learning to love her dearly.'

'A BEAUTIFUL CHILD, slender, dark-eyed, light-footed, very quiet, evidently observant, but saying little, affectionate, yet not demonstrative . . . No one indeed could know her without learning to love her dearly.' This description of Elizabeth Payson as a young child captured her personality perfectly. All her life she was petite, observant, softly spoken in company, reserved and yet deeply affectionate. And, throughout her life, she quickly won the love of those who met her.

She was born in Portland, Maine, New England, on Tuesday 26 October 1818, the fifth child of Dr Edward Payson and his wife Louisa. The day after her birth, Edward wrote to his mother, listing no less than six 'special mercies' associated with this happy event. Firstly, Louisa had survived. At that time all too many women lost their lives in childbirth. Next, the child was a girl. His wife had longed for another daughter since the tragic loss of their second daughter Caroline two years earlier. After listing four more mercies, the joyful father concluded:

> Still God is kind to us. Louisa and the babe continue as
> well as we could desire. Truly, my cup runs over with
> blessings. I can still scarcely help thinking that God is

preparing me for some severe trial; but if He will grant me His presence as He does now, no trial can seem severe. Oh, could I now drop the body, I would stand and cry to all eternity without being weary: 'God is holy, God is just, God is good; God is wise and faithful and true' . . . Could I sing upon paper I should break forth into singing, for day and night I can do nothing but sing . . . But I must close. I can not send so much love and thankfulness to my parents as they deserve. My present happiness, all my happiness I ascribe under God to them and their prayers.[1]

Elizabeth was a cherished baby, and she grew up as a dearly loved child. With an older sister Louisa, two older brothers Edward and Henry, and before long, three smaller brothers (one of whom died in infancy), the Payson home was full, noisy but happy. Edward Payson (1783–1827) was widely known as a great preacher and gifted pastor, but at home he was a dearly loved Papa, who enjoyed nothing more than playing games with his children, telling stories, listening to jokes, and joining in whatever fun was going on. He had a lively sense of humour and young people never found him dour or threatening.

He had come from a long line of distinguished ministers. Born in Rindge, New Hampshire, Edward's father, Seth Payson was a Harvard-educated Congregational minister, as were his three uncles and grandfather. His great-great-grandfather, Edward Payson, had arrived in America in the winter of 1635–6, and later married Mary Eliot (sister of John Eliot, the famous 'apostle to the Indians'). Edward's mother, Grata Payson was an extraordinarily gifted woman, and deeply pious.

After Edward Payson graduated from Harvard in 1803, he moved to Portland, Maine, to take charge of the Academy there. When his three-year contract expired, he moved back to Rindge, to prepare to enter the ministry, and was ordained to minister in the Second Church (Congregational), Portland, in 1807.

Portland, the leading harbour on the beautiful Maine coast, was built on two hilly peninsulas overlooking Casco Bay. With abundant timber close by (Maine is predominantly a forested state), Portland became an important shipbuilding and mast-building centre. By 1806 it was the sixth largest port in America. However, the town was going through a serious recession at the time Payson began his ministry. In December 1807 Congress imposed an embargo forbidding commercial dealings with foreigners until America's rights were respected (the Anglo-French naval war had resulted in disputes between Britain and America). This harmed America more than it did Britain; it 'wrecked Portland's once-brisk trade, driving the city's banks to ruin, its sailors to idleness, and its citizens to despair . . . With business thus waylaid, religion alone flourished.'[2] A spiritual hunger seemed to develop during this economic crisis and the people of Portland found the powerful ministry of the young Edward Payson to be deeply satisfying. Crowds flocked to hear him preach. Within six weeks of his arrival there was talk of extending his church meeting-house.

In 1811 Payson married Ann Louisa Shipman from New Haven, Connecticut. They set up home together close to the busy Portland wharves, where they enjoyed the wonderful views over Casco Bay towards the White Mountains. Louisa came from a wealthy and cultivated family.[3] She was well educated, intellectually able, and a great support to her husband in his ministry. Cheerful and positive, she beautifully balanced her husband's tendency to melancholy. She was also a gracious hostess, warm and welcoming towards their numerous guests.

For the Payson home was often full of visitors, and as Elizabeth grew older, she often sat quietly in a corner watching, listening, and forming her own (strong) opinions about the various topics of conversation being discussed. She sometimes appeared shy with strangers, but she loved observing people. From a young age she studied people in the way others studied books. Most of all she enjoyed being with her father, whom she idolized with all the force of her intense personality. When she was six, and Dr Payson was away, his wife wrote: 'The children all send a great deal of love, and Elizabeth says "Do tell Papa to come home."'

In a children's book written years later, Elizabeth based the character of Emily on her own life. She wrote how, one day, Emily came home from her best friend Anna's house, and scribbled Anna's name all over one side of her room, and all over all the blank pages in a beautiful Bible which she had been given for her seventh birthday. When her father saw it, he called her into his study, and gave her a whole ream of paper. He told her gently that she could write Anna's name to her heart's content on the paper – but that she should not write on her Bible in future:

> Emily [i.e. Elizabeth] felt very grateful. This little kindness on her father's part did her more good than a month's lecture could have done, and made her resolve never to do anything that could possibly grieve him again. She went away to her own little baby-house [play room] and wrote on one of the bits of paper, some verses, in which she said she had the best father in the world. When they were done, she read them over once or twice, and admired them exceedingly; after which, with a very mysterious air, she went and threw them into the kitchen fire.[4]

Elizabeth was a dark-haired child, small in frame, and weak in health. Nevertheless she did nothing slowly, loved games, and enjoyed chasing around with her brothers. She was very impressionable. Any sad news would affect her emotionally, and her father often joked that she would end up marrying a blind man or cripple out of sheer sympathy. To her family, she was always 'our Lizzy' – a pet name that stuck with her for the rest of her life. Julia Willis, who knew her throughout her childhood, later wrote:

> Combined with this wide and genial sympathy was another quality which helped to endear her to her companions, *viz.,* an entire absence of all attempt to show her best side, or put the best face on anything that concerned her. An ingenuous frankness about herself and her affairs – even about her little weaknesses – was one of her most striking traits . . . The Payson family was a delightful one to visit, all were so bright, and in the contest of wits that took place often between Lizzy and her merry brothers, it was sometimes hard to tell which bore off the palm.[5]

Elizabeth grew up in an atmosphere of deep and genuine piety. Three times a day the family prayed together, and it seems that Dr Payson ensured that these times were not tedious to the children. He believed strongly that it was not just formal teaching that mattered in the spiritual development of children. The daily demeanour of the children's parents mattered even more – whether they were kind, patient, and generous or impatient, harsh, and critical.

The services at the Second Church were profoundly serious and reverent, but also expectant and joyful. Dr Payson's preaching was powerful but when he prayed it seemed as if heaven opened. On occasions revival was a reality. In 1810, forty-two people were added to the membership. In April 1816, Edward wrote to his mother: 'I have conversed with about forty who entertain hopes, and with about sixty more who are inquiring. Twenty-three have joined the church since the year commenced.' In September he wrote: 'The revival, which I feared at an end, began again, and things now look as promising as ever. My meeting-house overflows, and some of the church are obliged to stay at home, on account of the impossibility of obtaining seats. I have, in the main, been favoured with great liberty for me, both in the pulpit and out.' By the end of 1816, seventy-two new members had joined the church, and a new meeting-house, seating five hundred worshippers, had been opened.

Further revivals occurred when Elizabeth was just three and eight years of age. She would have been present in the meeting-house during those days when her father preached with such power and directness that everyone felt as if he spoke to them alone. In another letter to his mother he described such services:

> No scene, on this side the bar of God, can be more awfully, overpoweringly solemn, than the scene which such an assembly exhibits. Then the Father of spirits is present to the spirits he has made; present to each of them, and speaking to each. Each one feels that the eye of God is upon him, that the voice of God is speaking to him. Each one therefore, though surrounded by numbers, mourns solitary and apart. The powers of the world to come are felt. Eternity, with all its crushing realities, opens to view, and descends upon the mind. The final sentence, though uttered by human lips, comes with scarcely less weight, than if pronounced by the Judge himself. All countenances gather blackness, and a stillness, solemn, profound, and awful, pervades the place, interrupted only by a stifled sob, or a half repressed sigh.[6]

During the years of her father's ministry, the average number of new additions to the church was more than thirty-five a year: in the year of his death (1827), seventy-nine new members joined the church. As she grew up there were constant visits to the manse from 'enquirers' and 'seekers', many of whom were converted. When she was five, her father set up a new Bible class for young people, fourteen years and over: about two hundred and fifty youngsters were in regular attendance.

At the heart of Payson's own spiritual experience and public ministry was a personal love to Jesus. As a very young minister he had written to his mother:

> I have sometimes heard of spells and charms to excite love and have wished for them, as a boy, that I might cause others to love me. But how much more do I now wish for some charm which would lead men to love the Saviour. Could I paint a true likeness of him methinks I should rejoice to hold it up to the view and admiration of all creation, and be hid behind it forever. It would be heaven enough to hear him praised and adored. But I cannot paint him, I cannot describe him, I cannot make others love him. Nay I cannot love him a thousandth part so much as I ought myself. O, for an angel's tongue, O for the tongues of ten thousand angels to sound his praises.[7]

Parsonage life did have its darker moments. Although Edward Payson was loved, even revered by his own congregation, his determined stand on spiritual and moral matters made him numerous enemies. Two years before Elizabeth's birth, arsonists had attempted to burn down the church. Various slanders were circulated about Payson. Most serious were the malicious rumours spread by a woman who had travelled on the same ship on a trip down to Boston. For a while it seemed as if his character and ministry would be destroyed. Eventually, the woman confessed that her slanderous story had been a lie.

The main cloud on the horizon of Elizabeth's otherwise happy childhood was her father's illness. By his fortieth birthday Dr Payson had fallen prey to tuberculosis – the great scourge of the age. He continued to minister as long as he could and even as he grew weaker he still made up games for his children. But by the time Elizabeth was eight, there was no disguising the reality of the critical state of her father's illness.

The last year of Payson's life was a harrowing time for all the family. They suffered with him as they witnessed the horrible coughing and decline characteristic of the disease. From the autumn of 1826 his right arm became withered and useless; the pain he suffered was acute. From March 1827 he could only preach once on a Sunday, but soon preaching had to be given up altogether. Elizabeth was probably present in church on 1 July 1827 when, after a sermon preached by the assistant pastor, her father stood before his congregation and delivered an unforgettable farewell message, including a solemn spiritual warning:

> I shall never behold another spring. And now, standing on the borders of the eternal world, I look back on my past ministry . . . We have lived together twenty years, and have spent more than a thousand Sabbaths together, and I have given you at least two thousand warnings. I am now going to render an account [of] how they were given, and you, my hearers, will soon have to render an account of how they were received. One more warning I will give you.[8]

From the end of August Edward Payson was housebound and then, from September, confined to his bed. He called groups of young people to his bedroom, where he gave them fatherly advice and spiritual counsel. His calm acceptance of his illness and death was remarkable:

O what a blessed thing it is to lose one's will. Since I have lost my will I have found happiness. There can be no such thing as disappointment to me, for I have no desires but that God's will might be accomplished. Christians might avoid much trouble if they would only believe what they profess, *viz.,* that God is able to make them happy without anything but Himself. They imagine that if is such a dear friend were to die, or such and such a blessing removed, they should be miserable, whereas God can make them a thousand times happier without them. To mention my own case, God has been depriving me of one blessing after another, but as every one was removed He has come in and filled up its place, and now, when I am a cripple and unable to move, I am happier than ever I was in my life before or expected to be, and if I had believed this twenty years ago I might have been spared much anxiety.[9]

During the final weeks, it seemed as if he were glimpsing heaven itself. Shortly before he died he wrote to his sister Eliza:

The celestial city is full in my view. Its glories beam upon me, its breezes fan me, its odours are wafted to me, its sounds strike upon my ear, and its spirit is breathed into my heart. Nothing separates me from it but the river of death, which now appears as an insignificant rill, that may be crossed at a single step whenever God shall give permission. The Sun of Righteousness has been gradually drawing nearer and nearer, appearing larger and brighter as he approached, and now he fills the whole hemisphere, pouring forth a flood of glory in which I seem to float like an insect in the beams of the sun, exalting yet almost trembling while I gaze on this excessive brightness, and wonder why God should deign thus to shine upon a sinful worm. A single heart and a single tongue seem altogether inadequate to my wants: I want a whole heart for every separate emotion and a whole tongue to express that emotion.[10]

On 21 Sunday October 1827 the family were called around his bedside. He was dying. But his dying agonies went on all day, all night, and all the next day. He finally passed away at sunset on the Monday, four days before Elizabeth's ninth birthday. When his body was laid out, for the congregation and friends to pay their respects, a piece of paper was pinned to his jacket, as he had directed: *Remember the words which I spake unto you while I was yet present with you.* The same words were inscribed on his coffin.

Elizabeth felt as if her life had literally been turned upside down. Up to that time she had been sweet-tempered and amenable. Now her pain and sense of loss led to terrible temper tantrums. She stormed and cried. She resented the streams of well-meaning visitors with their superficial condolences. She also found the drop in her family's standard of living a blow. Most of all she missed the father she had loved so much, and who had been devoted to her. All this must have been so difficult for her mother, who, of course, was battling with her own personal sorrow and sense of loss.

Fortunately, Louisa patiently bore with her tempestuous daughter and rose to the great challenge of leading the family. Although she had been used to a comfortable lifestyle, she managed the more austere budget efficiently, still giving regularly to others who were more needy. To supplement the family income she took in lodgers. Rather like 'Marmee' in *Little Women,* Louisa's children adored her, seeing in her the epitome of selflessness and faithfulness. Submissive and somewhat in the background during the life of her husband, she exhibited strength, resourcefulness, and initiative as a widow.

Most of all she relied on her God, with whom she communed often in prayer. In the last Bible study Elizabeth gave just before her death, she looked back to these early years: 'Accustom yourself to turn all your wants, cares and trials into prayer', she said. 'If anything troubled or annoyed my mother she went straight to the "spare room", no matter how cold the weather, and we children knew it was to pray. I shall never forget its influence over me.'[11]

But however much Elizabeth loved her mother, the death of her father left a huge void. Throughout her life she always kept a small picture of him nearby. She often recalled his transparent godliness. She never forgot the time when, as a young child, she rushed into a room and found him flat on his face on the floor, totally absorbed in prayer. Indeed, the legacy Edward Payson left to his family, his church, his community, and even his nation, was the reality of his spiritual experience. He was remembered as 'the seraphic Payson'. One writer compared him to 'an angel standing in the sun'. His biography, published posthumously, became the most popular ministerial memoir of the first half of the nineteenth century. Hundreds, if not thousands, of baby boys born in America during these years were named 'Edward Payson' in his honour. That was later; but for now, his small daughter sometimes cried herself to sleep, missing the kind Papa who would never tell her bedtime stories again.

2

'DAILY NEARER GOD'
1828-40

'Those words "daily nearer God" have an
inexpressible charm for me.'

EDWARD PAYSON'S DEATH in 1827 inevitably led to major
changes for his family. Even before his death, they had moved
into a smaller house so that they could get used to their new
surroundings while he was still with them. Now his widow,
two daughters and four sons had to make the necessary adjustments to life without his income. For the next few years,
the older daughter Louisa tried to support the family through
teaching, while her mother was fully occupied with caring
for the family. Six-and-a-half years older than Elizabeth,
Louisa was an intellectually brilliant and spiritually intense
young woman. As a child she had never found it easy playing
with other youngsters: she was happier buried in a book. She
recorded many of her discussions with her late father in *The
Pastor's Daughter*, written when she was just sixteen years of
age.[1] Fluent in several modern languages, she could also read
Hebrew, Greek, and Latin.

Shortly after her father's death, Louisa moved to Boston,
where she attended a good school for a year in order to
improve her prospects for a teaching career. While there, she
stayed with close friends of the family, the Willises. The

Willises were one of the leading literary families of nine-teenth-century America. Nathaniel Willis had moved to Portland in 1803 at the age of twenty-three, to edit the *Eastern Argus*. He had been involved in publishing and writing from an early age. When Edward Payson began his ministry at the Second Church, Nathaniel's wife Hannah began attending the church's prayer meeting and was soon converted. In 1808 Nathaniel was also converted and became a member of the church.

Nathaniel and Hannah Willis had nine children. Their oldest son, another Nathaniel, was to become one of the country's best-known poets and editors. Their daughter Sara was also to achieve fame as a columnist and novelist under the pseudonym Fanny Fern.

In 1812 the Willis family moved to Boston, where they settled in a large, square, painted brick home on Atkinson Street (later Congress Street). They settled into the well-known Park Street Church, where the father, Nathaniel Sr., became a deacon. In 1816 he founded *The Boston Recorder*, a regular paper for the Congregationalists. At this time, the Congregational churches were the leading denomination in New England, and thus Nathaniel Willis exerted a widespread influence. This influence extended to the young people of the churches when in 1827 he founded *The Youth's Companion*, a regular magazine for children. For many years, when the Willises visited Portland, they stayed with the Paysons, and when the Paysons went to Boston, they stayed with the Willises. Mrs Willis was a delightful, motherly person and the Payson children loved her dearly. Elizabeth became particularly friendly with two of their daughters, Julia and Ellen.[2]

Although nine-year-old Elizabeth wrote to her sister regularly, only one letter survives. In it she tells Louisa of the tedium of her own days at school:

Portland, May 18, 1828,

My dear sister: I thank you for writing to such a little girl as I am, when you have so little time. I was going to study a little catechism which Miss Martin has got, but she said I could not learn it. I want to learn it. I do not like to stay so long at school. We have to write composition by dictation, as Miss Martin calls it. She reads to us out of a book a sentence at a time. We write it and we write it again on our slates, because we do not always get the whole; then we write it on a piece of paper. Miss Martin says I may say my Sunday-School [lesson] there. Mr Mitchell has had a great many new books. I have been sick. Doctor Cummings[3] has been here and says E. [Edward] is better and he thinks he will not have the fever ... G. [George] goes to school to Miss Libby, and H. [Henry] goes to Master Jackson. H. sends his love. Good-bye.

Your affectionate sister,

E. Payson.[4]

When Elizabeth was nearly twelve, she fell ill and nearly died. Despite everyone's fears, she recovered and Mrs Payson wrote in her journal that she felt God had let Elizabeth live so that she could one day serve him.

The Payson family continued to worship at the Second Church, Portland. Lyman Beecher (revival preacher and father of Harriet Beecher Stowe) preached at the induction of Dr Payson's successor in the ministry, Bennet Tyler. In 1830 Louisa started out on a new venture when she opened a girl's school in New York. While the days of mass immigration still lay in the future, the city had already grown to about 250,000, and Louisa reckoned that her school would have greater opportunity for success here than in smaller, more provincial

Portland. The family moved down to join her and Elizabeth was able to attend her sister's school.

Shortly after the move to New York, Elizabeth professed faith in Christ, and became a member of the Bleecker Street Presbyterian Church at the tender age of twelve in May 1831. Although sincere in her profession, she would look back in years to come and seriously question whether she had been truly converted at that time. As with many children from Christian homes, her conversion was a gradual process. Throughout her teenage years she vacillated: at some points she felt very sure of her faith, was diligent in Bible reading and prayer, and devoured Christian books; at other times she would become completely absorbed in novels, poetry, music, drawing, clothes, and friends. Days if not weeks would pass by without her praying at all and she would miss church on the slightest pretext.

This process was exacerbated by the natural intensity of Elizabeth's personality. She did nothing by halves. When she was feeling spiritually minded, she would throw herself into religious pursuits as if her life depended on it. When she was feeling 'worldly' she would go all out for whatever leisure pursuit she enjoyed at the time. At such times, she would inwardly despair of her spiritual state, and feel that she never had been truly converted. But when she was on a spiritual high, she felt as if all she ever wanted to do was to please God.

New York evidently did not suit the Paysons because late in 1831 the family moved back to Portland, where Louisa started another school. Mrs Payson often took in some of her pupils as boarders to supplement the family income.

By the spring of 1832 the thirteen-year-old Elizabeth had a new friend called Carrie. The two girls were members of the same Sunday School class, taught by one of Bennet Tyler's daughters, and they both lived on Franklin Street in the town.

They enjoyed long walks beside the ocean, and spent many happy hours looking out over the sea.

Carrie later vividly remembered a conversation they had in one of their favourite haunts. In the old cemetery on Congress Street they would sit on one of the highest tombs - a vantage point which afforded wonderful views of the harbour. One dark spring day Elizabeth was telling her friend about a book she had been reading, the *Memoir of Susanna Anthony*. It recorded how Susanna had suffered greatly. Carrie was outraged: 'I do not see how it is right for God, who can control all things, to permit such suffering!' She never forgot Elizabeth's reply or the sweetness of her voice as she said: 'Well, Carrie, we can't understand it, but I have been thinking that this might be God's way of preparing his children for very high degrees of service on earth or happiness in heaven.' Years later, Carrie would say that this belief that God uses suffering for the good of his people was always a 'corner-stone' of Elizabeth's faith.

In the spring of 1833, Louisa opened her new school in Portland. Elizabeth and Carrie sat next to each other in class, and walked to and from school together every day. Elizabeth was already a prolific writer: she would often greet Carrie on a Monday morning with at least four 'notes' she had composed for her over the weekend, and was quite aggrieved when Carrie only managed one for her.

Reading opened new worlds to Elizabeth. Now that she was fourteen, her mother decorated 'the blue room' for her. There, seated at her father's old writing desk and surrounded by her many books, Elizabeth spent many happy hours. In her vivid imagination she was transported to the highlands of Scotland as she was caught up in the romance of Walter Scott's novels; she pounced on each new Dickens instalment the moment it was published; lost in the poetry of Wordsworth, Tennyson, and Longfellow she could forget the practicalities of everyday life; she revelled in the devotional verse of George Herbert. She studied her Bible, using the Puritan commentaries available to her. A voracious reader, Elizabeth lent Carrie her favourite books, persuading her to read such works as John Owen's *Exposition of the 130th Psalm*[5] and John Flavel's *Fountain of Life*.[6] The two girls often discussed the books they had read.

In 1834 the two friends changed school together when Louisa Payson took a new job as assistant principal of the Free Street Seminary, run by the Rev. Solomon Adams. The next summer, Elizabeth had the opportunity to spend a term away from home at a girl's school in Ipswich, which enjoyed the reputation of being the best school of its kind in New England.

In a pre-television era, families made their own entertainment. Amusing verses were composed and read aloud and word games were played. Absent relatives wrote long letters full of chat which were read aloud for the enjoyment of all. This culture of 'parlour literature' was a boon for youngsters blessed with literary skills. They could write for an audience that was friendly and unthreatening; they could hear what their compositions sounded like when read aloud; they could find a voice for themselves. Elizabeth thrived in this environment. By her mid-teens she was a prolific author of poems, essays, and long letters to friends. Without her prior knowledge, one of her siblings or friends sometimes sent off a piece Elizabeth had written to a magazine. It was not long before Elizabeth got used to seeing her name in print, and at the age of sixteen she was commissioned by Nathaniel Willis, Sr., to provide regular contributions to *The Youth's Companion*.

The articles that flowed from her pen were lively, funny, and imaginative as well as morally instructive. She loved children, and seemed to know instinctively what would appeal to them.

The Payson parlour welcomed all kinds of interesting visitors: scholars, ministers, and literary figures. This was partly due to the respect in which the memory of her father was held, partly because her older sister Louisa was well-known for her writing, and partly because her mother was such a well-educated, cultured, and charming hostess. The family were not well-to-do, but they were highly respected for their conversation and piety. Those who called in order to spend time with Louisa, often found themselves entranced by her younger sister.

In the spring of 1837, when Elizabeth was eighteen, her mother sold the Franklin Street home, and the family moved into rented accommodation: part of an old, ugly, and uncomfortable house in the upper part of town. Elizabeth nicknamed it 'the pumpkin house', but revelled in its glorious setting, overlooking Casco Bay and the White Mountains. They were within a few minutes of Deering's Oaks where Elizabeth spent a great deal of time walking alone or with friends. She enjoyed a wonderful summer that year, spending much of the time in the open air.

In the autumn of 1837, a supply minister, Cyrus Hamlin, came to the Second Church, Portland. His preaching attracted many young people and regular discussion meetings were organized for inquirers. Elizabeth urged her friends to attend these meetings, including her best friend Carrie, who later recalled:

Elizabeth besought me, with all possible earnestness and affection, to 'go to Mr Hamlin's meeting.' One day she came to see me a short time before the hour, saying that I was ever on her mind and in her prayers, that she had talked to Mr Hamlin about me, nor would she leave until I had promised to attend the meeting. I did so; and from that time we were united in the strong bonds of

Christian love and sympathy. What a spiritual helper she was to me in those days! What precious notes I was all the time receiving from her! The memory of her tender, faithful friendship is still fresh and delightful, after the lapse of more than forty years.[7]

Elizabeth recorded her own thoughts about this time:

During the time in which she [Carrie] was seeking the Saviour with all her heart, I was much with her and had an opportunity to see every variety of feeling as she daily set the whole before me. The affection thus acquired is, I believe, never lost. If I live for ever, I shall not lose the impressions which I then received – the deep anxiety I felt lest she should finally come short of salvation, and then the happiness of having her lost in contemplation of the character of Him whom she had so often declared it is impossible to love.[8]

A letter written by Cyrus Hamlin to a mutual friend conveys the esteem in which he held the young woman.

I should like to write a long letter about dear Elizabeth. I have seen her more since Louisa left, and I love her more. She has a peculiar charm for me. I think she has a quick and excellent judgement, refined sensibilities, and an instinctive perception of what is fit and proper . . . It seems to me there is a great deal of purity – of the *spirituelle* – about her feelings. But I can not tell you exactly what it is that makes me think so highly of her. It is a nameless something resulting from her whole self, from her sweet face and mouth, her eye full of love and soul, her form and motion. I do not think she likes me much, I have paid so much attention to Louisa and so little to herself. Yet she is not one of those who claim attention, but rather shrinks from it. She may have faults of which I have no knowledge. But I am charmed with everything I have seen of her.[9]

In 1838 the Paysons moved once again, purchasing a house on Cumberland Street, which was suitable for taking in lodgers. Elizabeth was again given her own room, which she decorated and furnished to her own taste. Her prized possession was a good collection of books. Shortly afterwards, she was thrilled when a young relative came to stay with them and took over some of the domestic chores, allowing her sufficient time to start a school of her own in the house. Beginning with about eight little girls, it quickly grew to about thirty pupils. This was a lot more interesting than spending her days 'making and mending' for her brothers. One of the few careers open to young women was teaching and at that time no formal teaching qualifications were required.

Once Elizabeth started teaching, she threw herself into it with enthusiasm. She was uninhibited in her affection for her pupils, and they loved her dearly in return. When her friend Julia Willis came to stay, she was astonished to see the enthusiasm with which all the girls rushed to greet their teacher and pull her into the classroom. Elizabeth was so devoted to her youngsters that she taught the same group on Sundays at 'Sabbath School'.

Although Elizabeth probably seemed to be a paragon of virtue to her pupils, she battled with a quick temper, which often led to harsh and hurtful words to those closest to her. She wrote in 1841:

> As to a hasty temper, I know that anybody who ever lived with me, until within the last two or three years, could tell you of many instances of outbreaking passion. I am ashamed to say how recently the last real tempest occurred, but I will not spare myself. It was in the spring

of 1838, and I did not eat anything for so long that I was ill in bed and barely escaped a fever. Mother nursed me so tenderly that, though she forgave me, I *never shall* forgive myself.[10]

In the summer of 1838, when Elizabeth was nineteen, a new minister, Jonathan Condit, came to the Second Church, and a local revival took place. The Church's young people were deeply struck with spiritual realities and many experienced profound conviction of sin. One by one they professed conversion. There was a real sense of anticipation each Saturday when the younger women gathered for their prayer meeting. They prayed earnestly for the conversion of friends and relatives and expected to see answers to their prayers almost immediately. Many of the youngsters now read only spiritual books and the main themes of their conversation were the Bible and salvation. This was a memorable time. Elizabeth had the great joy of leading several of her Sabbath School class to a personal assurance of faith. She had prayed for each pupil as she prepared her Bible lesson each week, and now those prayers were being answered.

Yet, completely unknown to her pupils, or even her closest friends, Elizabeth was experiencing a period of intense doubt at this time. She had a personality that tended to extremes and she swung from being exultantly happy and incredibly busy to being full of despair and listless inactivity. Of course, this kind of personality could not but affect her spiritual experience. Throughout her life she knew days of unusually intense joy and a very real sense of the love and presence of God, but she also went through days of deep darkness when she felt totally deserted by God.

During the winter of 1837–8, while she was leading others to faith in Christ, she lost the assurance that she herself was a Christian. In the midst of her busy teaching responsibilities she managed to suppress her doubts during the spring and summer of 1838, but by the autumn she had given up private prayer and experienced intense conviction of sin for a period of about four months:

> Sometimes I tried to pray, but this only increased my distress and made me cry out for annihilation to free me from the agony which seemed unsupportable . . . It was in vain that I sought the Lord in any of the lofty pathways through which my heart wished to go. At last I found it impossible to carry on the struggle any longer alone. I would gladly have put myself at the feet of a little child, if by so doing I could have found peace. I felt so guilty and the character of God appeared so perfect in its purity and holiness that I knew not which way to turn. The sin which distressed me most of all was the rejection of the Saviour. This haunted me constantly, and made me fly first to one thing and then another, in the hope of finding somewhere the peace which I would not accept from Him. It was at this time that I kept reading over the first twelve chapters of Doddridge's 'Rise and Progress'[11] . . . So great was my agony that I can only wonder at the goodness of Him who held my life in His hands, and would not permit me in the height of my despair to throw myself away.[12]

Elizabeth's spiritual distress contributed to a breakdown in her health and she was confined to her room for several weeks during the winter of 1839. She tried talking to her pastor but he did not know how to help her. However, one of his sermons, preached on Sunday 19 April 1840 on 'Christ's ability to save to the utmost', broke through all her defences:

> While listening to it my weary spirit rested itself, and I thought 'Surely it cannot be wrong to think of the

Saviour, although He is not mine'. With this conclusion
I gave myself up to admire, to love and to praise Him,
and to wonder why I had never done so before, and to
hope that all the great congregation around me were
joining with me in acknowledging Him to be chief
among ten thousand and the One altogether lovely . . .
From this time my mind went slowly onward, examin-
ing the way step by step, trembling and afraid, yet filled
with a calm contentment which made all the dealings of
God with me appear just right. I know myself to be perfectly helpless. I can not promise to do or to be anything;
but I do want to put everything else aside, and to devote
myself entirely to the service of Christ.[13]

During the summer of 1840, George Shipman,[14] Elizabeth's cousin (her mother's nephew) came to stay in Portland
for a few weeks. Although two years younger than Elizabeth,
he had a spiritual maturity beyond his years. He was easy to
talk to and was a source of encouragement in her spiritual
struggles. Indeed, during the next two years George was the
person from whom Elizabeth received most spiritual help
(the extracts above relating to her spiritual experience were
taken from her letters to him). Two further extracts from her
letters to George also illustrate the peace she enjoyed subsequent to her spiritual recovery in April 1840.

August 25, 1840. Those words *daily nearer God* have an
inexpressible charm for me. I long for such nearness to
Him that all other objects shall fade into comparative
insignificance, – so that to have a thought, a wish, a
pleasure apart from Him shall be impossible.

September 12 1840. At Sabbath-school this morning,
while talking . . . with my scholars about the Lord Jesus,
my heart, which is often so cold and so stupid, seemed

completely melted within me, with such a view of His wonderful, wonderful love for sinners, that I almost believed I had never felt it till then. Such a blessing is worth toiling and wrestling for a whole life. If a glimpse of our Saviour here upon earth can be so refreshing, so delightful, what will it be in heaven![15]

It seems that the twenty-one-year-old Elizabeth dated her conversion to this time of crisis in her life and felt that this was the beginning of the 'life of faith in her soul'. However, when, in later years, she shared these matters with her husband, he came to the conclusion that she had been genuinely converted in her childhood, and that this was a 'crisis experience' after which she was always willing to put God's will before her own. It is possible that Elizabeth eventually came to agree with him.[16] Certainly, her family and friends regarded her as a sincere believer in her earlier years. Her close friend, Ann Louisa Lord, was convinced that she was a genuine Christian throughout her teenage years, but believed that what she experienced at this time brought her on to a 'higher plane of religious experience and enjoyment'. As is common with many children from devout Christian homes it is probably impossible to put a precise date on her conversion.

Whether she had experienced conversion or a significant deepening of her faith in 1840, this was to prove a turning point for Elizabeth Payson. Previously there had been tension between her love for Christ and the world: 'Once earthly joys I craved, sought peace and rest.' Now she felt the matter was settled and that she was liberated from this draining conflict. She also knew how powerless she had been when battling against her temper. Now there were new resources of self-control. Elizabeth had suffered months of conviction of sin: now she was assured that her sins were forgiven and she was full of joy.

3

TEACHING IN RICHMOND
1840-43

'I can't think what makes my scholars love me so.'

ONE RESULT OF ELIZABETH'S CONVERSION was her enthusiasm
for foreign missions. She resolved to volunteer for missionary
service in Asia. When she made her thoughts known, her
mother was so distressed that the idea was quickly abandoned.
Mrs Payson had already lost her husband; her eldest daughter
was soon to marry and move far away from the family home.
The boys had left or would soon leave her too. Elizabeth was
all Mrs Payson had left. Missionaries to Asia were issued with
one-way tickets, and often never returned to see their home-
land again. The thought of losing her daughter was simply
unbearable.

This was a decision Elizabeth did not regret. On later
reflection, she honestly believed that her first duty was to her
own mother, and then to mission.[1] However, circumstances
dictated that a move away from home became necessary for
Elizabeth; albeit not to the other side of the world. Mrs
Payson was finding it difficult to pay for her sons' education.
Louisa had done as much as she could, firstly through school
teaching, then through writing. Elizabeth, too, had contributed to the family income through teaching. But now an
opportunity arose to take up a teaching position in Richmond,Virginia, with better pay than anything Elizabeth could

expect in Portland. It was with much trepidation that she applied for the post.

During this period the number of female academies in Richmond was increasing rapidly. The public schools provided free elementary education, but many people looked to the (fee-paying) academy system to provide secondary education. Between 1776 and 1870 (when public high schools were introduced) seventy-one academies for girls were chartered in Richmond, one of which was run by Mr Persico, an Italian artist, and his American wife. Persico had met and married his wife in Philadelphia, but her fragile health had led them south to the warmer climate of Virginia. The Persicos had recruited Susan Lord, one of Elizabeth's friends from Portland to be senior teacher in their Academy. Now Louisa Lord (Susan's younger sister) and Elizabeth were to join the staff. Once they had arrived, five out of the six teachers (apart from the Principal and his wife) were from Maine.

Before Elizabeth left Portland, she had to make 'calls' on all her family friends to say good-bye as she reported to cousin George:

> September 17, 1840. You will believe me if I own myself tired, when I tell you that I made fourteen calls this afternoon. But even the unpleasant business of callmaking has had one comfort. Some of the friends of whom I took leave, spoke so tenderly of Him whose name is so precious to His children that my heart warmed towards them instantly, and I thought it worth while to have parting hours, sad though they may be, if with them came so naturally thoughts of the Saviour. Besides, I have been thinking since I came home, that if I did not love Him, it could not be so refreshing to hear unexpectedly of Him . . . I did not know that mother had anything to do with your father's conversion, and

when I mentioned it to her she seemed much surprised and said she did not know it herself. Pray tell me more of it, will you? I have felt that if, in the course of my life, I should be the means of leading one soul to the Saviour, it would be worth staying in this world for no matter how many years.[2]

The farewells to her own family were very emotional and Elizabeth became ill whilst on a stop over in Boston, suffering paroxysms of pain from her chest across to her left shoulder and arm. It was thought to be *angina pectoris*, but it was probably partly triggered by the stress of leaving home. Looking back on her departure, she said 'No words can describe the anguish of my mind the night I left home; it seems to me that all the agony I had ever passed through was condensed into a small space, and I certainly believe that I should die, if left to a higher degree of such pain.'

But that was Elizabeth: she was either in the heights or the depths. She recovered her spirits on the journey by train from Boston to Richmond. At midnight the passengers were evicted from the train: a bridge had been destroyed by fire, and so they had to climb down a steep bank on a rocky pathway, before climbing up the opposite side using roughly cut steps in the ground. Hastily lit bonfires illuminated their way. For Elizabeth this was the stuff of real adventure. She arrived at the school at the 'tip top of excitement', only to plunge into gloom the next morning, when she awoke and viewed her surroundings in the daylight. Elizabeth always loved beautiful things, and was taken aback by the shabbiness of the room she was to share with Louisa. It was a low attic, with 'no carpet, whitewashed walls, loose windows that have the shaking palsy, fire-red hearth, blue paint instead of white, or rather a suspicion that there was once some blue paint here.'[3] 'My first thought was "I can never be happy in this miserable hole"; but in a second this wicked feeling took flight, and I reproached myself for my ingratitude.'

Elizabeth arrived in Richmond in late September 1840, and stayed until August 1841. This was the furthest she had been from home, and the longest time she had stayed away. The move from the bracing climate and sea air of Maine to the warm inland situation of Richmond was certainly a change. Culturally, the capital of Virginia was far wealthier and more sophisticated than Portland. 'The South lifts up its wings and crows over the North', she commented. Elizabeth felt like a country girl besides some of the glamorous and wealthy daughters of the owners of large plantations whom she was to teach. The greatest shock to her was the contrast between the Christian ethos of New England and the scepticism of a number of her students. The youngsters of Portland and Richmond were so different, she wrote, that you might believe them to be another race of beings. But she cared deeply for her pupils, and in the course of the year they became devoted to her.

There were a hundred and twenty five girls in the Academy, organized into four classes, one of which was Elizabeth's responsibility. Some of the girls were day students and some were boarders; they ranged in age from about ten to eighteen. Each morning Elizabeth and Louisa rose at six for their private devotions, well before classes began at nine. There was a thirty-minute break at mid-day, after which lessons resumed until three. Saturdays were free. On Sunday mornings staff and students went to church and in the evening Elizabeth taught a Bible class for the girls in the Academy. In a letter to her cousin George in December she wrote:'How I thank you for the interest you take in my Bible class. They are so attentive to every word I say that it makes me deeply feel the importance of seeking each of those words from the Holy Spirit. Many of them had not even a Bible of their own until now, nor were they in the habit of reading it at all ... I wish I could give you a picture of them, as they sit on Sabbath evening around the table with their eyes fixed so eagerly on my face, that if I did not feel that the Lord Jesus was present, I should be overwhelmed with confusion at my unworthiness.'

As well preparing her lessons, Elizabeth endeavoured to improve her French and to learn Italian. She read at least twenty pages of French each day with Louisa. French was also spoken at all meals (as was quite common in girls' schools at the time). Much time was also set apart for Bible study.

Elizabeth felt quite intimidated by the responsibility of these teenagers, many of whom appeared to be more sophisticated than her. She strongly disliked the way the older girls were always reading romantic stories and giggling about boys. But she shared their schoolgirl sense of humour, and was always willing to share a laugh and join in the fun, sometimes even playing her own practical jokes on the girls. One of the other teachers, a narrowly religious lady, found her sense of humour a cause for worry and a sure sign of a lack of grace. Elizabeth did not worry about these censures and was convinced that her colleague would be a better Christian if she could but cultivate her own sense of humour.

Elizabeth loved youngsters and was full of idealism. She was also tender-hearted and found the exercise of discipline anathema: she preferred to lead by example. Any girl with special needs received Elizabeth's particular interest. When one girl with a severe stammer joined her class, Elizabeth gave her a hug, and told her that she had a close friend who had the same problem, and that she understood how difficult it was for her. When the pupil wept with gratitude to find such sympathy, her teacher couldn't help but cry too.

The Principal of the Academy gently mocked Elizabeth's theories. Of course they found support among the girls who wanted to learn, but what about those who were constitutionally lazy or disobedient? He warned her that her youthful enthusiasm would soon give way to cynicism. But she stoutly defended her philosophy of education, arguing that you cannot truly 'educate' anyone by using force: the will has to be persuaded. In a letter to Anna Prentiss, a friend from Portland and the sister of her future husband, she wrote:

> I can't think what makes my scholars love me so. I'm sure it is a gift for which I should be grateful, as coming from the same source with all the other blessings which are about me. I believe my way of governing is a more fatiguing one than that of scolding, fretting and punishing. There is a little bit of a tie between each of these hearts and mine – and the least mistake on my part severs it forever; so I have to be exceedingly careful what I do and say. This keeps me in a constant state of excitement and makes my pulse fly rather faster than, as a pulse arrived at years of discretion, it ought to do. I come out of school so happy, though half tired to death, wishing I were better, and hoping I shall become so; for the more the scholars love me, the more I am ashamed that I am not the pink of perfection they seem to fancy me.[4]

Mr Persico took the opportunity of testing out this resolve; at the beginning of January 1841 he asked her to take care of a child on whom everyone else had given up. Eleven-year-old Nannie was undisciplined and deceitful. She was spoilt at home, everyone found fault with her at school, and she responded with wild and rebellious behaviour. Elizabeth and Louisa were asked if Nannie could move into their room, so that they could keep a constant eye on her. 'I receive her as a trust from God', wrote Elizabeth, 'with earnest prayer that we may be enabled to be of use to her.' Nannie tried her patience on numerous occasions, but Elizabeth's prayers were answered. This little girl had been goaded into rudeness and disobedience by constant criticism. When treated gently and with love, she was won over eventually. By the end of January her father admitted that Nannie had changed beyond all recognition and said that Miss Payson had done wonders. Most importantly to Elizabeth, Nannie began to show a keen interest in spiritual things, sometimes almost driving her teacher to distraction with perpetual questions.

During this year in Richmond Elizabeth enjoyed many extended times of prayer and reflection. Although she did not have her own room, she contrived to find quiet corners where she could study her Bible; alternatively she went out for long walks just to be alone with her thoughts. Each morning she got up early, sometimes as early as five, and taking her Bible with her into the corridor, she would sit in a corner by one of the windows and spend time in private prayer. In later years, when surrounded by the demands of a young family, she looked back with nostalgia to this time when she was able to manage her devotional life without babies crying or children calling for her attention.

She shared some of her aspirations with her cousin George, with whom she maintained regular correspondence until he left for Europe in the spring of 1841. She also shared many of her thoughts in frequent letters to Anna Prentiss. However, it is in her private journal that we find her innermost feelings most freely expressed.

> January 1, 1841. Oh, how dissatisfied I am with myself. How I long to be like unto Him into whose image I shall one day be changed when I see Him as He is! I believe nobody understands me on religious points, for I can not and, it seems to me, *need* not parade my private feelings before the world . . . I do dislike the present style of talking on religious subjects. Let people pray –

earnestly, fervently, not simply morning and night, but the *whole day long,* making lives one continued prayer; but, oh, don't let them tell of, or let others know *half* how much of communion with Heaven is known to their own hearts. Is it not true that those who talk most, go most to meetings, run hither and thither to all sorts of societies and all sorts of readings – is it not true that such people would not find peace and contentment – yes, blessedness of blessedness – in solitary hours when to the Searcher of hearts alone are known their aspirations and their love? . . . there is not enough of real, true communion with God, not enough nearness to Him, not enough heart-searching before Him; and too much parade and bustle and noise in doing His work on earth.[5]

Elizabeth thoroughly enjoyed the spring in Virginia; flowers bloomed much earlier here than in Maine, and the surrounding countryside looked exquisitely beautiful. But as the oppressive heat of summer approached, Elizabeth's health began to suffer. 'I feel as if I were in an oven with hot melted lead poured over my brain.' The pains experienced in her chest and shoulder during the previous year returned and she missed home more and more. Worse still was the loss of that close sense of the presence of God which she had enjoyed during the winter and spring. But she was learning not to put so much store on how she felt. She wrote to her cousin on 12 July:

While suffering from my Saviour's absence, nothing interests me . . . I see now that it is not always best for us to have the light of God's countenance. Do not spend your time and strength in asking for me that blessing but this – that I may be transformed into the image of Christ in His own time, in His own way.[6]

Early in August, the term ended and, with a sense of relief, Elizabeth returned home. She was physically and mentally exhausted, but she helped her mother to organize Louisa's wedding to Professor Albert Hopkins of Williams College, Williamstown. Although Louisa had been engaged for some time, the wedding had been delayed until her sister returned from Richmond. It seems that adrenalin kept Elizabeth going until the big day; when it was over she collapsed, and spent some weeks more or less confined to her bedroom, feeling sick, giddy, and nervously overwrought.[7]

She was not strong enough to return to Richmond in September, but by October she was able to resume her Sabbath School class in Portland. During this winter she spent a good deal of time helping her mother with the house work, visiting sick and elderly people, and furthering her own studies:

14 December, 1841. Busy all day. Carried a basket full of 'wittles' [i.e. vittals, victuals, food] to old Ma'am Burns, heard an original account of the deluge from the poor woman, wished I was as near heaven as she seems to be, studied, sewed, taught T. and E., tried to be a good girl, and didn't have the blues once.

20 December, 1841. Spent most of the afternoon with Lucy, who is sick. She cried, held my hand in hers and kissed it over and over, and expressed so much love and gratitude and interest in the Sunday School that I felt ashamed.

24 December, 1841. Helped mother bake all the morning, studied in the afternoon, got into a frolic, and went out after dark with G. [brother George] to shovel snow, and then paddled down to L.'s with a Christmas pudding, whereby I got a real backache, leg ache, neck ache and all over ache . . . I was in the funniest state of mind all afternoon.

25 December, 1841 [Christmas Day]. Got up early and ran down to Sally Johnson's with a big pudding, consequence whereof a horrible pain in my side. I don't care, though. I do love to carry puddings to good old grannies.[8]

Her mother tried to encourage her to mix with young people of similar age, but Elizabeth often preferred to stay at home:

December 1, 1841. I went to the sewing circle this afternoon and had such a stupid time! Enough gossip and nonsense was talked to make one sick, and I'm sure it wasn't the fault of my head that my hair didn't stand on end. Now my mother is a very sensible mother, but when she urges me into company and exhorts me to be more social, she runs the risk of having me become as silly as the rest of 'em. She fears I may be harmed by reading, studying and staying with her, but heaven forbid I should find things in books worse than things out of them. I can't think the girls are the silly things they make themselves appear. They want an aim in life, some worthy object; give them that, and the good and excellent which, I am sure, lies hidden in their nature, will develop itself at once. When the young men rushed in and the girls began to look unutterable things, I rushed out and came home. I can't and won't talk nonsense and flirt with those boys![9]

Louisa returned to spend a few weeks at home over Christmas 1841. By this time she had become attracted to the views of the 'perfectionists'. The early 1840s saw a growth in the influence of Phoebe Palmer (1807–74) and several others who taught a popularized version of John Wesley's teaching on 'Christian perfection'. Wesley insisted that Christians should aspire to a state of 'perfect love'. His teaching, in brief, was that the mature or 'perfect' Christian can attain to loving God with heart and soul and strength before death, and so overcome all inbred sin that sinning may be said to have ceased. To describe this attainment he used several terms: 'full sanctification', 'pure love', 'Christian perfection', and less commonly, the 'second blessing'. This condition might be received by faith in an instant: 'Full deliverance from sin, I believe, is always instantaneous.'[10] Phoebe Palmer believed she had had an experience of 'entire sanctification' on 27 July 1837. She taught that any believer who surrendered all to God would experience the same. Their duty thereafter was to testify of this blessing.[11]

The 'holiness movement' spread quickly across America. Many believers, who found the ongoing conflict with sin troublesome and tiring, were attracted by the offer of entire sanctification without the struggle. However, Christians have always maintained that perfection in this life is an unattainable goal and that an ongoing battle against sin is a necessary feature of Christian sanctification. The two sisters had many long discussions on this point of doctrine. Elizabeth was un-convinced by the perfectionist arguments: she knew only too well the deep-seated sinfulness of her own life.

Elizabeth remained in Portland for the first eight months of 1842. Impulsive and enthusiastic, she threw herself into her studies and good works before paying the price in terms of exhaustion and depression. After a time of rest and recovery the intense activity of her daily routine was resumed and she became as busy as ever. She went through similar cycles in her spiritual and devotional life. Sometimes she felt guilty after engaging in 'worldly' activities, such as reading novels, social-izing, playing music; under a sense of guilt she would then restrict herself to what she believed to be 'spiritual' activities. When she began to feel better physically and emotionally she would then lapse back into 'worldly' reading and activities.

Alarmed by the cold and weak state of her spiritual life, she would once again make all sorts of rigorous resolutions.

The Paysons continued to supplement the family income by receiving lodgers. Their Cumberland Street home was pleasant and spacious, and the kind of people who lodged with them were often devoted Christians and interesting company. For example, a Lieutenant Henry Thatcher had been stationed at Portland in order to recruit young men for the navy. He and his wife were delighted when someone recommended they seek lodgings with Mrs Payson, and they 'moved from a noisy hotel to the quiet of that most desirable retreat.' Lieutenant Henry had a younger brother, James, who had trained as a lawyer, but who had taken a post in the navy as a purser. Also stationed temporarily in Portland, Mrs Payson invited him to spend Sundays in her home, where he could enjoy the day with his brother and sister-in-law. The inevitable happened: James fell helplessly in love with Elizabeth.

She admitted that he was 'one in a thousand' – in character, integrity, gifts, and piety. But, although admiring him enormously, she did not love him. Refusing his proposal was one of the most difficult things she had ever done: she was devastated to see his distress. Worse was to follow. James was suddenly ordered to join the U.S. schooner *Grampus*, which was docked off the coast of Virginia. On the night of 20 March 1843 a violent gale resulted in the loss of the *Grampus* with all its crew. Elizabeth deeply mourned the loss when she received the terrible news of James' death, for she regarded him as a dear friend.

Back at the beginning of the fall semester of 1842, Mr Persico found himself short of teaching staff and so wrote to Elizabeth, begging her to return for another year. Reluctantly she agreed to do so. This second year at Richmond was not nearly as happy as her first. Mrs Persico, who had always been the organiser and a good influence on her husband, had died and he seemed helpless without her. It was not long before he fell into debt. Morale at the school plummeted as teachers' salaries went unpaid. Not surprisingly some of the staff left. Elizabeth soon realized that she would never receive full payment for her services, but she remained at her post throughout this difficult school year out of a sense of loyalty to her unfortunate employer and affection for her pupils.

Not long after her arrival in Richmond a letter to her friend Anna Prentiss hints at the beginning of an attachment to Anna's brother, George:

November 26, 1842. When I reached Richmond last night, tired and dusty and stupefied, I felt a good deal like crawling away into some cranny and staying there the rest of my life; but this morning, when I had remembered mother's existence and yours and that of some one or two others, I felt more disposed to write than anything else. Your note was a great comfort to me during two and a half hours at Portsmouth, and while on my journey. I thought pages to you in reply. How I should love to have you here in Richmond, even if I could only see you once a month, or *know* only that you were here and never see you! With many most kind friends about me, I still shall feel very keenly the separation from you. There is nobody here to whom I can speak confidingly, and my hidden spirit will have to sit with folded wings for eight months to come. To whom shall I talk about you, pray? On the way hither I fell in love with a little girl who also fell in love with me, and as I sat with her over our lonely fire at Philadelphia and in Washington, I could not help speaking of you now and then, till at last she suddenly looked up and asked me if you hadn't a brother, which question effectually shut my mouth.[12]

In the summer of 1843 the school closed for the last time. Elizabeth left Richmond on 18 July and took a long and leisurely trip home, stopping off with friends and family along the way. A happy fortnight was spent at Williamstown with her sister Louisa, brother-in-law Albert, their new baby, and also Mrs Payson. A highlight was listening to Albert deliver an impressive address to a gathering of alumni. Then a few days were spent in Boston catching up with the Willises, before finally reaching Portland on 22 August. The next day Elizabeth was inundated by a flood of nineteen different visitors – the second of whom was George Prentiss. A brief diary entry summed up her feelings: 'Came home, oh so very happy! Dear good home!'

4

COURTSHIP AND MARRIAGE
1843–45

'My heart is dancing and singing and making merry.'

EXACTLY THREE WEEKS after arriving home, on 11 September 1843, Elizabeth accepted a proposal of marriage from George Prentiss. She kept this anniversary without fail for the rest of her life. A year later, looking back on that day, she wrote to him: 'I have had such happy thoughts and prayers to-night! You should certainly have knelt with me in my little room, where, for the first time a year ago this evening, I asked God to bless *us;* and you too, perhaps, then began first to pray for me. Oh, what a wonderful time it was!'

She had always threatened that if she were ever to fall in love, it would be with a vengeance: 'If I ever fall in love I dare say I shall do it so madly and absorbingly as to become in a measure and for a season forgetful of everything and every-one else.' Moreover, she had always resolved that she would never marry just for the sake of it. Apart from anything else, she was clear-sighted enough to see that a wife needed 'oceans of self-sacrificing love' and only a union with a real 'soul mate' would make that sacrifice worthwhile. 'Oh, I won't talk nonsense and flirt with those boys!' she had confided to her journal. 'Oh, what is it I do want? Somebody who feels as I feel and thinks as I think; but where shall I find that somebody?' At times indeed she had wondered whether she would ever find somebody compatible:

> I don't open myself to anybody on earth; I cannot; there is a world of something in me which is not known to those about me and perhaps never will be; but sometimes I think it would be delicious to love a mind like mine in some things, only better, wiser, nobler. I do not quite understand life. People don't live as they were meant to live, I'm sure. I want soul. I want the gracious, glad spirit that finds the good and the beautiful in everything, joined to the manly, exalted intellect – rare unions I am sure, yet possible ones. Little girl! Do you suppose such a soul would find anything in yours to satisfy it? No – no – no – I do not. I know I am a poor little goose which ought to be content with some equally poor little gander, but I *won't*. I'll never give up one inch of these the demands of my reason and of my heart for all the truths you tell me about myself – never![1]

Elizabeth believed she had found her ideal: both 'soul' and 'intellect'. George Prentiss was committed to God, and could understand her passion and commitment. He was also intellectually brilliant. This was more important to her than physical appearance. In a letter to cousin George she wrote: 'He is not handsome, though he has a fine expression of both intellectuality and goodness . . . he was pleased to love me years ago, before going to Europe.'[2]

George traced his ancestry to a Henry Prentice (the spelling was later modified), who had settled in Cambridge, Massachusetts, before 1640. George's father, William Prentiss, was a sea captain, based in Portland. He was away from home for long periods, but on his return was always laden with exotic presents, and full of exciting tales of storms, hurricanes, pirates, and shipwrecks. William and his wife were converted under the ministry of Edward Payson, and became members of the Second Church. The Prentiss family regarded their pastor with the utmost affection, seeing in him a saintly father figure.

When war broke out between America and Great Britain in 1812, maritime trade was seriously disrupted and the consequences were disastrous for Portland's traders including William Prentiss. He, his wife, and two young sons, Seargent (born 1808) and Samuel (born 1811), moved about eight miles out of Portland, to Gorham, a pleasant farming town. There, they lived with George's maternal grandparents, the Lewises. Abby was born in 1814, George in 1816, Anna in 1818, and Mary in 1821. Gorham was blessed with an excellent academy, and the Prentiss children received a good education. The young students were also expected to help on their grandfather's farm, although Seargent was limited in what he could do because of a paralysed leg. The youngest child, Mary, suffered a severe head injury when just an infant, and was permanently brain-damaged. George later commented that her tragic disability 'gave a particular tenderness to family life'. The family cared for her with exemplary devotion.

When George was a lad of nine, his father died. 'How well I remember the wintry day, the sad scene, the burial service in the village church, and the lonely sleigh ride back to our desolate home', he recalled. The family were now to struggle with poverty. Seargent, who had just graduated from Bowdoin College, studied law for a year, and then set out for what was then the far west in order to make his fortune. He succeeded. Within ten years he was one of the richest men in Mississippi, and had achieved fame as a lawyer and orator. With great generosity he used his new wealth to support his family back in Maine.

It seems that George had a simple and sincere faith from a young age. As a child he attended Methodist camp meetings, and was deeply moved by the fervent preaching and prayers. In 1831, when he was fifteen, he professed conversion and joined the church. From that time in his life he sensed a call to Christian ministry. The next year he left home to attend Bowdoin, a prestigious college where Henry Longfellow was one of the professors. Two of George's fellow students, Cyrus Hamlin and Henry Boynton Smith, were to become his life long friends. George's time at Bowdoin was overshadowed by intermittent illness. Never physically robust, George's serious bouts of ill health raised doubts as to his ability to enter the ministry at all.

George's older brother Seargent, who took a fatherly interest in his academic progress, financed his studies at Bowdoin. Upon graduating from college George returned to Gorham to teach in the academy there. At that time a gifted woman called Hannah Lyman was the Principal of the girls' section of the academy. She was to be another of George's life-long friends. In 1836 George spent some time visiting Seargent in Mississippi and was deeply disturbed by the slavery so prevalent in that southern state: 'It is a system full of iniquity, accursed of God and deserving universal reprobation.'

The following year, Seargent provided the funds necessary for the family to move from Gorham into a large house in Portland. George described Portland as 'this beautiful city by the sea'. In retrospect, he said 'I have never seen a community more deeply imbued with the ancestral New England spirit, fuller of business energy and enterprise, richer in happy, well-ordered homes or marked by more solid worth or a more generous, refined and wholesome culture.'[3]

Once settled into their new home, the family decided to join Portland's High Street Church, but on occasions also visited the Second Parish Church, where they had previously worshipped. Four decades later, George could look back and remember how he 'saw her [Elizabeth] for the first time late in the summer of 1837. The hour and the lovely vision I recall, as if but a week, instead of three and forty years had since passed over me.' He was smitten, but knew that he had no reasonable prospects of marriage for some time. He continued with his plans for further study, which included the possibility of several years in Europe.

That autumn, George's friend Cyrus Hamlin came to take up the pastorate at the Second Church. George saw a lot of him, as well as of his friend Henry Smith, who was also from Portland.

At that time of the Prentisses' removal to Portland, Elizabeth was seventeen, about the same age as George's sister Anna. The two young women had several things in common: they both suffered the death of a father; their mothers experienced the financial struggle of widowhood; but above all, Elizabeth and Anna proved to be kindred spirits in their intellectual and spiritual interests. By 1840 when Elizabeth took up her teaching post in Richmond, she and Anna were very close friends.

In 1838 George left Portland to read German and Hebrew at university in New York, and in the following year travelled to Europe to continue his studies there. Prentiss was to join his friend Henry Smith who had already departed for Germany. Smith had spent a year studying at Halle, where something of an evangelical awakening was taking place under the teaching of Friedrich Tholuck (1799–1877). Tholuck befriended the young American student and introduced him to many of the leading theologians and philosophers of the day. When Smith moved on to Berlin for his second year of studies, he became close friends with Ernst Hengstenberg (1802–69) and Johann Neander (1789–1859), as well as the widow of the philosopher Hegel. When Prentiss arrived in Germany, he too was introduced and quickly accepted into the circle of these Christian leaders.

At that time German universities were considered to be at the cutting edge of theological and philosophical studies. Many friends back in America were concerned about sending young students like Smith and Prentiss to Germany to study, fearing that they would become influenced, and even infected, by the new critical ideas. Smith had initially struggled with all the challenges presented to his faith, but he worked through his doubts, and became one of the first American theologians to fully grasp current German thinking while still maintaining his strong belief in the authority of Scripture. What he gained from his time in Germany was a conviction that Christ had to be central to any theological 'system'. In later years his theological works 'expressed the traditional New England theology in terms of the vital Christocentric principles that he had appropriated from Tholuck and the German evangelicals.'[4] Prentiss too appropriated some of the emphases of German evangelicalism, while sceptical about German critical thought: 'In these mines are deep veins of purest gold. In it also are poisonous gases, full of menace to sane, fruitful thinking.' He was determined to hold on to his 'simple' faith, even amid the dizzying cocktail of new ideas. In a letter to Smith from this period he told his friend:

> How many and great are my causes of thankfulness to my Heavenly Father! The greatest . . . such an insight into the blessed and adorable mystery of the redemption through Christ as I never had before, and has at times quite overpowered me with amazement.[5]

George Prentiss had left America young and rather diffident, but his travels in Europe transformed him. While in the old world he was received by the Pope (who, he noted with amazement, took snuff throughout the interview); was given tea and a guided tour of part of England's Lake District by

William Wordsworth; was entertained to breakfast in Oxford by Dr Pusey and was also received by John Henry Newman, the leader of the Oxford Movement (George's view of which was that it was 'false and dangerous'). He attended worship services in a whole range of denominations: worshipping with the Moravians at Herrnhut, Germany, observing Mass at Rome, attending Anglican services in England. He saw the sights of Italy, Austria, and England. In London he attended debates in the Houses of Parliament, saw Queen Victoria on several occasions, and was received in fashionable society. Through all these experiences he gained immeasurably in confidence and poise and returned to America with his intellectual and social graces in place.

Although Prentiss maintained his basic commitment to New School Congregationalism/Presbyterianism, this European trip laid the foundations of his increasing willingness to cultivate friendships with those of other religious persuasions.

During these years abroad, George had pushed thoughts of marriage to the back of his mind. He could not realistically plan to marry while he was dependent on his brother for financial support. He would have to wait until he was able to support himself.

By the time he returned to Maine in October 1842, Elizabeth was about to leave for her second stint of teaching in Richmond. The following September was therefore the earliest George could realistically commence courting Elizabeth. By that time he was sure he would enter the ministry rather than continue his studies abroad. Wasting no time, he proposed marriage on 11 September 1843 and Elizabeth accepted.

This was a wonderfully happy time for Elizabeth. 'My heart seems to me somewhat like a very full church at the close of the services – the great congregation of my affections trying to find their way out and crowding and hindering each other in the general rush for the door. Don't you see them – the young ones scampering first down the aisle, and the old and grave and stately ones coming with proud dignity after them?'

Her only reservation about courtship and marriage was a lurking fear of growing cold in her love for God. On this point, she wrote to cousin George:

> You know how by circumstances my affections have been repressed, and now, having found *liberty to love,* I am tempted to seek my heaven in so loving. But, my dear cousin, there is nothing worth having apart from God; I feel this every day more and more and the fear of satisfying myself with something short of Him – this is my only anxiety. This drives me to the throne of His grace and makes me refuse to be left one moment to myself. I believe I desire first of all to love God supremely and to do something for Him, if He spares my life.[6]

A few days before George proposed to Elizabeth, his sister Anna had announced her engagement to Jonathan Stearns, minister at Newburyport (a coastal town between Portland and Boston). Anna and Jonathan began planning their wedding straight away and Elizabeth was fully involved in all the excitement. Her own wedding would take place after George's ordination. George had planned to spend the winter of 1843-44 with his brother Seargent in Mississippi, much to Elizabeth's disappointment. Seargent was now married and the proud father of a little girl, and George thoroughly enjoyed this time of getting to know his niece Jeannie.

Elizabeth's letters to her fiancé were long, frequent, and very affectionate. During his absence she tried to keep herself busy. Great excitement followed the birth of a son to Louisa and Elizabeth was delighted to be an aunt for the first time. When her sister brought little Eddy to stay at Portland for three months, Elizabeth gladly shared the care of the child. During this period she also took up learning German. Already fluent in French and Italian, she now began an intensive course in German literature. Soon she was reading long sections of Schiller and Goethe. George had a large collection of German theological works and was widely read in German literature. She wrote to him about what she was reading, and he encouraged her in these studies. The works of the French mystic François Fénelon were of particular attraction to her and she developed a love for his writings (in the original French) that never left her.

George's absence was hard to bear and Elizabeth's winter was overshadowed by pain caused by a tumour on her shoulder. There was also bad news from Boston. Mrs Hannah Willis was seriously ill. Her youngest, newly married, daughter Ellen had given birth to a premature still-born baby. Ellen died shortly afterwards aged just twenty-three. The tragedy devastated the Prentisses who considered the Willis family among their closest and oldest friends.

Shortly after this, George wrote to say he was soon to return to Portland. Elizabeth was beside herself:

February 21, 1844. Are you in earnest? Are you in earnest? Are you really coming home in March? I am afraid to believe, afraid to doubt it. I am crying and laughing and writing all at once. You would not tell me so unless you really were coming I know . . . And you are coming home! (How madly my heart is beating! Lie still, will you?) I almost feel that you are here and that you look over my shoulder and read while I write. Are you sure that you will come? . . . I wouldn't have the doctor come and feel my pulse this afternoon for anything. He would prescribe fever powders or fever drops or something of the sort, and bleed me and send me to bed, or to the insane hospital; I don't know which. I could cry, sing, dance, laugh all at once. Oh, that I knew exactly when you will be here – the day, the hour, the minute, that I might know to just what point to govern my impatient heart – for it would be a pity to punish the poor little thing too severely . . . Dear me; there's the old clock striking twelve, and I verily meant to go to bed at ten, so as to sleep away as much of the time as possible before your coming, but then I fell into a fit of loving meditation, and forgot everything else. You should have seen me pour out tea tonight! Why, the first thing I knew, I had poured it all into my own cup till it ran over, and half filled the waiter [tray], which is the first time I ever did such a ridiculous thing in my life. But, dearest, I bid you goodnight, praying you may have sweet dreams and an inward prompting to write me a long, long, blessed letter, such as shall make me dance around the house and sing.

February 22, 1844. Oh, I am frightened at myself, I am so happy! It seems as if even this whole folio would not in the least convey to you the gladness with which my heart is dancing and singing and making merry. The doctor seems quite satisfied with my shoulder, and says 'it's first rate'; so set your heart at rest on that point. I hope there'll be nobody within two miles of our meeting. Suppose you stop in some out of the way place just out of town, and let me trot out there to see you? Oh, are you really coming?[7]

During the spring of 1844 George was licensed by the Cumberland Congregational Association, and began preaching in various churches. Elizabeth was there to hear him when he preached for the first time at the Second Church where her father had ministered. The church was packed, and she was understandably nervous. So was he. But it went well, and her friends had a great time teasing her afterwards about how fortunate she was. Elizabeth wrote to her mother, who was out of town at the time:

> Sunday afternoon, in spite of a sick headache, I would go to hear George preach. He looked finely, but was a good deal agitated . . . The house was crowded full. The sermon was admirable throughout . . . George came back here to tea and was hungry as a bear. I forgot to tell you how dreadfully he misses you . . . The truth is you know how to express your satisfaction and I don't. I do believe George thinks I liked him only a little. But I can't help it.[8]

In April, Elizabeth's doctors decided that the lump on her shoulder had to be removed. In the days before anaesthetics, all operations, however minor, were horrific. This one was mercifully quick, but even so, Elizabeth was not able to sleep for a week afterwards, and lost an alarming amount of weight for someone who was so slender. Worst of all, the wound did not heal properly and she continued to suffer pain throughout the summer. In September she and her mother travelled down to Boston, where a leading surgeon, Dr John Warren, agreed to operate again. He told her that the operation would take about five minutes – a bad enough prospect. Instead, it took an hour and a quarter. Julia Willis was with the Elizabeth throughout, and was awestruck at the patient's self control. Elizabeth spoke only once during the procedure. 'After the knife was laid aside and the threaded needle was passed through the quivering flesh to draw the gaping edges of the wound together, she asked, after the first stitch had been completed, in a low, almost calm tone, with only a slight tremulousness, how many more were to be taken.'

Mrs Payson wrote to tell George that the operation had been much worse than anticipated, but that her daughter had behaved like a heroine. He rushed down to Boston to join them. Elizabeth was thrilled to see him, and was deeply gratified by the many letters, cards, and good wishes sent to her, but she vowed that she'd rather die than have to undergo such pain ever again. Fortunately, this time the operation was a success. However, the doctors put her on to a strict diet which left her feeling half-starved. On the return journey home, she spent a few days resting at the Newburyport manse of George's sister Anna and brother-in-law Jonathan.

Elizabeth spent a quiet winter, recuperating and preparing for her spring wedding. She treasured this time spent with her mother, knowing that soon she would be moving away from the family home for good: she dreaded the separation almost as much as she longed for the marriage. Much of her time was spent in prayer for George and their future ministry together. Some pastors' daughters resolve never ever to marry a minister: they have seen too much of the stresses and strains of manse life: not so Elizabeth. She understood her vocation from God was to be a support to her husband in his ministry. Elizabeth fell in love with George and his calling. As they thought and prayed about where he should minister, she argued that they should not make human considerations, such as a pleasant home, congenial society, or lovely scenery, their priority. They should simply look for a place where he could minister to a congregation in order to train them 'heavenward'. 'And if you are happy at the North Pole shan't I be happy there too?' she asked. 'I shall be heartily thankful to see you a pastor with a people to love you. Only I shall be jealous of them.'

George accepted a unanimous call from the South Trinitarian Church (Congregational) at New Bedford, Massachusetts. 'They offer me a liberal salary and six weeks holiday', he told Elizabeth. He was ordained on 10 April 1845. Elizabeth was not present at his ordination, but wrote a note to reach him just before the final 'examination.' He replied:

> Well, it is all over, and I am an ordained minister of Christ's blessed Gospel. Pray for me, dearest, that God would strengthen me with all might by his Spirit in the inner man . . . The people are very glad I'm not going to be absent over the Sabbath, [i.e. George and Elizabeth were not going away on honeymoon], and I am glad too. You cannot think how delighted I was to get your note by Father Cummings; he gave it to me just as my examinations commenced, and it made me so happy that I could have stood quietly before a Council of Apostles! Such power is in a little love note! I do believe my heart was saying all the time, 'I love Lizzy Payson; isn't it a most blessed thing?' May the peace of God, dearest, keep our hearts and minds in the knowledge and love of God.[9]

The wedding took place in Portland the following week, on Wednesday 16 April 1845. Elizabeth, radiantly happy, wore a traditional point lace veil and masses of orange blossom in her hair. Elizabeth's wedding was small in comparison to that of her sister Louisa with Albert Hopkins, a well-respected university professor; only about fifty close family and friends were present, as she explained to cousin George:

> We had a very pleasant wedding. Not a smashing party like sister's, but a quiet, friendly and affectionate set; and our two mothers not only did not cry on the occasion, but none of the family shed a tear when we left next morning, owing, as sister says, to the 'sunshiny face' with which my new husband carried me off.[10]

The happy couple travelled down to Boston on Thursday morning, where they spent a couple of nights, before getting to New Bedford in time for Sunday 20 April, when George preached twice to his new congregation. Initially they stayed in a hotel, while the house they were to rent was repaired and decorated. Shortly after the wedding, George wrote to his brother Seargent:

> We have now been married more than a week and I believe both of us are *perfectly satisfied* with our new life and a little more. Our only regret is that it didn't begin years ago. It seems just as natural for us to live in 'holy matrimony' as for the birds to sing on a bright summer morning, and I wonder beyond measure how long we contrived to live so long apart.[11]

Once more Elizabeth found herself beside the ocean: New Bedford was an important whaling centre. The church had a number of whalers in the congregation, men of huge energy and endless stories of adventures at sea. Elizabeth wrote to a friend on 28 April:

> 'We have been here ten days, and very happy days they have been to me, notwithstanding I have had to see so many strange faces and to talk to so many new people. And both my sister and Anna tell me that the first months of married life are succeeded by far happier ones still, so I shall go on my way rejoicing.'[12]

Elizabeth loved the church and enjoyed the responsibilities of being the minister's wife. Visiting the sick came naturally to her. She was shy with large numbers of people, but came alive when speaking with individuals and small groups. Even in those situations, however, she did not feel able to lead in prayer, something she often regretted. Perhaps this had something to do with her upbringing, or perhaps it was her almost morbid fear of hypocrisy. She never wanted to appear more spiritual than she actually was. Later in life she became much more relaxed about praying audibly in prayer meetings.

George was industrious and threw himself into his preaching and pastoral work. After a few months in the ministry he became somewhat discouraged when he realized that the congregation appeared content to 'wait for revival' and had little expectation of an ongoing work of conversion. Elizabeth's mother wisely advised him to work for conversions 'one at a time', by praying for and discipling individuals. He took her advice. The first young man he began speaking to about spiritual things was soon converted, and later entered the Christian ministry. George continued with this policy of spiritually mentoring individuals.

Soon after the marriage, George paid a visit to Portland, which gave Elizabeth the chance to write to him:

> How I do love you! It already seems to me that you have been gone a week, and how will it seem tomorrow, I wonder? My heart has been as full of love and thankfulness as it could hold ever since you went away. Oh, how much better I love you than I did before you were my own husband; how infinitely more I admire and respect and esteem you! . . . Ever since our marriage I have half wished you would sometime go away that I might write and tell you as I never can when with you, how every hour and every moment I am running over with love.[13]

Seven months after his marriage, George wrote to his mother: 'It would do your heart good to see how happy and contented we are together.'[14] Then, the following January when Elizabeth visited Portland, he wrote: 'I miss her dreadfully; it seems almost as if my soul had left my body! We have never been so happy since our marriage as for the last two months; we have been in better health, and our life has been a continual honeymoon.'[15]

Caught up in the whirl of domestic and church duties, Elizabeth had no time to compose stories for magazines. But

ELIZABETH PRENTISS

she did not stop writing altogether. A constant stream of letters to female friends and relations communicated the minute details of her life. In an age before telephone and e-mail, when women wanted to communicate with family and friends and to share their lives, letters were the only means. Elizabeth's letters did not merely convey information; they described life. Atmospheres, feelings, emotions, the minutiae of household doings, were conveyed as if the correspondents were speaking to each other. The tone is natural, conversational. For example, in November 1845 she wrote to one of her girl friends:

> I was in Portland after you had left, and got quite rested and recruited after my summer's fatigue, so that I came home with health and strength, if not to lay my hand to the plough, to apply it to the broom-handle and other articles of domestic warfare. Just what I expected would befall me has happened. I have got immersed in the whirlpool of petty cares and concerns which swallow up so many other and higher interests, and talk as anxiously about good 'help'[16] and bad as the rest of 'em do. I sometimes feel really ashamed of myself to see how virtuously I fancy I am spending my time, if in the kitchen, and how it seems to be wasted if I venture to take up a book. I take it that wives who have no love and enthusiasm for their husbands are more to be pitied than blamed if they settle down into mere cooks and managers . . . We have had right pleasant times since coming home; never pleasanter than when, for a day or two, I was without 'help', and my husband ground coffee, and drew water for me, and thought everything I made tasted good. One of the deacons of our church – a very old man – prays for me once a week at meeting, especially that my husband and I may be 'mutual comforts and enjoyments of each other,' which makes us laugh a

little in our sleeves, even while we say *Amen* in our hearts. We have been reading aloud Mary Howitt's 'Author's Daughter,' which is a very good story indeed – don't ask me if I have read anything else. My mind has become a complete mummy, and therefore incapable of either receiving or originating a new idea. I did wade through a sea of words and nonsense on my way home in the shape of two works of Prof. Wilson – 'The Foresters' and 'Margaret Linsay' – which I fancy he wrote before he was out of his mother's arms or soon after leaving them. The girls in Portland are marrying off like all possessed. It reminds me of a shovel full of pop corn, which the more you watch it the more it won't pop, till at last it all goes racketing off at once, *pop, pop, pop;* without your having time to say Jack Robinson in between.[17]

In this letter we see Elizabeth's sense of fun, comparing the rapid marriage of so many of her girl friends with the explosion of pop corn. We see the way that she and George shared the same sense of humour, giggling to themselves over the old deacon who prays that they should be 'mutual comforts and enjoyments to each other', but each agreeing with the sentiment of the old man's prayer. Most of all, we see her determination that in becoming a wife, she should not simply fulfil the role of a 'cook and manager'. She wanted to organize a happy home, as well as keeping up her reading, so that she could provide intelligent and spiritual companionship to her husband.

George, for his part, was delighted and grateful to be married and settled in the ministry at last: 'Everything now seems to have a touch of *Lizzy* about it, what I think, feel and do – and that makes it all delightful. And yet it seems so natural that I can hardly believe I have not been married for many years!'[18]

5

'GOD NEVER MAKES A MISTAKE'
1846–52

'What a world of new sensations and emotions come with the first child!'

EVER SINCE she was a little girl Elizabeth loved babies. Looking back, her friend Carrie noted that one of Elizabeth's most striking traits as a teenager was 'a perfect passion for babies'. She 'revelled in tending, kissing and playing with them'. She was overjoyed when her first child, Annie, was born in December 1846, a year and a half after her marriage to George. Like many new mothers, she lay awake at nights just to watch and marvel at her beautiful daughter. She wrote to a friend:

> What a world of new sensations and emotions come with the first child! I was quite unprepared for the rush of strange feelings . . . I dare say the idea of Lizzy Payson with a baby seems quite funny to you, as it does to many of the Portland girls, but I assure you it doesn't seem in the least funny to me, but as natural as life and . . . as wonderful, almost. She is a nice little plump creature, with a fine head of dark hair which I take some comfort in brushing round a quill to make it curl, and a pair of intelligent eyes, either black or blue, nobody knows which. I find the care of her very wearing, and have

cried ever so many times from fatigue and anxiety, but now I am getting a little better and she pays me for all I do. She is a sweet, good little thing, her chief fault being a tendency to dissipation and sitting up late o'nights. The ladies of our church have made her a beautiful little wardrobe, fortunately for me.[1]

Since Elizabeth was quite a distance from her own mother, several of the older women in the church took a motherly interest in her, making sure she had everything she needed and visiting often with little treats for her as well as gifts for the baby.

Sadly, Annie's arrival was overshadowed by the critical illness of George's older sister Abby. Only thirty-two years old, she had been ill for some time with tuberculosis. She was near to death when Annie was born and Elizabeth was unable to travel up to Portland to say her final farewell. George was called up to his old home in January. He wrote to Elizabeth:

I found dear Abby still alive, and [she] rejoiced beyond expression to see me. She had had a very feeble night, but brightened up towards noon, and when I arrived seemed entirely like her old self, smiling sweetly and exclaiming 'This is the last blessing I desired! Oh, how good the Lord is, isn't He?' It was very delightful . . . Mother is wonderfully calm and happy, and the house seems like the very gate of heaven . . . I so wish you could have seen Abby's smile when I entered her room. And then she enquired so affectionately for you and baby. 'Now tell me everything about them.' She longs and prays to be gone. There is something perfectly child-like about her expressions and feelings, especially towards mother. She can't bear to have her leave the room and holds her hand a good deal of the time. She sends ever so much love.[2]

Abby died on 30 January 1847, nearly two months after Annie was born. Elizabeth had loved Abby dearly, and grieved much for her loss, but she also felt deeply for her husband, his other sister Anna, and the other members of the family. She wrote to Anna expressing her feeling that Abby's loss had taken away her own youth and that she could never again be so light-hearted and carefree as before. For a time she dreamed about Abby every night.

On 11 April 1847 George noted that he 'Baptized Anna Louisa, who behaved sweetly. It was a great joy to Elizabeth and myself, thus publicly to dedicate her to the Lord.'

In the autumn, George made an extended visit to Maine to preach as well as to see family. Elizabeth sorely missed him and wrote (at length!) daily:

Friday, September 3, 1847 Yesterday forenoon I was *perfectly wretched*. It came over me, as things will in spite of us, 'Suppose he didn't get safely to Brunswick!' and for several hours I could not shake it off. It had all the power of reality, and made me so faint that I could do nothing and fairly had to go to bed. I suppose it was very silly, and if I had not tried in every way to rise above it might have been even wicked, but it frightened me to find how much I am under the power of mere feeling and fancy. But do not laugh at me. Sometimes I say to myself, 'What *madness* to love any human being so intensely! What would become of you if he were snatched from you?' and then I think that though God justly denies us comfort and support for the future, and bids us lean upon Him *now* and trust Him for the rest, He can give us strength for the endurance of His most terrible chastisements when their hour comes.[3]

Twenty-one months after the birth of Annie, Elizabeth gave birth to a little boy whom she named Edward Payson after her late father. This second pregnancy had been over-shadowed by the critical illness of her mother. Mrs Payson spent the final months of her life in Williamstown, being cared for by her older daughter Louisa. She suffered greatly, and Elizabeth fretted constantly. She feared that her mother's real condition was being concealed from her – which it was. Mrs Payson went downhill rapidly just at the time that Eliza-beth gave birth to Eddy in October 1848. Within three weeks of the birth, Mrs Payson died, and Elizabeth was distraught that she had been unable to go and say goodbye. The shock of her mother's death contributed, she believed, to her own incapacity to nurse her baby satisfactorily, and his subsequent weakness. She felt strongly that it had been wrong to deceive her as to her mother's true condition. In future she always advocated honesty in such situations. Elizabeth now dreamed about both her mother and sister-in-law Abby every night.

Her mind was also filled with worries for her brothers. In 1848 gold was discovered on the banks of the Sacramento river in California, and there followed a mass migration of men from the northern states hoping to make their fortune in the west. Among them were three of Elizabeth's four brothers. Life was rough and hard, but for some the rewards were great. Elizabeth fretted about the conditions they worked in, the rough company they kept, and all the tempt-ations of these primitive mining communities. It just made her flesh crawl, she wrote, to think of them involved in such gruelling physical labour all day.

All this stress was compounded by her baby boy's chronic colic. It seemed that he screamed incessantly for months. His exhausted parents tried everything they could think of but usually resorted to walking up and down with the infant. Elizabeth recalled years later: 'Your sister's allusion to *Watts and Select Hymns* reminds me of ages long past, when I used to sing the whole book through as I marched, night after night through my room, carrying a colicky baby up and down for fifteen months until I became a living skeleton.'

Such few hours of relief as they enjoyed were only achieved by giving Eddy laudanum (opium, commonly used at that time for pain relief). These trying months sapped what little strength Elizabeth had, her weight dropping to less than seven stone (45 kg). Her sleep patterns were permanently broken and she suffered from insomnia for the rest of her life. She found the demands of day and night exhausting. No longer could she maintain her routine devotional times. In a letter to Anna she wrote: '*By far* the greatest trial I have to contend with, is that of losing all power to control my time. A little room of my own, and a regular hour morning and night, all of my own would enable me, I think, to say '*Now let life do it's worst!*' Lamenting the poverty of her spiritual state she began to miss those rich devotional hours of her time in Richmond. George tried to comfort her, telling her that the Richmond years had been the time for contemplation: this season of her life was for action. God would not demand of her a consistency in prayer that was simply impractical. But despite her husband's best efforts Elizabeth still felt miserable.

Throughout her life Elizabeth felt a desolation of spirit if she could not enjoy communion with God. Space and time for reflection and prayer was necessary she believed if she was to have such closeness with her Lord. When illness or sleeplessness interrupted her routine, she seemed to suffer what can only be described as physical withdrawal symptoms.

When Eddy was eight months old he was still hardly sleeping, and the doctor ordered that Elizabeth be allowed to get away from home for a while. Unless she could get some rest, he feared for her life. She agreed to go away for a week, but ended up staying away for a month. Eddy was left in the care of relatives, neighbours, and a nurse. (At that time, middle class families often employed a 'nurse', if they could afford to, to care for young children. These women were not trained nurses as we think of them today. They were unqualified, and varied enormously in their commitment and efficiency. We would probably refer to them as 'nursemaids').

One of the weeks away was spent with Anna and her family at Newburyport, with George and Annie joining them. Seargent came up from his home in the south with his wife Mary, and their four children.[4] Mrs Prentiss, George's mother, was also there, making it a most enjoyable family reunion. But when Elizabeth, somewhat stronger, returned home, Eddy was no better. She realized that he was seriously unwell, and at this point she gave him over to God. When he rallied and regained strength, she felt as if another child had been restored to her – not her own child, but God's. From that time on every day was precious. Each morning, Elizabeth thanked God that Eddy was still alive. She kept a journal of all he did, and as he began to talk, all he said as well. She sensed that she would not have him much longer, and would need tangible reminders of his brief life.

Eddy was a delightful toddler. Once he was walking, it seemed as if he was everywhere all at once, quick as lightning in his movements and full of enthusiasm. 'It is worth a good deal to see his face', wrote his mother proudly; 'it is so brimful of life and sunshine and gladness.'

Even though the family employed a nurse to look after the children, Elizabeth did not really get much stronger. Her hands reminded her of claws, they looked so scrawny. On average, three days of every week was spent prostrated with a sick headache. In such a condition she could not eat and began to worry about how the household was going to pieces around her. She also fretted about the family finances, as her ill health meant that more was being spent on 'help' than they could afford. However, even in these depressing circumstances she did not lose sight of God's plan for her life. Writing to George she confessed:

I can truly say that I have not spent a happier winter since our marriage, in spite of all my sickness. It seems to me I can never recover my spirits and be as I have been in my best days, but what I lose in one way perhaps I shall gain in another. Just think how my ambition has been crushed at every point by my ill-health, and even the ambition to be useful and a comfort to those about me is trampled underfoot, to teach me what I could not have learned in any other school![5]

Having lost his older sister, George was faced with the loss of his older brother at the age of just forty-two. Seargent was eight years older than George and had achieved national fame as a powerful orator and gifted lawyer. If it had not been for his financial support and ceaseless encouragement, George would not have been able to enter the ministry. Seargent's death was a bitter blow for the whole family. Elizabeth was with her mother-in-law when the news came through. 'Poor mother weeps incessantly', she reported in a letter to George.

After five-and-a-half happy years in New Bedford, George took up an associate pastorate at the Second Presbyterian Church, Newark, New Jersey, in October 1850. [6] The minister, Jonathan Condit, previously Elizabeth's pastor in Portland, had been ill and was in need of help in the work. For the next few months the two men shared the Sunday services with Jonathan taking the morning and George the evening services. This arrangement enabled George to support his mother as she mourned her eldest son. Mrs Prentiss had moved in with her daughter Anna and son-in-law Jonathan Stearns, who by this time was minister of the First Presbyterian Church, Newark. George visited his mother every day, except for Sundays.

Elizabeth was glad to be able to support her mother-in-law at this time but greatly missed her New Bedford friends and found the climate of Newark harsher than the coastal town she had been used to. It wasn't long before both Elizabeth and George suffered attacks of rheumatism and she was quick to note that 'everyone has a horrible cold, or the rheumatism, or fever and ague'. That winter was indeed hard as George suffered depression brought on by the death of his brother. All the old cheerfulness, which had eased their way through the hard times, evaporated. It was as if the iron had entered into his soul. There was nothing Elizabeth could do about it, and his gloom almost inevitably affected her.

But there were lighter moments too. Newark was close enough for them to go across to New York City for concerts. In September 1850 the famous Swedish singer, Jenny Lind (1820–87), made her American debut in New York and caused quite a stir. Europe had already been caught up with 'Jenny Lind fever' and it was reported that even Queen Victoria had been entranced by her 'exquisite, powerful, and really quite peculiar voice, so round, soft, and flexible.' On 2 November the Prentisses had the opportunity to hear her sing. 'A pleasure to remember for the rest of one's life', wrote Elizabeth. 'If anything, she surpassed our expectations.' The evening, however, nearly ended in tragedy. An accident meant that the passengers had to leave their railway carriages and walk about a mile. Crossing an unlit bridge the passengers did not see a large hole in the way and Elizabeth fell into it: 'I think if I had been walking with Mr Prentiss I should not only have gone in myself but pulled him in too; but I had the arm of a stronger man, who held me up until I could extricate myself.'

When Jonathan Condit's health recovered, in the spring of 1851, George was free to accept a call from Mercer Street Presbyterian Church, New York City. The church was actively engaged in City Mission Work and half of the gallery was always filled with orphans from a nearby institution. Mercer Street Church was also closely connected with Union Theological Seminary and its pulpit was therefore one of great significance. The move opened up all sorts of opportunities for George in both the denomination and the Seminary.

Mercer Street Presbyterian Church had many leaders of business, education, and philanthropy within its membership, and thus George and Elizabeth began to move within wealthy and cultured circles. One of the deacons, William G Bull, ensured that the new pastor and his family moved into a large cool house (fitted with the most up-to-date bathroom), a facility that would make hot and humid summers a little more bearable. He also ensured that the family had everything they needed, and willingly put at their disposal his own holiday cottage each summer. (The oppressive heat meant that Elizabeth and the children often moved out of the city to the country during the hottest months, while George remained in the city with the church. Air conditioning was invented only in 1911).

The Prentisses were now resident in the greatest industrial city, port, and financial centre in America. Situated at the mouth of two navigable rivers that flow into the Atlantic, New York's harbour played a key role in transatlantic trade. In 1825 the Erie Canal opened. This linked the city with the Great Lakes and gave access to the mid-west. During the 1830s, huge numbers of Irish and German immigrants poured into the city, providing an abundant supply of cheap labour. Poor housing sprang up rapidly on both the east and west sides of Manhattan Island. Industry boomed. Innumerable workshops supplied the ever-increasing demand for consumer goods. Wall Street became the nerve-centre of America's financial markets. Fortunes were made (and lost) rapidly.

In this great metropolis the arts flourished. The wealthy found ever more spectacular ways of exhibiting their riches and power. Grandiose buildings were erected. Elegant and glittering shops and hotels catered for the expensive tastes of the great magnates and their families. Efficient public transport systems were put in place: horse-drawn omnibuses from the 1830s; elevated railways from the 1870s. Elizabeth relished the freedom which public transport afforded. She wrote to her youngest brother in August 1851:

> I have improved fast in health since we came here. Yesterday I walked two and a half miles with George, and a year ago at this time I could not walk a quarter of a mile without being sick after it for some days. When I feel miserably I just put on my bonnet and get into an omnibus and go rattlety-bang down town; the air and the shaking and the jolting and the sight-seeing make me feel better and so I get along. If I could safely leave my children I should go with George. He hates to go alone and surely I hate to be left alone; in fact instead of liking each other's society less and less, we every day get more and more dependent on each other, and take separation harder and harder. Our children are well.[7]

There was always plenty to see and do. Elizabeth enjoyed taking the children to see Barnum's Museum:

> They were delighted, particularly with 'The Happy Family' which consisted of cats, rats, birds, dogs, rabbits, monkeys, etc. etc. dwelling together in unity. I observed that though the cats forbore to lay a paw upon the rats and mice about them, they yet took a melancholy pleasure in looking at these dainty morsels, from which nothing could persuade them to turn off their eyes.[8]

Alongside the wealth and conspicuous consumption there was also the ever-present blight of poverty and squalor with the city. The rural poor and vast numbers of overseas immigrants were drawn to New York in the hope of finding employment. In 1854, 427,833 new immigrants arrived. Not all stayed in New York, but many did. Most of them had endured appalling conditions on their journey across the Atlantic. On one voyage 108 German passengers died out of a total of 544.[9] On arrival, the new immigrants had to be processed through the Castle Garden reception centre. Friends or relatives would then meet the fortunate ones, but many immigrants had little choice but to pay extortionate sums for wretched lodgings, before facing the challenge of finding work and making a new life. Men, women, and children often found nothing better than poorly paid piecework with long hours in shocking conditions. Families were crammed into tenements: four, five, six, or more, people to a small room, with shared facilities. Not surprisingly, disease spread rapidly, and conditions became a national scandal.

These huge contrasts between luxurious wealth and crushing poverty greatly upset the sensitive Elizabeth. The suffering of so many in the city sickened her and where possible she sought to bring help. After taking care of one poor little girl she wrote: 'What a drop in the great bucket of New York misery, one such child is! Yet somebody must look out for the drops, and I am only too thankful to seize on this one.'[10]

George was of necessity taken up with his pastoral duties, and was also becoming increasingly involved with Union Theological Seminary, where his friend Henry Boynton Smith had just started lecturing. Union had been founded in 1835 chiefly to serve the 'New School' Presbyterian grouping.[11] Within just five years the Seminary had a board, a faculty, a building, and a student body; it also had considerable debts. Mercer Street Church was one of its most generous supporters. By 1850 the Mercer Street Church was providing about $4,000 a year to help meet the Seminary's $11,000 annual operating costs. That same year, Thomas H. Skinner, George's predecessor as pastor of Mercer Street, left the pastorate to teach at the Seminary.

George was committed to the cause of providing good theological training for prospective ministers of the gospel. In one of his first sermons at Mercer Street in 1851 he made an impassioned appeal for the ongoing financial support of Union Seminary. The sermon was published and widely circulated. As a result, a special meeting was held at the home of Charles Butler, a lawyer who had acquired a fortune through his real estate and railroad interests. Decisions taken at this meeting effectively placed the Seminary on a firm financial footing. The prospects for the Seminary were encouraging: new buildings were acquired and among the new members of the faculty were scholars of international repute, such as the respected church historian Philip Schaff. George was invited to take a place on the board of the Seminary.

As a board member a considerable amount of his time was spent on administering the affairs of the Seminary. During this time George became very close friends with Dr Skinner. George and Elizabeth were also able to continue their close friendship with Henry Boynton Smith and his wife Elizabeth. Over the coming years, Elizabeth would find Mrs Smith's loyal support a great encouragement.

In the summer of 1851, George went up to Hapswell, Maine, to stay for a short time with a friend. Elizabeth wrote to him every day and among her letters was one from their daughter Annie:

I was delighted with the nice letter you were so kind as to write me. I was sitting in Mamma's lap, pale and disconsolate, when it came. Mamma had just sent a letter to you. I have been out to Newark to see Grandma, and Una[12] and we played together every day and loved each other dearly. I did not want to come home *ever*, but I was sick and Mamma would make me come. I have had the nose bleed three times. The last time Mamma was frightened and so was I. I thought I should bleed to death, and Mamma would have sent for a doctor if she could have spared Margaret to go. I never was so frightened in my life, and I cried and said, 'Oh, I wish my dear papa would come!' Then I had a great plaster on my chest;[13] it hurt me dreadfully, but I did not cry and so Mamma let me pare a peach for her and gave me a slice.

Papa, don't you think we have got two little kittens! One is Eddy's and one is mine. I wish I could see the pretty things you told me about in your letter. When Mamma read the last part where you said 'God bless you', I cried a little. Mamma talks to me about you every hour. I told her yesterday I thought she loved you pretty much and she said she guessed she did.

I send a *great deal* of love to you, my own self; and I thank you for that nice letter. I must now bid you good night, my dear papa, and go to bed.[14]

During their first autumn in New York, Elizabeth was overjoyed to see her three brothers, returned from their prospecting for gold in California. The Prentiss home was large enough for several visitors. George and Elizabeth also regularly took the children over to Newark to visit George's mother.

By December, Eddy's health was giving cause for concern and Elizabeth was consumed with anxiety about her son. He grew weaker and weaker. By January he had succumbed to what seems to have been meningitis. He did not sleep at all for the last week of his life. This was a terrible time for all the family. They all knew what was coming. Even Annie tried to comfort her little brother in the face of death. When he said 'I don't want to die', his mother replied, 'Why? You know it is a great deal pleasanter in heaven than it is here . . . Little boys don't have the headache there. I should love dearly to go if God said I might.' 'Yes', Annie joined in, 'Don't you know how we used to sing about the happy land?' Eddy kept asking for Annie, but his sister got so distressed that they didn't always let her see him. There are harrowing day-by-day descriptions of Eddy's last days in Elizabeth's book, *How Sorrow Was Changed into Sympathy*.[15] His suffering was exacerbated by the treatments prescribed by the doctors, including the application of painful mustard plasters. Part of Elizabeth's journal reads:

> On Sunday morning, January 4, not being able to come himself, Dr Buck sent Dr Watson in his place. I told Dr W. that I thought Eddy had water on the brain; he said it was not so, and ordered nothing but a warm bath. On Thursday, January 8, while Margaret [the nursemaid] was at dinner, I knelt by the side of the cradle, rocking it very gently, and he asked me to tell him a story. I asked what about, and he said, 'A little boy', on which I said something like this: 'Mamma knows a dear little boy who was very sick. His head ached and he felt sick all over. God said, I must let that little lamb come into my fold; then his head will never ache again, and he will be a very happy little lamb.' I used the words little lamb because he was so fond of them. Often he would run to his nurse with his face full of animation and say, 'Marget! Mamma says I am her little lamb!' While I was telling him this story his eyes were fixed intelligently on my face. I then said, 'Would you like to know the name of this boy?' With eagerness he said, 'Yes, yes, Mamma!' Taking his

dear little hand in mine, and kissing it, I said, 'It was Eddy.' Just then his nurse came in and his attention was diverted, so I said no more.

On Friday, January 16, his little weary sighs became more profound, and, as the day advanced, more like groans; but appeared to indicate extreme fatigue, rather than severe pain. Towards night his breathing became quick and laborious, and between seven and eight slight spasms agitated his little feeble frame. He uttered cries of distress for a few minutes, when they ceased, and his loving and gentle spirit ascended to that world where thousands of holy children and the blessed company of angels and our blessed Lord Jesus, I doubt not, joyfully welcomed him. Now we were able to say, 'It is well with the child!'[16]

The funeral was held the following Monday, and Dr Skinner led the service. The choir sang 'Thy will be done', which Elizabeth said was 'like cold water to thirsty souls.'[17] She was submissive, writing the well-known words in her journal: '"Oh", said the gardener, as he passed down the garden-walk, "who plucked that flower?" His fellow-servants answered, "The Master!" And the gardener held his peace.' She was also grateful for the support which friends and family had given. Her young cousin Louisa Shipman had been there for her throughout, and Mrs Bull moved in during the final week or so to provide nursing care at night. She later said 'I used to think I could never endure to lose a child, but you see how it is. God does carry us through whatever he pleases.'[18]

Despite the love and care of family and friends, Elizabeth was terribly weakened by her grief. She was six months pregnant when Eddy died, and had not recovered by the time her next child was delivered. On the 17 April 1852, just three months after Eddy's death, she gave birth to a baby girl. She was named Elizabeth after her mother, but was called Bessie. In common with many mothers of the time, Elizabeth suffered a postnatal infection. It was not yet realized that germs carry disease and all too often the doctors attending women in labour carried infections with them. For a couple of weeks Elizabeth hung between life and death. She rallied, but was temporarily unable to walk because of a painful abscess on her hip joint. The worst of her case was that she was too weak to care for Bessie. The baby was kept in a different room and was looked after by a nurse. Elizabeth only saw her for a few brief moments once a day. Frustration at not being able to hold and nurse her own baby so upset her that her recovery was delayed.

When Bessie was one month old, Elizabeth was able to hold her briefly. Cuddling the little girl close for the first time, she was convinced the child was seriously unwell. She had an overpowering premonition that Bessie would soon die. She wept all afternoon, but when George got in he dismissed her fears, saying that her own illness was giving rise to these morbid feelings. The next morning, 19 May, Elizabeth insisted that Bessie be brought to her. The child had a burning temperature. A doctor was summoned, he prescribed some medicine, but at eleven o'clock the nurse reported that a swelling on baby's head now had a black spot on it. Elizabeth begged that the baby be brought to her; the nurse said she was too sick to be moved, and in desperation Elizabeth crawled on her hands and knees to the nursery. She found a scene of chaos. Everything was all over the place, medicines were on the floor, the baby was giving the most heart-rending moans. George came in at this moment and fearful for his wife's life, got her back to her bed. He had to go out again, and made her promise not to leave the room until he returned.

The next few hours were the most terrible of Elizabeth's life. She could hear Bessie's cries, but could do nothing, as she had promised not to leave her own room. Eventually, in a state of almost total hysteria, she dragged herself over to her chest of drawers and pulled out the clothes she planned for the little one's funeral. When her cousin Louisa Shipman called in the afternoon, she found the distraught mother clutching at her baby clothes and weeping. Elizabeth begged Louisa to go to the nursery and find out what was going on. Louisa found the doctor there, and he confirmed that the child was dying. At last, George arrived back home. Elizabeth later wrote:

> I crawled once more to the nursery, and snatched my baby in fierce triumph from the nurse. At least once I would hold my child, and nobody should prevent me. George, pale as death, baptized her as I held her in my trembling arms; there were a few more of those terrible, never to be forgotten sounds, and at seven o'clock we were once more left with only one child. A short, sharp conflict and our baby was gone. Dr B. came in later and said the whole thing was to him like a thunderclap – as it was to her poor father. To me it followed closely on the presentiment that in some measure prepared me for it. Here I sit with empty hands. I have had the little coffin in my arms, but my baby's face could not be seen, so rudely had death marred it. Empty hands, empty hands, a worn-out exhausted body, and unutterable longings to flee from a world that has had for me so many sharp experiences. God help me, my baby, my baby![19]

She could only repeat over and over to herself something that one of her friends had said when calling on that last dreadful day. 'God never makes a mistake.' Somehow she clung on to that truth.

Though Elizabeth always believed that God had overruled, with hindsight one cannot but be struck by the appalling mismanagement of this death. Where was George all that day? Why was Elizabeth left alone, distraught, bound by her promise to her husband not to leave her room? Why could she not have had her child with her during its dying hours? It is certain that the sheer trauma of that terrible day deeply scarred Elizabeth and hindered her recovery still further. That summer, she went away with Annie to Portland, and began to regain her strength. But 19 May 1852 would remain engraved on her memory for the rest of her life. Left with one daughter, Annie, Elizabeth penned the following:

> One child and two green graves are mine
> This is God's gift to me;
> A bleeding, fainting, broken heart –
> This is my gift to Thee.

6

'More Love to Thee'
1852–58

'I trust that in this hour of sorrow you have with you that Presence, before which alone sorrow and sighing flee away. God is left; Christ is left; sickness, accident, death cannot touch you here. Is this not a blissful thought? . . . May sorrow bring us both nearer to Christ!'

NEVER ONE TO SHOW HER FEELINGS publicly, Elizabeth somehow managed to get through the funeral of baby Bessie. Annie, still just five years old, had to be loved and cared for. George grieved the loss of his two younger children too, but of necessity had to throw himself back into his pastoral duties. He also felt a measure of gratitude and relief that at least his wife's life had been spared: she had come so very close to death.

Perhaps only George knew how broken his wife was in the weeks and months following that fateful day in May. At the happiest family moments, suddenly her grief would come crashing in again and overwhelm her. It was something of a relief for Elizabeth to get away for much of the summer of 1852. She was able to stay with the family up in Portland and also enjoyed some weeks in the beautiful setting of Ocean House at Cape Elizabeth on the Maine coast. Back in New York in the autumn, she resumed her various church duties of visitation and hospitality.

To distract her from her grief she began to record some of the stories she told to Annie. Elizabeth felt frustrated to be so weak physically – she desperately wanted to minister to others in some way. There was so much suffering all around and she felt so limited in what help she could offer. But investing in the spiritual lives of the younger generation was something she could do.

She aimed to write books that would attract children to Jesus. Writing for them came naturally to her. She believed that children brought up in Christian homes would grow to love God from an early age if encouraged to do so. This assumption lay behind all her children's stories.

She wrote her first book, *Little Susy's Six Birthdays*, in just ten days early in 1853. This was a series of simple stories, light and fresh in style. As she wrote, she read out each chapter to George, Annie, and her brother who was staying with them at the time, and they encouraged her on.

For a different kind of relief, Elizabeth turned to poetry. Some women would have wanted to express their sense of loss by talking to female friends. Always introspective, Elizabeth turned to prayer, putting her prayers into verse. Many of the poems later gathered into the collection entitled, *Golden Hours: Hymns and Songs of the Christian Life*, are dated from this time, although they were not originally intended for eyes other than her own.

Elizabeth always remembered her father's testimony that he had 'lost his own will' during his illness, and wanted only the will of God. Many of her poems pick up this theme. Others express her conviction that times of suffering are the times when Christians are driven closer to God. Looking back on the deaths of Eddy and Bessie, she later said that she and George would not change a thing. They had been forced into a radical dependence on God which may not have come about in any other way. Elizabeth was convinced that her children went immediately to heaven when they died. They were now in a sinless world with no suffering, and had been spared much pain: 'I can truly say that I feel myself a favoured mother to have been permitted to send two of my children away from my own poor training, my mistakes and my follies, to the very bosom of the Good Shepherd. Of those two I may feel assured that they will never sin against God.'[1] She was also convinced that these dark losses were all in the purpose of God. She drew comfort from the eternal perspective. This life is all about 'a closer walk with God'. The deeper the sorrow, the closer the walk.

Some would find this emphasis on God's ordination of his children's suffering for his own wise purposes somewhat overdrawn, and even morbid. For example:

> Yes, blood-drops ooze from many a rent that Thou
> Thyself has torn, and I am faint and sore;
> I feel a death-like moisture on my brow
> And on my dizzy brain wild voices roar.
>
> But oh I waver not! Thou knowest well
> I meant that Thou shouldst take me at my word,
> The bitter waves of anguish rise and swell,
> But heed them not, my Master and my Lord.
>
> Keep what Thou hast in wise and tender grace,
> Snatched from my deepest depths, nor left to me
> Option or choice; love shines upon Thy face,
> Thou knowest best what I can spare for Thee.
>
> But oh, by all this pain, this bleeding heart,
> Subdue, control, beat down and lay me low;
> New knowledge of Thyself to me impart,
> Jesus, my Saviour, let me learn to know.

I smart, I writhe, I bleed – and still I cry –
Lo that Thou hast is Thine, is mine no more;
Thou Master of my treasures are, and I
In this new poverty Thy name adore.[2]

Suffering is regarded as the means God employs to bring his people closer to himself: suffering breaks the idolatrous love of the creature. A potential danger in this thinking is that it almost glorifies suffering. And yet one must make due allowance for the fact that many of these verses were written during the times of Elizabeth's greatest agony. She was only able to come through these dreadful times by clinging to the perspective that God was using them to draw her closer to himself. The themes of many of the poems from this period express the grief at the loss of little ones:

As I have seen a mother bend
With aching, bleeding heart,
O'er lifeless limbs and lifeless face –
So have I had to part.

With the sweet prattler at my knee,
The baby from my breast,
And on the lips so cold in death,
Such farewell kisses prest.

If I should live a thousand years
Time's hand cannot efface,
The features painted on my heart
Of each beloved face.

If I should bathe in endless seas
They could not wash away
The memory of these children's forms;
How fresh it is to-day.

Ah, how my grief has taught my heart
To feel another's woe!
With what a sympathetic pang
I watch the tear-drops flow!

Dear Jesus! must Thou take our lambs,
Our cherished lambs away?
Thou hast so many, we so few –
Canst Thou not let them stay?

Must the round limbs we love so well,
Grow stiff and cold in death?
Must all our loveliest flowerets fail
Before his icy breath?

Nay Lord, but it is hard, is hard –
Oh, give us faith to see,
That grief, not joy, is best for us
Since it is sent by Thee.

And oh, by all our mortal pangs
Hear Thou the mother's plea –
Be gracious to the darling ones
We've given back to Thee.[3]

In the summer of 1853, Elizabeth went to stay with her friends the Warner sisters, Susan (1819–95) and Anna (1827–1915). They lived with their father and aunt on Constitution Island, near West Point. The stock market crash of 1837 had resulted in the ruin of Mr Warner's business. Previously a family of great wealth and well used to a life of luxury, by the late 1840s they were reduced to wondering where their next meal would come from. Susan wrote her novel *The Wide, Wide World* in the hope of making some money. It was published in 1850, and became the first best-seller in American history, going through fourteen editions in two years.[4] A central theme of the novel is the way Ellen (the heroine) learned to submit to the will of God through a whole series of severe trials, beginning with a cruel separation from her mother at a young age, and then her mother's death.

Elizabeth, still feeling raw from her own bereavements, experienced not only the warmth of welcome in the Warner home, but also a deep empathy from the sisters. She found Susan and Anna (author of well known hymn, *Jesus loves me*) to be 'kindred spirits' who held in common the belief that trials draw the Christian closer to God.

Later that summer, Elizabeth, George, and Annie spent a delightful holiday with several of the church families at White Lake, Sullivan County. On arrival, the whole party was weighed: Elizabeth, a couple of pounds short of seven stone (forty-five kilograms) being by far the lightest of the adults. Six weeks of fresh air and exercise did her a huge amount of good, and she returned to New York feeling far stronger.

During the autumn, one of Elizabeth's brothers came for an extended stay, as did her young cousin, Louisa Shipman. Louisa was a delightful teenager: cheerful, attractive, and always singing. She seemed a picture of health and energy. Louisa and Elizabeth especially enjoyed a day out at the grand new Crystal Palace, where they were dazzled by the fantastic array of goods on display at the First International Exhibition. During October, while George was away in New Bedford, Louisa was suddenly struck down with small-pox and died soon after the symptoms appeared. The family had to be vaccinated immediately and the whole house disinfected. Little Annie was next to catch the disease, before Elizabeth's brother also succumbed. In fact he became so ill that he was not far from death. Elizabeth nursed both of them through their two months of quarantine. During this time they were not allowed to see anyone apart from the doctor. Elizabeth wrote to her mother-in-law:

I am not allowed to see anyone – am very lonesome, and hope Anna will write and tell me every little thing about you all. The scenes I have lately passed through make me tremble when I think what a fatal malady lurks in every corner of our house. And speaking after the manner of men, does it not seem almost incredible that this child, watched from her birth like the apple of our eyes, should yet fall into the jaws of this loathsome disease? I see more and more that parents must leave their children to Providence.[5]

The winter of that year was another dark one for Elizabeth: grief at Louisa's premature death; on-going mourning for little Eddy and Bessie; fear for Annie's life; the toil of nursing the sick. But at the end of the year her first book, *Little Susy's Six Birthdays,* arrived from the publisher. This event was enormously exciting for her and the book was well received. Letters came in from children and parents saying how much the book had meant to them. This encouraged her to press on with her writing.

The Flower of the Family, a book for girls, was published in 1854.[6] It tells the story of Lucy Grant. The second of ten children, Lucy longs for an education, but poverty forces her to stay at home and help her mother with domestic chores. The opportunity to leave home and go to school eventually comes, but after a year she is forced to return home. Through all the various trials, she grows in her love for God, and in the virtues of patience and self-control. The book throws an interesting light on Elizabeth's own frustrations with the mundane nature of domestic duties during the early years of motherhood and her conviction that times of frustration are 'Christ's school' in which humility and grace are taught.

Elizabeth wrote to her old friend Carrie about her aspirations for this book:

> I long to have it doing good. I never had such desires about anything in my life; and I never sat down to write without first praying that I might not be suffered to write anything that would do harm, and that, on the contrary, I might be taught to say what would do good. And it has been a great comfort to me that every word of praise I ever have received from others concerning it has been 'it will do good', and this I have had from so many sources that amid much trial and sickness ever since its publication, I have had rays of sunshine creeping in now and then to cheer and sustain me.[7]

The book was well received, and soon translated into French and German. Elizabeth quickly began work on her next children's book, *Henry and Bessie, or What they Did in the Country*.

Annie, now aged seven, was overjoyed when a little sister, Minnie, was born on 23 July 1854. Elizabeth was deeply thankful, but Eddy and Bessie were never far from her thoughts. In the same year she received news of the death of Carrie's two young children. As a young teenager Elizabeth had suggested to Carrie that suffering might be all part of God's purpose. Now she wrote to her out of her own experience of suffering:

> Is it possible, is it possible that you are made childless? I feel distressed for you my dear friend, I long to fly to you and weep with you; it seems as if I must say or do something to comfort you. But God only can help you now and how thankful I am for a throne of grace and power where I can commend you, again and again, to Him who doeth all things well. I never realize my affliction in the loss of my children as I do when death enters the

house of a friend. Then I feel that I can't have it so. But why should I think I know better than my Divine Master what is good for me, or good for those I love? Dear Carrie, I trust that in this hour of sorrow you have with you that Presence, before which alone sorrow and sighing flee away. God is left; Christ is left; sickness, accident, death cannot touch you here. Is this not a blissful thought? . . . May sorrow bring us both nearer to Christ! I can almost fancy my little Eddy has taken your little Maymee by the hand and led her into the bosom of Jesus. How strange our children, our own little infants, have seen Him in his glory, whom we are only yet longing for and struggling towards![8]

Another sweet daughter has been lent to me of the Lord. Lent, LENT, let me repeat to myself in remembrance of my own sorrow and of yours.[9]

Twenty-nine years later, Carrie could look back on that time after the death of her second child when she had collapsed with grief. For days she lay on her bed wanting to die. Then Elizabeth's letter arrived. 'I was fairly aroused, lifted up, placed upon my feet, and by the grace of God have continued to this day.'[10]

George struggled with his health during 1854, and in August Dr Buck sent him to Sharon Springs, a popular spa resort. He took the waters and spent time walking. On 22 August he wrote to Elizabeth:

Here I am, scribbling these lines to the dearest, loveliest little wife on earth. How I wish you could see some of the sweet thoughts I had about you as I walked in the woods alone today! Loving you makes me so contented and happy. N.B. I am finding out more clearly than ever why I love you so. To be sure, I have always known a thousand ample reasons, but there is ONE – however I think I will not tell you what it is. Guess! Guess! But you wouldn't guess it in a hundred years. It is too much to your praise. But I do love you as profoundly as I fancy it is right to love a mortal. And yet the best part of our love, I trust, is as immortal as ourselves. Is it not so?[11]

The autumn was difficult as Minnie was continually unwell and Elizabeth was worn out. The doctor ordered her to give up nursing Minnie, and employ a wet-nurse. The baby slept with the nurse at night, 'while I, poor anxious mother, am turned out of my nursery that a stranger might do what I most delighted in doing and for want of which I feel lost'.[12]

The year 1855 saw Elizabeth's thirty-seventh birthday pass uneventfully. Another long and happy summer was spent by the sea: in Portland throughout the whole of July, followed by six weeks at the Ocean House, Cape Elizabeth. Elizabeth and Annie (now aged eight) both enjoyed having a baby to love and care for. George joined them for some of the time at the Ocean House and Elizabeth's brother George was part of their company as well. For her husband, this was a genuine break from the work and one on which he looked back with great delight:

> After all these many years I cannot recall those weeks at the Ocean House in 1855 without fresh delight. Your Uncle George[13] kept us company; and he was very bright and genial. We wandered up and down the wild shore; we climbed upon the high rocks and watched the in rushing waves when the tide had turned; we bathed, bowled, read and slept at our own sweet will; we betook ourselves to the adjoining woods and made charming little excursions; we sat still betimes and looked off upon the wide Atlantic where the ships were passing. I had just sent back the proofs of the last chapter of your uncle's

Memoir; my Church Extension report had been finished and adopted; the hardest year's work of my life was over and every day was a holiday. I do not think that ever before, or after, was I more happy to rest awhile. I felt, too, that the privilege had been fairly earned. And then, to crown the whole, I made repeated visits to my native town, and revived there the dear, childish memories.[14]

Elizabeth's third book, *Henry and Bessie; or What They Did in the Country* was published in this same year. George reckoned that this was one of her best children's books. Perhaps her writing reflected the joy she was experiencing with her own children and the measure of relaxation and refreshment she enjoyed during this summer; perhaps, too, in writing she was able to capture her happy, albeit brief, memories of Eddy and Bessie.

In January 1856, Minnie, aged just a year and a half, fell critically ill. She then seemed to make a recovery. However, one evening while Elizabeth and George were out, they received word that Minnie had taken ill again. The anxious parents rushed home to find her unconscious. When the doctor arrived, they were informed that she was dying. George and Elizabeth sat with her for twelve hours as she fought for every breath, purple in the face, and suffering terribly. But amazingly she pulled through. More than ten years later, when writing *Stepping Heavenward*, the memory of this traumatic night was still etched in Elizabeth's memory. The following description of Katy's agony at her daughter's illness surely reflects Elizabeth's own willingness to surrender even her beloved children to God. (Note the language of sacrifice: 'I gave my ewe lamb . . . as my free-will offering to God'):

We watched over her till far into the night, scarcely speaking to each other, but I know by the way in which Ernest held my hand clasped in his that her precious life was in danger . . . What a night it was! God only knows what the human heart can experience in a space of time that men call hours. I went over all the past history of the child, recalling all her sweet looks and words, and my own secret complaints at the delicate health that has cut her off from so many of the pleasures that belong to her age. And the more I thought, the more I clung to her . . . Alas, my faith seemed, for a time, to flee, and I could see just what a poor, weak human being is without it. But before daylight crept into my room light from on high streamed into my heart, and I gave even this, my ewe-lamb, away, as my free-will offering to God. Could I refuse Him my child because she was the very apple of my eye? No indeed, then, but let me give to Him, not what I value least, but what I prize and delight in most. Could I not endure heart-sickness for Him who had given His only Son for me! And just as I got to that sweet consent to suffer, He who had only lifted the rod to test my faith laid it down. My darling opened her eyes and looked at us intelligently, and with her own loving smile.[15]

For a few days Elizabeth was in shock: exhausted, she was unable to do anything, even to pray. The child had not fully recovered and gave the family much anxiety for months to come. It was to be several more years before she was fully well.

To distract her from this continual gnawing anxiety about her youngest child, Elizabeth started work on a new book, *Little Susy's Six Teachers*.

That summer Elizabeth and the children spent three full months at Westport on the coast, hoping the fresh sea air would build up the baby's strength. They lodged at a farm, and spent happy days out walking, or at the beach, and strawberry picking. Minnie grew stronger and Elizabeth felt almost

like her old self. Times of solitude and reflection were alike
essential to her, without which she could not function properly. Above all else she craved the sense of being close to God
and the busyness of city life, with the constant calls on her
time to receive guests and make visits to others sapped her
physical, emotional, and spiritual energies. The summer re-
treats by the sea left her feeling refreshed and replenished.

George was of the opinion that it was probably during this
year that Elizabeth wrote her well loved hymn 'More Love to
Thee'. She may well have written it during the summer
months when she enjoyed this quiet time of reflection. Having scribbled out the lines hastily, they lay aside for several
years, until George discovered them and insisted that they be
printed in order to freely share them with others.

> More love to Thee, O Christ, more love to Thee!
> Hear Thou the prayer I make on bended knee;
> This is my earnest plea,
> More love, O Christ, to Thee,
> More love to Thee, more love to Thee!
>
> Once earthly joy I craved, sought peace and rest;
> Now Thee alone I seek; give what is best:
> This all my prayer shall be,
> More love, O Christ, to Thee,
> More love to Thee, more love to Thee!
>
> Let sorrow do its work, send grief or pain;
> Sweet are Thy messengers, sweet their refrain,
> When they can sing with me,
> More love, O Christ, to Thee,
> More love to Thee, more love to Thee!
>
> Then shall my latest breath whisper Thy praise;
> This be the parting cry my heart shall raise,

This still its prayer shall be,
More love, O Christ, to Thee,
More love to Thee, more love to Thee!

These extracts from Elizabeth's journal capture her delight at having so much time to devote to prayer during this summer of 1856:

June 30, 1856. I am finding this solitude and leisure very sweet and precious; God grant that it may bear the rich and abundant fruit it ought to do! Communion with him is such a blessing, here at home in my own room, and out in the silent woods and on the wayside.

July 7, 1856. I do trust God's blessed, blessed Spirit is dealing faithfully with my soul – searching and sifting it, revealing it somewhat to itself and preparing for the indwelling of Christ. This I do heartily desire. Oh God! search me and know me, and show me my own guilty, poor and meagre soul, that I may turn from it, humbled and ashamed and penitent, to my blessed Saviour. How very thankful I feel for this seclusion and leisure; this quiet room where I can seek my God and pray and praise, unseen by any human eye – and which sometimes seems like the very gate of heaven.

July 27, 1856. Today I gave way to pride and irritation, and my agony on account of it outweighs weeks of merely earthly felicity. The idea of a Christian as he should be, and the reality of most Christians – particularly myself – why, it almost makes me shudder; my only comfort is, in heaven, I can not sin! In heaven I shall see Christ and see Him as He is, and praise and honour Him as I never do and never shall do here. And yet I know that my dear little ones need me, poor and imperfect mother as I am; and I pray every hour to be made willing to wait for their sakes. For at the longest it will not be long. Oh, I do believe it is the sin I dread and not the suffering of life – but I know not; I may be deluded. My love to my Master seems to me very shallow and contemptible. I am astonished that I love anything else. Oh that He would this moment come down into this room and tell me I never, never shall grieve Him again![16]

She returned to New York in the autumn, to face a flurry of domestic duties. She had to shop for winter clothes, get the home organized again, and catch up with the parishioners. Fortunately, Minnie's weaning, which Elizabeth had dreaded, went remarkably smoothly. In December she fell pregnant again, aged thirty-nine. Having regained her strength in the summer, Elizabeth now lost ground and her health collapsed.

By March 1857 she was critically ill and her doctors thought that there was little hope of recovery. Her husband was distraught, and although two-year-old Minnie hardly knew what was going on, this was a terrible time for Annie, now aged ten. It seemed all too likely that her mother was going to die. And Elizabeth longed for death. Lying in bed, so weak that she was unable to speak, she heard George and her doctor discussing the medicine that was her 'last chance'. If they could manage to give the medicine to her then maybe she might just pull through; but otherwise not. Elizabeth remembered how she debated within herself whether to co-operate and take the medicine. She felt that she had reached the gate of heaven. She wanted simply to 'go home', but re-lented, took the medicine, and recovered.

In May, she was able to resume her journal. Her thoughts on the recovery she made express her willingness to 'go home':

May 24, 1857. Now, contrary to my hopes and expect-ations, I find myself almost well again. At first, having got my heart set toward heaven and after fancying myself almost there, I felt disappointed to find its gates still shut against me. But God was very good to me and taught me to yield in this point to His wiser and better will; He made me, as far as I know, as peaceful in the prospect of living as joyful in the prospect of dying. Heaven did, indeed, look very attractive when I thought myself so near it; I pictured myself as no longer a sinner but a blood-washed saint; I thought I shall soon see Him whom my soul loveth, and see Him as He is; I shall never wound, never grieve Him again, and all my companions will be they who worship Him and adore Him. But not yet am I there! Alas, not yet a saint! My soul is oppressed, now that health is returning, to find old habits of sin returning too, and this monster Self usurping God's place, as of old, and pride and love of ease and all the infirmities of the flesh thick on me . . . Indeed, I do thank my dear Master that He does not let me alone, and that He has let me suffer so much; it has been a rich experience, this long illness, and I do trust He will so sanctify it that I shall have cause to rejoice over it all the rest of my life. Now may I return patiently to all the duties that lie in my sphere. May I not forget how momentous a thing death appeared when seen face to face, but be ever making ready for its approach. And may the glory of God be, as it never yet has been, my chief end. My love to Him seems to me so very feeble and fluctuating. Satan and self keep up a continual struggle to get the victory. But God is stronger than either. He must and will prevail, and at last, and in time far better than any I can suggest, He will open those closed gates and let me enter in to go no more out, and then 'I shall never, never sin.'[17]

Baby George was born safely in August 1857. Following the birth, Elizabeth recovered her strength quickly, but by now her husband was totally drained. George's typical week consisted of two sermons, one lecture, one or two funeral addresses, a church extension planning meeting, fifteen to twenty pastoral calls, plus two or three sick people to visit regularly, a ministers' meeting, two or more invitations to tea or dinner, the writing of letters, plus occasional extra engagements. The workload plus the family traumas sapped his already fragile health. He struggled through the winter of 1857. In Spring 1858 he wrote to Joseph Howland, one of his closest friends, who was then in Nice:

> Sometimes I feel a kind of assurance that I shall yet be well before I die; but I am willing to leave it with my Master. You and I have both learned by sad experience that we must not 'pick and choose' for ourselves. I hope we don't wish to do so. . . This has been a glorious winter's day. I hardly ever saw a finer one. I had a noble congregation in the morning, and it would have done your eyes and heart good to see how the people listened. I preached on the connection between faith in Christ and everlasting life. In the afternoon I preached to young Christians on cultivating high and reverential thoughts of their calling of God in Christ Jesus.

> February 7, 1858. I have just had my dear wife and children about me and committed us all to Him who loves us infinitely better than we love ourselves. What a blessed thing is prayer and a family altar! What a blessed thing is a Christian Sabbath! What a blessed thing is faith in Jesus Christ! What a blessed thing is the hope of everlasting life through and in Him! Oh, how do men get through this world and pass into eternity without Christ! Isn't it a wonder of wonders? If I were compelled to give up my belief in Him, it seems to me that the heavens would turn black over my head. I think I should

want to be annihilated. How I wish you could be with us next Sabbath. It is our Communion Sunday and a number of young persons are to make confession of their faith. There is an unusual religious interest in the country, and thousands are pressing into the kingdom far and near. It is a great comfort at a time when our public affairs wear so discouraging an aspect.[18]

1858 was a year of revival in New York and beyond. Thousands professed faith in Christ. The central feature of this revival was preaching on the Cross of Christ. 'One thought – one feeling – is absorbing this work. It is the Cross of Christ . . . The nearer the speaker gets to the Cross, the more he carries his hearers with him.'[19] During this year, Old School and New School Presbyterians, Methodists, Baptists, Low Church Episcopalians – all joined in prayer meetings and engaged in evangelism. George Duffield, Jr. (1818–88), a New School minister, wrote the famous hymn 'Stand up, Stand up for Jesus' at the very height of the revival, and the Christocentric emphasis encapsulates its message. The revival was a source of great joy to George Prentiss but increased his workload tremendously. 'Tens of thousands of conversions, which bear every mark of reality are occurring all over the land', he wrote. 'My pastoral labours too, growing out of the present unusual religious interest, have scarce left me a minute's leisure.'[20] In the spring his doctors told him that he had to stop working. With great reluctance he resigned his pastorate in April 1858.

This was a bleak time. George felt that he had been called into pastoral ministry, and now he was having to withdraw from it at a time of boundless opportunities. His whole future looked uncertain. Elizabeth felt that he had given his strength and energy to support her and the children through their illnesses and feared that she had failed him.

The only consolation during this dark time was the love and generosity of the Mercer Street Church family. They rallied round and raised funds for the family to travel to Switzerland, making it clear that they would be welcomed back among them if and when George was able to resume the work. In cases of serious illness, before the development of effective drugs, a period of time in the pure mountain air of Switzerland was commonly prescribed for those who could afford to go. After an exhausting whirl of packing and good-byes, George, Elizabeth, eleven-year-old Annie, three-year-old Minnie, and baby George boarded a steam ship and sailed for France on 26 June 1858. They were helped on their way by George's brother-in-law, Jonathan Stearns, who was to join them for a couple of months, and by Isabella, a faithful domestic maid. Parishioners loaded them down with cakes and fruit and gifts for the journey. The two-week summer crossing of the Atlantic was cold, foggy, and wet.

Once the ship finally set sail and the family had settled into their quarters, Elizabeth found the time to take stock. She had been married for thirteen years. On her wedding day she had entertained such bright hopes for the future. She had wanted to support George in his ministry: praying for him, encouraging him, and providing the peaceful home that would facilitate his pastoral labours. She had dreamed of a table surrounded by cheerful little children. Far from being the crowning blessing on their marriage, it now seemed that their children had destroyed their health and brought George's ministry to a premature end. For eleven years they had been robbed of sleep; Elizabeth's strength had been sapped by five pregnancies and confinements; they both had passed through the valley of the shadow of death when Eddy and Bessie had been taken from them. Elizabeth had been unable to provide the calm and happy retreat for George of which she had dreamed. George, it seemed, had such a strategic and fruitful ministry in New York; but now, as they sailed away from that great city, his broken health raised a serious doubt as to whether he would ever be able to preach again.

Elizabeth could easily have sunk down into total despondency. But she could not afford to do so. If she gave way to depression, there would be even less prospect of George recovering. She had to keep cheerful for his and the children's sakes. Looking at Annie, a lovely girl, mature beyond her years, serious and thoughtful, and beautiful little Minnie beside baby George, she could not regret her calling to be a mother. Yes it had cost her the bitterest anguish, but it had also brought her the deepest joy.

7

EUROPE
1858–60

*'I do trust that in the end we shall come forth from this
troublous time like gold from the furnace.'*

ONE OF THE RESULTS of the increasing wealth of the American
middle classes was the sudden increase in European tourism
from the 1840s onwards. Those who could afford it were
anxious to send their sons and daughters to France, England,
and Italy. The 'Continental' experience was considered to be
of benefit to one's education (improving one's mastery of the
French, German, and Italian languages); culture (seeing
Europe's antiquities); health (the pure mountain air of Switzerland was prescribed for all manner of ailments); and
even spirituality (the Romantic movement gave rise to the
notion that one could get 'closer to God' when surrounded
by natural beauty).[1]

Continental tourism enjoyed a further boost when the
introduction of steam ships reduced the time taken to cross
the Atlantic from about six to two weeks. Samuel Cunard
founded the first transatlantic steamship company in 1839.
Travelling conditions were safer and much more comfortable
than in the days of sail. Numerous American travellers carried
with them the immensely popular *Sunny Memories of Foreign
Lands* (1854). This was Harriet Beecher Stowe's own record
of visits to Britain, France, Switzerland, and Italy, which was
often employed as a nineteenth-century travel guide.

Several members of the Mercer Street Church had already taken trips to the Continent. In fact Dr and Mrs Buck had gone ahead of the Prentisses to Switzerland in order to organize lodgings for the first-time visitors.

The major excitement during the voyage was the celebration of Independence Day on 4 July. This anniversary was commemorated in style with a grand dinner, patriotic speeches and toasts. George fully entered into the spirit of the day and 'ran up and down the saloon like a war-horse', getting so excited that Elizabeth feared he would faint.

After two weeks at sea the family were delighted to disembark at Le Havre. The weather in Normandy was grey and drizzly, but could not dampen the spirits of those who were so glad to be back on *terra firma*. Their arrival in Europe came a decade after the dramatic and violent 'year of revolutions'. The fall of King Louis-Philippe of France in 1848 had triggered off a series of upheavals throughout Germany and Central Europe. Although the uprisings were quelled in the short term, the lasting result was the abolition of serfdom and greater mobility for peasant workers. In France, universal suffrage was achieved and Napoleon I's nephew was elected President of the Second Republic. Four years later he took the title of Emperor Napoleon III. By July 1858 all was relatively stable and quiet on the political front.

After spending a night in a Le Havre hotel, the family took the train to Paris. Blue skies and bright sunshine lit up the French countryside and Elizabeth was enchanted by the huge fields, straight lines of trees, old farmhouses, and ancient villages.

But all that was eclipsed by the glories of the historic sights of Paris. The Prentisses found hotel accommodation opposite the Tuileries gardens for a few days. Their rooms were on the fifth floor, so they had plenty of exercise toiling up and down stairs, as well as walking round the gardens and visiting some of the city's famous attractions. They were staying close to the massive Arc de Triomphe, erected by Napoleon I, between 1806 and 1808, to commemorate his epic victories. Huge bronze horses were placed on top of the arch (purloined by Napoleon from Venice but duly returned to that city after World War I). They admired the beautiful Palais Royal, and drove through the Bois de Boulogne. Paris was infinitely more beautiful than they had imagined and, to their surprise, much cleaner than New York.

After just a few days, they began the four-day train journey to Switzerland. As soon as they came in view of the mountains, the man-made splendours of Paris were forgotten. The weather was glorious when they reached Geneva. They stayed a night at Vevay, with rooms overlooking beautiful Lake Leman. Next morning, a horse-drawn *voiture* was hired to convey them and their goods to Château-d'Oex, twenty-two miles east of Lausanne, in one of loveliest parts of Switzerland.

The Bucks had secured them a place in a pension. This meant that they were staying with other guests in a boarding house and that all the catering would be provided for them. Breakfast (bread and honey) was served at eight, dinner at one, and 'tea' at seven. Sometimes the other guests provided considerable entertainment. Annie was fascinated by a Spanish couple. The wife had been 'married off' at the tender age of twelve to a husband of thirty-two. He had organized lessons for her until she was fourteen, when she had her first baby. The lady was very vivacious, full of talk and laughter, and gave hilarious imitations of the tantrums she threw when, refusing to do her lessons, she would throw her books at her husband.

The family had four rooms for their own use; they were simply furnished in the Swiss style with plain pine floors. They were able to unpack their books and other belongings

– including Elizabeth's prize possession, a sewing machine. This was installed in a little summerhouse outside the pension, and Isabella began work on winter clothes for the family. Local people quickly heard of this American novelty and many came to take a look.

On Sundays, the family went to the little Protestant chapel in the village nearby. They became very fond of Pastor Panchaud, a gentle and godly man. Elizabeth found the services very different. There were no children, and the women came dressed in the most dismally dark clothes, with long 'bloomers' on their heads rather than bonnets.

The house was located up a little winding path and was only accessible by foot. A small stream ran down alongside the path. Glorious views were to be had in every direction. Each afternoon the older visitors followed the path up beyond the chalet for a walk through the higher alpine meadows.

Given that the whole purpose of the holiday was the restoration of George's health, Elizabeth anxiously watched to see how he was responding to the enforced rest. George's chronic fatigue was a condition that, under these favourable conditions, allowed him to regain a certain degree of strength, and with that sense of renewed vigour, the desire to do more. But after attempting longer hikes in the afternoon or more demanding hours in the study, George would often be left feeling sick, giddy, and weak.

The continual ups and downs were emotionally draining for both of them. George took one or two longer trips with his brother-in-law Jonathan, but, again, these exertions brought on relapses of total exhaustion. However, overall this period of rest and relaxation in the fresh mountain air of Switzerland was of great benefit to the ailing patient. One of George's trips was to Zurich. As always, he wrote to his wife daily. Having received two of his letters, Elizabeth replied as follows:

Château-d'Oex, August 20, 1858. I got your two letters from Zurich, darling, just as I was going down to dinner and they enlivened me so that I don't know but they all thought at the table that I had been drinking wine. But I had been drinking love, you know, and that is just as bad! How kind you are to write so often. I wish I could do as much for your comfort and happiness as you do for mine. All you say quite humbles and frightens me; and yet it makes me very happy, too. I found it hard to listen to the sermon with necessary attention this morning, for my thoughts kept wandering to you. I felt grateful to God for having granted me the rich experience of *satisfied* affection, and almost tremble when I look my felicity in the face. What would have become of me if I had never known the happiness I have found in looking up to, leaning on, admiring and loving you! We ought to bless God every day for our daily joy and solace in each other – and so we do, yet not half enough. Do not talk about your faults: it pains me. If I had no more reason to do it than you have, I should be spared many hours of anguish. What a wonderful thing human love is! Think how by a breath, as it were, you can fill me with ecstasy![2]

George replied:

Zurich, August 26, 1858. It is a pleasant place and I have a nice room overlooking a magnificent lake—and landscape. How I do long to hear from you! It seems about four weeks, or rather months, instead of four days, since I left Château-d'Oex. How much I have thought of you and loved you, as I have sat or walked alone! Without you and the dear children near me I do not, indeed, seem to be living my own true life. Everything has an unreal and foreign air when I am away from you. Oh, if when with you, dearest, I could always in all things, great and small, do and be what is wisest, fairest, most unselfish and best! It is weakness and fault here, the thought of which fills me sometimes with a kind of terror. But do not suppose absence is necessary in order to make me feel so; such a feeling has been for years one of my most familiar experiences. No words can express my sense of the love and tenderness and homage which, a thousand times over, are due to such a wife as you have been to me. God bless and reward you! Since you became mine it seems as if my existence had increased in sweetness and in value an hundred-fold. To think of having never known you is almost to think of having never been born. And now with a blessing on you and the precious children, my dearest love, good night.[3]

By September the nights were getting really cold. Plenty of hot water bottles and thick Swiss duvets were needed to keep the family warm. In October, they moved to Montreux, at the east end of Lake Geneva, to spend the six months of winter. They continued walking as long as they could, and enjoyed the autumn colours. Elizabeth was delighted with the Swiss passion for flowers; brightly coloured window boxes still decorated the houses even through October. A teacher was employed to visit the home occasionally to give Annie some tutoring. Being away from other children of her own age was making the poor girl feel very lonely.

In November George travelled to Paris to meet with Benjamin F. Butler, one of the members of the Mercer Street Church who travelled to Europe with his two daughters. One of the girls had been ill and the trip had been prescribed by her doctor. Butler (1795–1858), a descendant of Oliver Cromwell, had served the United States as both Attorney General (1833–8) and Secretary of War (1836–7). A well-known statesman, he was also a much-loved member of

George's congregation. On the way to Paris George was stunned to receive news of his friend's sudden death at the age of sixty-three. When he arrived in Paris he did his best to console the two grieving daughters.

Time through the winter months dragged dreadfully slowly. The days were short and the dark nights were long. The family could not get out as much as they did during the warmer months and they knew so very few people whose company and conversation they could enjoy. George and Elizabeth spent the long evenings talking about home. Annie had no youngsters of her own age to mix with and nor did the little ones. Confined in the small house they grew bored and fretful. By this time Elizabeth was also expecting again and felt weary and ill. She was also beginning to feel apprehensive about whether she could cope with another infant.

In these circumstances the family felt homesick often: they looked forward so much to receiving letters from America and wrote many in reply. However, letters from home were not always full of cheering news. It seemed that one after another brought sad tidings of another bereavement. Such news felt harder to bear at such a distance: it was impossible to visit their friends and relatives to sympathize with them. Other letters were not very tactful: some were from church members who wrote to complain about their own personal struggles and who seemed to be somewhat resentful of the fact that the Prentisses were having a 'glorious free holiday' in Europe.

Filled with ongoing concern for her husband, often feeling poorly herself, and having to cope with bored and restless children, it was rather trying to have their situation so misunderstood by the folks back home. But Elizabeth had learned that misunderstanding is part of life. She had long before given up trying to defend herself against the criticism of others.

George spent some of his time in study. He wrote to his friend Joseph Howland:

Baby is bright as ever and almost boisterous in his expressions of astonishment at all the cows, horses, goats and dogs that catch his eye. He begins to talk French, too, I believe; at any rate he jabbers away in what I have no doubt is good baby French. As for M[innie] she has grown into a perfect lump of fat, and amuses us greatly (it doesn't take much to amuse parents) with her strange prattle about life and death and heaven. I wish her mother would write it all down in a little book; not because it is anything extraordinary, but because all the revelations of a child's soul are so extremely interesting and instructive.

I have been busying myself of late with the history and criticism – especially the destructive criticism – of the New Testament canon. For years I have felt the greatest interest in the subject, but never before had leisure thoroughly to study it. The German rationalists and infidels, you know, have expended immense talent, acuteness, and erudition in attempting to prove that most of the books of the New Testament were written long after the death of their supposed authors. No such assault was ever before made upon these sacred bulwarks of our faith. But I am surprised, on examination, to find how frivolous and morally discreditable much of this sceptical criticism is. Dear Joe, has it ever distinctly occurred to you what an amazing privilege and grace of God it is to have a hearty, complete and unshaken faith in the absolute *reality* of Christ's gospel? When I read the attempts of men vastly more learned and highly gifted than myself to prove the gospel a delusion, I am ready to exclaim with Paul, *No man can say Jesus is Lord* but in the Holy Ghost.[4]

Elizabeth's spirits lifted with the arrival of spring. As early as March, the fields were covered with flowers: primroses, daisies, crocuses, buttercups, and violets. The children were thrilled to be able to walk out and gather baskets of them. At the end of March, the family moved again, this time to a rented house at the campagne Genevrier, situated about two miles away from Vevay. Although they arrived in a fierce snowstorm, April brought warm sunshine. The children were wild with delight at being able to play outside in the large garden as much as they wished. Annie had been given a guinea pig, and it promptly produced seven babies, to the joy of the little ones. They were surrounded with glorious views of lake and mountains. They grew their own vegetables and had a bountiful supply of milk and cream from the neighbouring farm. Writing to her close friend Elizabeth Smith, Elizabeth described their new home:

April 7, 1859. You would fly here in a balloon if you knew what a beautiful spot we are in. We are surrounded with magnificent views of both the lake and the mountains, and can not turn in any direction without being ravished. The house is pretty, and in most respects well and even handsomely furnished; damask curtains, a Titian, a Rembrandt, and a Murillo in the parlour; the floors are waxed and carpetless, to be sure, but Mrs Buck has given us lots of large pieces of carpeting such as are used in this country to cover the middle of the rooms, and these will make us comfortable next winter.

We have quite a nice garden, from which we have already eaten lettuce, spinach, and parsley; our potatoes were planted a day or two ago, and our peas are just up. One corner of the house, unconnected with our part, is occupied by a farmer who rents part of the land; he is obliged to do our marketing, etc., and we get milk and cream from him. I wish the latter was as easy to digest as it is palatable and cheap. They beat it up here till it looks like pure white lather and eat it with sugar. The grounds about our house are very neat and we shall have oceans of flowers of all sorts; several kinds are in full bloom now. The wild flowers are so profuse, so beautiful and so various that A. and I are almost demented on the subject. From the windows I see first the wide, gravelled walk which runs round the house; then a little bit of a green lawn in which there is a little bit of a pond and a tiny *jet feau* which falls agreeably on the ear; beyond this the land slopes gently upward till it is not land but bare, rugged mountain, here and there sprinkled with snow and interspersed with pine-trees. The sloping land is ploughed up and men and women are busy sowing and planting; too far off to disturb us with noise, but looking, the women at least, rather picturesque in their short blue dresses and straw hats. On the right hand the Dent du Midi is seen to great advantage; it is now covered with snow. The little village of St Leger lies off in the distance; you can just see its roofs and the quaint spire of a very old church; otherwise you see next to no houses, and the stillness is very sweet. *Now* won't you come? The children seem to enjoy their liberty greatly, and are running about all the time. They have each a little garden and I hope will live out of doors all summer.[5]

The children were fit and well and happy for the next few months, but Elizabeth really struggled during the second half of her pregnancy. She could not sleep, and was also afflicted with bad headaches. But such was her delight in the surroundings that one day of good health and beautiful scenery almost made up for days or even weeks of sickness. Eventually, in August 1859, her sixth baby and fourth surviving child was born, following a long and difficult labour. His parents named him Henry, after their good friend, Henry Boynton Smith, who, shortly after the birth, paid them a visit, and was able to baptize his little namesake.

Henry Smith's arrival provided the family with much-needed conversation and news from home. He was a great conversationalist, and had a tremendous sense of humour. All the family enjoyed his company. He and George went on several excursions, sometimes taking Annie with them. Annie deserved some outings. She had cared for her sick mother and often looked after the little ones too. Although only twelve years old she had done all without complaint, but Elizabeth was thrilled that she could now receive some special attention and a little spoiling. Henry's sparkling presence among them must have been sorely missed after his departure at the end of August 1859.

In the middle of September Elizabeth was well enough to leave baby Henry with their maid, Isabella, and travel to see the glaciers at Mont Blanc with George and Annie. This was the first proper outing for sightseeing she had been able to undertake since arriving in Switzerland the previous year and it was an enormous success. To see such amazing alpine scenery seemed to make up for all the difficulties and frustrations of the past year or so. Elizabeth thrived on days spent in the fresh air and the exercise greatly benefited her. Travel plans included a return trip to Genevrier to check on the younger children before proceeding to do some more sightseeing in the Bernese Oberland. But when they arrived at Genevrier they were shocked to find baby Henry seriously ill with whooping cough. He was so poorly that he could not hold down any food, had lost much weight, and seemed to be all skin and bones. He was listless and all he could do was wail weakly. Elizabeth feared for his life. Then Minnie and little George succumbed as well.

The brief interlude of good health and the joy of sightseeing had come to an abrupt end. Now began six miserable months of illness. Elizabeth was effectively housebound, nursing her children. Not surprisingly her own health suffered on account of the broken nights of sleep and being shut up in the house, unable to take proper exercise. At times she feared they were going to leave one or more little graves in Switzerland. Seeing the wonderful sights of the magnificent Alps paled into insignificance before the greater task of fighting to save the lives of the children. She wrote characteristically to a friend: 'If I must choose between the two, I'd rather have the littlest baby in the world than see all the biggest mountains in it.'

The family decided unanimously that they could not possibly stay the whole winter in Switzerland. They had found the isolation and boredom of the previous winter very trying. So when George was invited to Paris in December, to take a temporary Chaplaincy at the American Chapel, it seemed to be an ideal opportunity. They all planned to go, but George would go ahead to secure suitable accommodation. Part of December was spent buying Swiss souvenirs to take home for friends. If Elizabeth had not intervened, George would have bought a bushel or two of wooden Swiss Chalets; and he bought 'leaf-cutters enough to stab all his friends to the heart. Most of our lady friends will receive a salad-spoon and fork from one or the other of us.'

Less than two days after her husband's departure, Elizabeth was appalled to find that little George had succumbed to scarlet fever. The common insistence was strict quarantine and isolation: the patient had to stay in the same room for forty days – six and a half weeks.

Such an imposition on little children when they had all been looking forward to the Paris trip was almost unbearable. They all craved the company of the Americans whom they knew to be in Paris at that time. Now, not only were they trapped in their own chalet, they sorely missed the comfort of their father's presence with them.

Elizabeth sent George the bad news. She knew that he would be inclined to give up the chaplaincy and return to Switzerland to help her nurse the children, but she urged him to stay in Paris. She knew that the long weeks of confinement in the chalet would put a huge strain on her. But if her husband returned she feared for his health. On balance, her concern was for him to get well. She reckoned that he desperately needed the stimulation of work in Paris, meeting new people and fitting in to a proper routine. 'I see but one thing to be done: for you to stay and preach and me to stay and nurse, each in the place God has assigned us . . . you must pray for me that I may be patient, and willing to have my coming to Europe turn out a failure as far as my special enjoyment of it is concerned.'

George was torn between the two but followed the advice of his wife and the family's doctor. He wrote to Joseph: 'Imagine my solicitude! Judge, too, what must be my conviction of duty when I tell you that I feel bound to stay here (though Mrs P. and the doctor both urge it), unless absolutely summoned back by more serious news still. But I am trying to do the Lord's work, and He I know will take care of my wife and lambs. It is however a terrible trial.'[6]

Little George was not too seriously ill, but when Minnie caught the scarlet fever she became very poorly. Elizabeth was completely taken up with nursing her, and had to leave baby Henry to Isabella. Annie just had to look after herself and Elizabeth felt particularly sorry for her. Annie had so set her heart on getting to Paris but, as usual, was sweet tempered in the midst of her disappointment. Elizabeth set about nursing Minnie, all the while wondering whether the child would pull through. She wrote to her husband:

I need not tell you what to ask for the dear child, but for me do pray that I may have no will of my own. All these trials and disappointments are so purely Providential that it frightens me to think I may have much secret discontent about them, or may like to plan for myself in ways different from God's plans. Yet in the midst of so much care and fatigue I hardly know how I do feel; I am like a feather blown here and there by an unexpected whirl-wind and I suppose I ought not to expect too much of myself. 'Though he slay me yet will I trust in Him,' I keep saying over and over to myself, and if you are going to write a new sermon this week, suppose you take that for your text . . . I do trust that in the end we shall come forth from this troublous time like gold from the furnace.[7]

Somehow they got through those long weeks of sickness and quarantine. Elizabeth's overwhelming feeling was one of exhaustion but also intense gratitude that all her children had survived the winter.

Meanwhile, early in February 1860, the British Baptist preacher, C. H. Spurgeon visited the American Chapel where George was acting chaplain, which proved a welcome diversion. Spurgeon, then just twenty-five years old, was already famous, and large crowds came to hear him preach, some travelling great distances. Spurgeon's preaching was reported in the newspapers and even the Catholic journalists were impressed by his oratory. George wrote to Elizabeth: 'I had a nice walk and talk with him yesterday, and dined with him at Mr Curtis's. He is certainly a remarkable man, and a faithful preacher of the Gospel.'[8] On 10 February George wrote:

Mr Spurgeon preached again in the American chapel at two o'clock yesterday, and again at eight o'clock in the Oratoire. Both sermons were good, but the first was one of the best in its kind that I ever heard. Not a sentence, or word, could have offended the most fastidious taste, while the matter and the delivery were alike admirable. It was on the passage in the twenty-third Psalm — *The Lord is my Shepherd, I shall not want.* The evening sermon was also very striking, and contained passages of great power and beauty, but it was marred by some terrible slaps at the Unitarians. On the whole Mr Spurgeon's visit has given me a great deal of pleasure, and has decidedly raised my opinion of his character and merits. I was introduced to Mrs Spurgeon after the morning service and received the most agreeable impression of her, too. She was educated partly in Paris, I am told, and no one could see and talk with her without being highly pleased.[9]

Elizabeth and the children finally arrived in Paris at the end of February 1860 and managed a bit of sightseeing despite incessant rain and further illness. On their arrival in the city following their months of quarantine in the Swiss mountains she wrote playfully to a friend:

We got here safe and sound with our little batch of invalids. They bore the journey very well and are heartily glad to get into the world again. I am chock-full of worldliness. All I think of is dresses and fashion, and, on the whole, I don't know that you are worth writing to as you were never in Paris and don't know the modes, and have perhaps foolishly left off hoops and long sleeves. I long, however, to hear from you and your new babby [sic], and will try to keep a small spot swept clear of finery in my heart of hearts, where you can sit down when you've a mind.[10]

The summer was spent in England, if one could call it a summer, continual rain rather dampened their efforts to enjoy the countryside and the sights. The family enjoyed London's Crystal Palace, 'a little fairyland', and did the rounds of the Tower, Westminster Abbey, Madame Tussaud's, the National Gallery, and so on. They were especially impressed by seeing Queen Victoria and Prince Albert at the review of 20,000 volunteers in Hyde Park, on 23 June 1860. They were vastly entertained by the 'stiff little grey wigs' worn by the judges in court. Concluding their European holiday, a couple of happy weeks were spent on the Isle of Wight. Then in mid-September the Prentiss family, now numbering six instead of five, embarked on the eleven-day voyage back across the Atlantic to New York, on board the steamship *Adriatic*.

8

THE WAR YEARS
1861–65

'I have felt for a long while greatly discouraged and
depressed, yes, weary of my life.'

THE FAMILY ARRIVED HOME in August 1860. The European trip
had been successful to the extent that George was sufficiently
recovered to be able to resume his pastorate. The members at
Mercer Street were delighted to have their pastor back
among them. Almost immediately George was involved in a
church planting project. A daughter congregation began
meeting in the upper part of New York City, on the corner
of Fifth Avenue and Twenty-Sixth Street. A huge amount of
his time and energy was invested in this work. George also
resumed his involvement with the Union Theological
Seminary.

Much as Elizabeth wanted to become fully involved with
the work of the church, her energies were largely consumed
with looking after her large family: Annie (13); Minnie (6);
George (3); and Henry (1). Her insomnia was now worse
than ever, exacerbated by the demanding care for her children
during their illnesses in Europe. But she was delighted to be
back in her own home, with her friends, and perhaps most of
all, the church where she could worship God in her own
language and listen to George preach again.

However, all church and family concerns were overshadowed by the tensions dominating the nation and by the impending war. Abraham Lincoln was elected President of the United States in 1860. Shortly after the election, South Carolina left the Union, only to be followed by six other Southern states. Civil War broke out in April 1861. The South was fighting for the right to determine its own future. The North was fighting in the first instance to preserve the Union. It was only later in the war that emancipation became a declared aim of the Union cause.

At the outbreak of hostilities in April 1861, no one could have fully realized just how long the war would drag on, or at what cost in human lives. This was the first 'modern' war, fought with all the resources of an industrialized nation; the newly constructed railroads meant that troops and supplies could travel unprecedented distances. Firearms were more lethal than in previous conflicts, and the casualties of this war were correspondingly high. This was the first war in which 'modern' weapons were used; but it was also waged before the advances of modern medicine had been discovered, and about twice as many men died of disease as were killed by direct combat. Cutting-edge photographic equipment captured the horrors of war and so, for the first time, non-combatants were able to receive some impression of just how gruesome and bloody were the casualties suffered by both sides. Field reporters sent back vivid accounts of the distress of wounded soldiers amid the inadequacies of medical supplies and care.

Both sides confidently expected the winning of a quick victory. The Union side (the North) possessed overwhelmingly superior industrial capacity, a more extensive transport network, and a greater potential for mobilizing troops. The Confederates (the South) hoped that their great resolution, as well as the wealth created by their production of cotton would pull them through. Both sides were certain of the rightness of their cause. Both sides contained individuals of outstanding piety and godliness.

As in every civil war, this conflict was the more terrible in that it was fought between 'brothers divided'. Many of the leaders on both sides had gone through West Point, the United States Military Academy. They had trained together, but now found themselves fighting against each other. In absolute terms, the Union side had far greater resources. But the Confederates had generals of outstanding quality such as Robert E. Lee and T. J. 'Stonewall' Jackson. These brilliant military leaders managed to inflict a succession of defeats on the Union side. By contrast, Lincoln was hampered by a succession of mediocre generals, until at last he found the man he needed in Ulysses S. Grant.

From the commencement of the conflict the Prentisses were unequivocally loyal to the Union side. George wanted to volunteer as a chaplain to the army, but was persuaded by his doctor that his health would not bear the strain of such a position. However, he eagerly followed every battle and was enormously excited to be invited by General Grant to attend a Grand Review of the troops. He was a fervent admirer of President Lincoln and was thrilled to be received by him when on a visit to the Capital, accompanied by Professor Schaff and Dr Stearns. His diary entry for 9 November 1864 summed up his feelings for the President: 'Mr Lincoln re-elected! *Annus Mirabilis!* Glory be to God most High! THE NATION IS SAVED!'[1]

The beginning of 1862 was overshadowed by the war, but Elizabeth's great anxiety was for her older sister Louisa, who lay critically ill. During the previous few years she had been virtually bed-ridden. Louisa's worst fear was that she might lapse into insanity. Her condition would have been far worse if it had not been for the continual and loving care of her husband Albert.

Often he would steal home from his beloved Observatory, where he had been teaching his students how to watch the stars, and pass a sleepless night at her bedside, reading to her, and by all sorts of gentle appliances trying to sooth her irritated nerves. And this devotion ran on, without variableness or shadow of turning, year after year.[2]

Louisa died, aged fifty, on 24 January 1862. It was a terrible loss for her husband and son. Long years of sickness had blighted what had started out as a life full of promise. Louisa had been an intellectually brilliant young woman. She had contributed literary reviews to some of America's most prestigious journals. Her company had been sought by the leading academics of the day. She had published several books, some of which had a wide circulation, before her health deteriorated.[3] She left behind her large quantities of notes, which she had never had the strength to prepare for publication. Elizabeth travelled in an open sleigh through a fierce blizzard to Williamstown to attend the funeral, and spent some time with her brother-in-law and eighteen-year-old nephew Eddy, in an attempt to comfort them.

Elizabeth and the family spent the summer of 1862 on the coast at Newport. They were again struggling with ill health themselves. George (5) and Henry (3) suffered terribly from dysentery. For a while it was touch and go as to whether George would pull through, and no sooner had he recovered, than Henry went down with the disease. Elizabeth lamented in a note at this time: 'Day after day of confinement and night after night of sleeplessness has pulled down my strength.' But the horrors of war put their own struggles in perspective. On 3 August she wrote to Elizabeth Smith:

Last night as I lay awake, too weary to sleep, I heard a harsh, rasping sound like a large saw. I thought some animal unknown to me must be making it, it was so regular and frequent. But after a time I found it was a dying young soldier who lives farther from this house than Miss H. does from our house in New York. His fearful cough! Oh this war! this war! I never hated and revolted against it as I did then. I had heard someone say such a young man lay dying of consumption in this street, but till then was too absorbed with my own incessant cares to hear the cough, as the rest had done. I never realized how I felt about our country till I found the terror of losing a link out of that little golden chain that encircles my sweetest joys, was a *kindred* suffering. Have the times ever looked so black as they do now? We seem to be drifting round without chart or pilot.[4]

Elizabeth and the children spent the month of September in Williamstown with her brother-in-law Albert, and his son. Albert was still desperately missing his late wife. In almost everything they did together he would instinctively think of how Louisa would have enjoyed it. Elizabeth tried her best to cheer him but she had fears about her own health too. In the autumn of 1862 she wrote to one of her sisters-in-law: 'I do not know as I ever was so discouraged about my health as I have been this fall. Sometimes I think my constitution is quite broken down, and that I never shall be good for anything again.'

One of her friends, Caroline, had a brother serving as a doctor with the Union troops. Elizabeth wrote on 19 September 1862:

Caro. H. read me yesterday a most interesting letter from her brother Henry, describing the scene at Bull Run[5] when he went there five days after the battle. It is very painful to find such mismanagement as he deplores. He gave a most touching account of a young fellow who lay mortally wounded, where he had lain uncared-for with his companions for five days, and whom they were obliged to decline removing, as they had only room for a portion of the most hopeful cases. After beseeching Mr H. to see that he was removed, and entreating to know when and how he was ever to get home if they left him, he was told that it was not possible to make room for him in this train of ambulances. As Mr H. tore himself away, he heard him say,

> Here, Lord, I give myself away;
> 'Tis all that I can do.

The torture of the wounded men in the ambulances was so frightful, that Mr H. gave each of them morphine enough to kill three well men. They 'cried for it like dogs and licked my hands lest they should lose a drop', he adds. As a contrast to this letter, some of the new recruits came into the Professor's [Albert's] grounds yesterday to get bouquets.[6]

Elizabeth was so moved by this letter, that she worked the account of the abandoned soldier into one of her more sentimental short stories, *Why Satan Trembles*. In her story, the young soldier lies dying, remembering his misspent youth, but also remembering his mother's prayers. The spirits of evil hover, waiting their prey. But then he remembers that 'one refuge alone awaited him [and] cried in his despair: "Here, Lord, I give myself away; 'Tis all that I can do." And as the words died on his lips, the two evil spirits stepped aside and gave place to the angels who came to bear the new-born soul into the presence of its Redeemer.'[7]

President Lincoln announced the Preliminary Emancipation Proclamation on 23 September 1862. It was simply a measure to liberate those slaves in the states that were in rebellion against the Union, but was greeted with enormous enthusiasm by all those who like Elizabeth looked eagerly towards total abolition. The Proclamation was finalized on 1 January 1863.

Back in New York City for the winter, Elizabeth settled once more into church life. The writers, Susan and Anna Warner, came to stay for a fortnight, which she greatly enjoyed. 'They grow good so fast that there is no keeping track of them', she wrote. When they returned to their home on Constitution Island, Anna packed up and sent a trunk of mosses and cones to Elizabeth as a gift. Elizabeth promptly wrote back:

I wanted to write a book when the trunk came this afternoon; that is, a book full of thanks and exclamation marks. You could not have bought with money anything for my Christmas present, that could give half the pleasure. I shut myself up in my little room up-stairs (I declare I don't believe you saw that room! did you?), and there I spread out my mosses and my twigs and my cones and my leaves and admired them till I had to go out and walk to compose myself. Then the children came home and they all admired too, and among us we upset my big work-basket and my little work-basket, and didn't any of us care. My only fear is that with all you had to do you did too much for me. Those little red moss cups are *too* lovely! and as to all those leaves how I shall leaf out! G. asked me who sent me all those beautiful things. 'Miss Warner' quoth I absently. 'Didn't Miss Anna send any of them?' he exclaimed. So you see you twain do not pass as one flesh here . . . I have outdone myself in picture-frames since you left. I got a pair of nippers and some wire, which were of great use in the operation. I am now busy on Mr Bull, for Mr Prentiss' study.[8]

Although Elizabeth tried hard to keep things at home happy at Christmas, especially for the children, she and George were desperately concerned about the national situation. Despite having overwhelming superiority of numbers at Fredericksburg on 13 December 1862, General Burnside only managed, in Lincoln's scathing words, to snatch defeat from the jaws of victory. Union losses totalled 12,653, and Confederate casualties 5,377. Elizabeth wrote:

> Was there ever anything so dreadful as the way in which our army has just been driven back [at Fredericksburg]? But if we had had a brilliant victory perhaps the people would have clamoured against the emancipation project, and anything is better than the perpetuation of slavery.[9]

Eventually the tide turned for the North in July 1863 with the Union's victory at Gettysburg[10] and the fall of Vicksburg. But heavy Union losses continued and led to Lincoln having to draft men into the army. This unpopular measure aroused much opposition, especially because rich men could buy their way out of military service. There was also a proportion of people in the North who deeply resented Lincoln's Emancipation Proclamation. Opposition to the Draft and Emancipation boiled over during 1863. Riots broke out in New York City on 13 July and raged for four days. Buildings were burned (including an orphanage), stores were looted, soldiers were beaten, and a total of 119 people killed. Elizabeth and the children were safely out of the way in Rockaway, Long Island, but it was fearful to hear of the violence raging within the city where they had so many friends.

Elizabeth and the children spent some of the summer of 1863 in Rockaway (as usual, George worked on in New York, while the family sought relief from the heat of the city in the country). These letters, written to Elizabeth Smith, describe their stay.

July 24, 1863. We were glad to hear that you were safely settled at Prout's Neck, far from riots, if not from rumours thereof. We have as convenient and roomy and closetty [sic] a cottage as possible. We are within three minutes or so of the beach, and go back and forth, bathe, dig sand, and stare at the ocean according to our various ages and tastes. I really do not know how else we spend our time. I sew a little, and am going to sew more when my machine comes; read a little, doze a little, and eat a good deal. The butcher calls every morning, and so does the baker with excellent bread; twice a week clams call at thirty cents the hundred; we get milk, butter, and eggs without much trouble; and ice and various vegetables without any, as Mrs Bull sends them to us every day, with sprinklings of fruit, pitchers of cream, herring and whatever is going. We either sit on the beach looking and listening to the waves, every evening, or we run in to Mrs Bull's; or gather about our parlour-table reading. By ten we are all off to bed. George does nothing but race back and forth to New York on Seminary business; he has gone now. I went with him the other day. The city looks pinched and woebegone. We were caught in that tornado and nearly pulled to pieces.

July 27, 1863. You will be sorry to hear that our last summer's siege with dysentery bids fair to be repeated. Yesterday, when the disease declared itself, I must own that for a few hours I felt about heart-broken. My own strength is next to nothing, and how to face such a calamity I knew not. Ah, how much easier it is to pray daily, *Oh, Jesus Christus, wachs in mir!* [O Jesus Christ, dwell Thou in me!][11] than to consent to, yea rejoice in, the terms of the grant! Well, George went for the doctor. His quarters at this season are right opposite; he is a

German and brother of the author Auerbach. We brought G.'s cot into our room and George and I took care of him till three o'clock, when for the first time since we had children, I gave out and left the poor man to get along as nurse as he best could. I can tell you it comes hard on one's pride to resign one's office to a half-sick husband. I think I have let the boys play too hard in the sun. I long to have you see this pretty cottage and this beach.[12]

On 19 November 1863, at a memorial service for those who had fallen at Gettysburg, President Lincoln gave a brief but unforgettable address which captured his vision for the struggle. 'Four score and seven years ago our fathers brought forth, on this continent, a new nation, conceived in liberty and dedicated to the proposition that all men are created equal . . .' He urged the Union to keep fighting, to honour the memory of those who had fallen, and so that this 'government of the people, by the people, for the people shall not perish from the earth'. This memorable speech was tremendously effective. It led to a muting of anti-war sentiment, and a fresh kindling of patriotism.

Having lost his wife, Elizabeth's brother-in-law Albert Hopkins was soon to lose his only child as well. Eddy was killed on 11 May 1864. He was leading a cavalry charge at Ashland, in the Battle of the Wilderness. His father was devastated but was reconciled to his death because he believed so strongly in the cause for which Eddy had fought. Hearing the accounts of the Christian testimony Eddy had maintained among his fellow soldiers also comforted him. Albert wanted to bury his son with dignity and so travelled to Ashland in June 1865 in an attempt to recover the body. This proved impossible because Eddy had been buried in a shallow grave with many other soldiers and his remains could not be identified. A friend of the family noted how the failure of this sad trip aged Albert by about ten years. However, he did not give up hope. In December 1865 he travelled south again, this time accompanied by experts, and managed to identify his son's body. He brought Eddy back to Williamstown to be interred with due honours next to Louisa's grave.

One event in the summer of 1864 brought real joy to the Prentiss family; Annie made a public profession of her faith and was received into the membership of the church. 'I can hardly realize my felicity', wrote Elizabeth. 'I seem to myself to have a new child.' The morning service when Annie and other young people were received into the church provided welcome relief during this trying year.

In July 1864 Elizabeth wrote from her holiday home to Elizabeth Smith, describing how she had adorned her portrait of General Grant with great festoons of evergreens, 'conjuring him all the while not to disappoint our hopes but to take Richmond'. In fact, he would not take the Confederate capital until April 1865. But once Richmond fell, the war was effectively over. General Lee formally surrendered his troops to General Grant on Sunday 9 April 1865 at Appomattox Court House, Virginia.

For many soldiers, horribly maimed by their injuries, the homecoming was a bitter experience as fiancées or girl-friends turned away from their deformities in disgust. Elizabeth was appalled at this heartless attitude. Her novel *Aunt Jane's Hero* picks up this theme. The heroine, Maggie, is sickened when one of her girl-friends breaks off her engagement to a soldier because of his wounds. 'To think what sacrifices he had made for his country, and . . . how thankful a girl with the very least speck of heart would have been to spend her whole life in making him forget what he had lost.'[13] Maggie herself ends up marrying Horace, an amputee.

In the aftermath of the war both sides suffered a measure of shock as they came to terms with the sheer enormity of their losses. This was the bloodiest and most terrible war in America's history.[14] Hopes of the reconstruction of the Union and reconciliation between the opposing sides, as well as hopes of peaceful emancipation of the slaves, were pinned on President Abraham Lincoln. But on 14 April 1865 Lincoln was assassinated in a theatre in Washington. The news broke on the nation like a thunderbolt.

George's diary entry for Saturday 15 April read simply: 'Dreadful day. Mr Lincoln murdered!! Oh, horror of horrors!' That morning Elizabeth was ill in bed. George judged that she should not be given the news in her fragile condition. But when one of the children went into her room and burst into tears, the news could not be kept from her any longer. Like tens of thousands of others, she saw the President as a father figure and felt a personal devastation on hearing news of his violent death. This national tragedy totally overshadowed what should have been the celebration of her twentieth wedding anniversary on 16 April. George had the difficult task of leading his congregation in worship at a time when all were preoccupied with the affairs of state: 'A sad and trying Easter Sunday', he wrote. 'Everybody overwhelmed with grief and amazement.'

In the midst of all the drama surrounding Lincoln's assassination, a happier event marked the end of April 1865. Mercer Street Church's newly planted daughter congregation – 'The Church of the Covenant' – dedicated its magnificent new building on Park Avenue on the last Sunday in April. The Prentisses moved closer to the new church building, taking up residence in 70 East Twenty-Seventh Street. 'The rent is *enormous*', wrote Elizabeth, '$1,000 having been just added to an already high price. Our people have taken that matter in hand, and no burden of it will come on us.'[15] The family remained in this rented home until the beautiful new parsonage on Thirty-Fifth Street was ready.

The dedication of the new building marked a significant turning point in the lives of the Prentisses. George and Elizabeth would minister there for the next eight years, until 1873. These were happy years. Annie, now a church member, became fully involved in the various activities of the young people. The younger children too had plenty of companions.

By the spring of 1865, Elizabeth's insomnia and neuralgia (pain along the course of a nerve) had worsened. Her friends were seriously worried and persuaded her to visit Dr Schieferdecker, a well-known hydropathist. At first she was a little reluctant about this course of action. When she wrote to inform her cousin that she was considering the 'water cure' (details of which are given below), she asked that the possibility should not be mentioned to anyone else. However, not long after beginning the treatment in the spring of 1865, her energy levels increased, she slept better, and soon she became convinced of its benefits.

Now aged forty-six, Elizabeth had suffered various bouts of ill health since she was a young child. The commonly prescribed treatments for all manner of ailments often only made matters worse and caused lasting harm. Throughout her life, she complained of intermittent neuralgia. She also experienced a severe shaking of her hands, which at times left her unable to write. In the first half of the nineteenth century doctors routinely prescribed 'blue pills' to children for various sicknesses. These were made of calomel (mercurous chloride, an inorganic compound of mercury). Symptoms of mercury poisoning include headaches (neuralgia), shaking hands, lethargy and mental confusion. Elizabeth suffered from all of these symptoms, as did her sister Louisa. It is possible, perhaps even likely, that these resulted from the medicine they had been given since childhood.

While conventional medicine often made matters far worse for everyone, women's health problems in particular were exacerbated by pregnancy and childbirth. Poor standards of hygiene led to a high incidence of post-natal infection. Even if a new mother escaped infection, several weeks of bed rest were routinely prescribed after confinement. This left her feeling enfeebled and unfit.

By the mid-nineteenth century, various 'alternative' practitioners had launched an understandably violent attack on conventional medicine. Among the various alternative therapies, the 'water cure' became one of the most popular.[16] It began with the teaching of Vincent Priessnitz (1799–1851), who founded a spa in Austrian Silesia. He taught that we are naturally healthy, but become diseased when foreign matter enters the body. Traditional 'cures' such as bleeding, purging, and drugs, he argued, made things worse. He advocated giving up conventional medicine, rich food and alcohol. Patients were told to live on simple food (coarse bread and milk), drink twelve glasses of water a day, and exercise rigorously in fresh air (his motto was, *People need mountains*'). He offered a range of water therapies at his spa: head baths, wet stomach packs, cold showers (internal douches, as well as external icy showers from a height of twenty feet), and wrapping patients in cold wet sheets.

Not surprisingly, the therapy delivered impressive results. Patients whose systems were poisoned with mercury drugs, or with too much alcohol, whose bodies were overloaded with the rich food commonplace at the time, or who were weakened through lack of fresh air and exercise, benefited from being taken off the traditional medicines and adopting the healthy lifestyle.

The ironic thing is that, then as now, a simple idea was packaged expensively and became a lifestyle directed at the middle and upper classes. Many today will pay large amounts for 'detox' treatments of various kinds (the equivalent of the 'water cure'), when drinking water is free.[17]

The best known water-cure establishment in America was the Brattleboro Water-Cure spa, opened in 1845 on the banks of the Connecticut River. Clients enjoyed the pleasant buildings situated in the glorious rural setting. Various forms of entertainment were provided: billiard rooms, bowling alleys, parlours for music and conversation, and an attractive open piazza. Separate-sex dormitory accommodation meant that women could relive their boarding-school experiences and intimate friendships flourished. Women far outnumbered men at the Water Cure, as many doctors found that prescribing time away from domestic duties and children was the only hope weary mothers had of regaining their strength.

Elizabeth followed the new regime for some years, aiming to walk at least four or five miles a day. In 1869 she wrote: 'No tongue can tell how much I am indebted to him [Dr Schieferdecker]. I am like a ship that after poking along twenty years with a heavy load on board, at last gets into port, unloads, and springs to the surface.' Her insomnia was never fully cured, but it was considerably relieved.

George's mother, having lived to the grand age of eighty-three, passed away in August 1865. She had remained mentally alert to the end and had been a loving grandmother to the children.

Elizabeth and the family spent the summer of 1865 at Newburgh, as did a number of close friends. Evenings were spent together enjoying the 'home made' entertainment of games and readings. Elizabeth was always brilliant at word games and puzzles, and enthusiastically participated in such social activities. She was already beginning to feel some of the positive effects of the water treatments commenced in the spring. The war was over. The church was settled in the new building. The family were settled in their new home. It seemed as if she were, at last, emerging from a long tunnel of sleeplessness, illness, and anxiety. She was ready to throw herself into her duties as a pastor's wife, and she was also eager to take up her pen once more and write.

FAMILY TREE:
Elizabeth Payson Prentiss

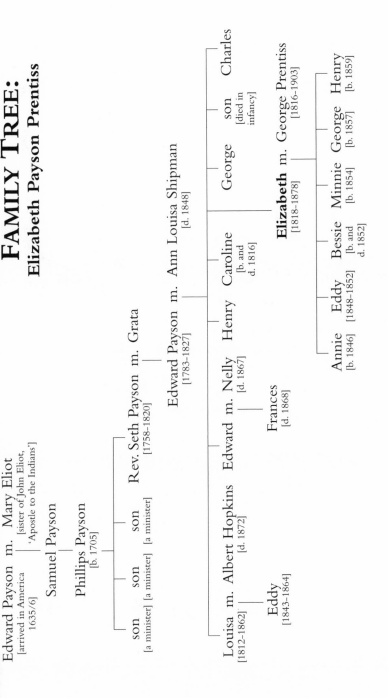

Edward Payson m. Mary Eliot
[arrived in America [sister of John Eliot,
1635/6] 'Apostle to the Indians']

Samuel Payson

Phillips Payson
[b. 1705]

Rev. Seth Payson m. Grata
[1758–1820]

son son son son
[a minister] [a minister] [a minister] [a minister]

Edward Payson m. Ann Louisa Shipman
[1783–1827] [d. 1848]

Henry Caroline George son Charles
[b. and [died in
d. 1816] infancy]

Edward m. Nelly Louisa m. Albert Hopkins Elizabeth m. George Prentiss
[d. 1867] [1812–1862] [d. 1872] [1818–1878] [1816–1903]

Frances Eddy
[d. 1868] [1843–1864]

Annie Eddy Bessie Minnie George Henry
[b. 1846] [1848–1852] [b. and [b. 1854] [b. 1857] [b. 1859]
d. 1852]

Family Tree of Elizabeth Prentiss

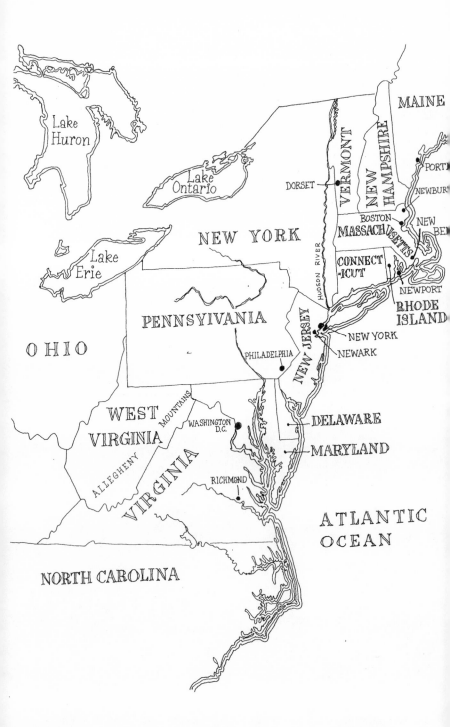

Map of places relating to Elizabeth Prentiss's life.

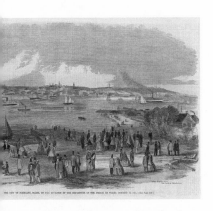

graving depicting the City of Portland,
circa 1860. Elizabeth's father Edward
as pastor of the city's Second Church and
lizabeth was born here in 1828.

Rev. Edward Payson, D.D

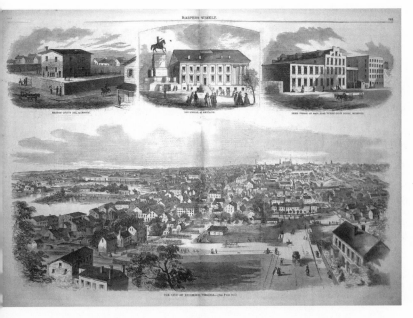

*An engraving of Richmond, Virginia before the Civil War. Elizabeth
spent two years teaching here between 1840 and 1843.*

An engraving depicting Château d'Oex, Vaud, Switzerland. The Prentiss fam
stayed in a pension within a 'typical Swiss chalet' for several months in 185

An engraving of La Maison des Bains, near Montreux on Lake Leman, whe
the Prentisses spent the winter of 1858-9.

An engraving of 'Kauinfels', the Prentiss's Dorset home. George Prentiss organised the construction of this house, which was eventually completed in 1869.

'Kauinfels' as it is today. Photo used by kind permission of Alec Marshall.

The Dorset Mountains

The Mill and Pond at Dorset

Barnum's Hippodrome was the venue for D. L. Moody's New York Mission in 1876. Vast crowds attended the evangelist's meetings. Elizabeth Prentiss was one of the many Christian volunteers who gave their assistance to the Mission.

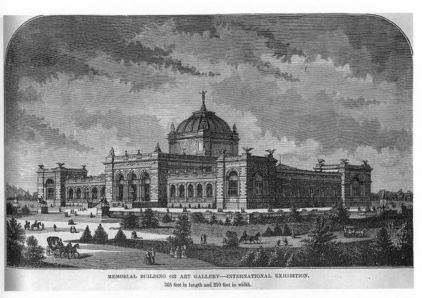

MEMORIAL BUILDING OR ART GALLERY—INTERNATIONAL EXHIBITION.
365 feet in length and 210 feet in width.

The Memorial Building or Art Gallery of the Centennial Exhibition in Philadelphia. The Prentisses spent a very enjoyable week visiting the Exhibition in May 1876.

*Elizabeth Prentiss, taken from the frontispiece of
Life and Letters of Elizabeth Prentiss, compiled
by her husband, George Prentiss (New York:
Randolph & Co., 1882)*

*Elizabeth Prentiss © Robert Nettles
2006*

9

'CHRIST IS IN MY SOUL; HE IS MINE' 1866–68

'You can't think how sweet it is to be a pastor's wife; to feel the right to sympathize with those who mourn, to fly to them at once, and join them in their prayers and tears.'

'You can hardly understand how I feel, as a pastor's wife, toward our people. Their sorrows come right home.'

ELIZABETH REGARDED HER MINISTRY TO HER FAMILY as taking precedence over any other demands upon her time, whether in the form of service in the church or opportunities for writing. Thus far, motherhood had presented her with as many sorrows as joys and had drained Elizabeth of much of her strength. But as she took stock on New Year's Day, 1866, things looked somewhat brighter. She had now been married to George for more than twenty years and they had weathered the storms of bereavement and illness together. They also shared a deep love, had an unshakable confidence in the goodness of God, and, through it all, they kept a sense of humour. Of course, Elizabeth's heart still ached for Eddy and Bessie, but she had a real sense that they had simply gone before her to heaven. Annie was now a young woman of nineteen, strong in faith and active in the church. She took care of schooling Minnie, George and Henry at home and was able, when necessary, to take full care of them, which was an enormous help to Elizabeth. Minnie had come through years of ill health and was now a lovely little girl of ten.

George (8) and Henry (6) were full of energy and life. They were happiest during the summer months when they could run wild in the country. Elizabeth hoped that now, at last, aged forty-seven, she would be well enough to play her part in church life, visiting, giving hospitality, and caring for the sick. Her years of suffering had equipped her particularly well for a ministry of comfort to the ill and bereaved.

By the beginning of 1866, George was back where he loved to be, caught up in the busy affairs of church and seminary life. He was taking a leading role in his ministers' fraternal, where discussion of a reunion with Old-School Presbyterians was top of the agenda for the next few years. The war had led to a breaking down of the barriers between Old-School and New-School Presbyterians. The national crisis had put some of the past disputes into perspective. When ministers had worked together, some of the Old-School Presbyterians realized that the New-School men were not as unorthodox as they had often suspected.[1] When, in 1862, the Old School General Assembly voted to recognize New-School ministers, reunion became a possibility. Henry Boynton Smith became one of the leading proponents of reunion and George fully supported the move towards it.

Church life kept both husband and wife busy. A typical day included receiving several visitors and making several calls. There were nearly always sick people to visit, funerals to attend, or grieving relatives to comfort. The church included many very wealthy people, including several millionaires, and the Prentisses would be expected to attend grand dinner parties. Constant emotional energy was needed. One night they would dress up to eat the successive courses of a stately banquet, not returning home until about midnight. The very next morning they would often be called on to visit a poor grieving family. One day they would attend a hugely expensive wedding and the next they would be at a funeral.

Elizabeth and George remained level-headed amidst the extremes of wealth and poverty they encountered every day. The spiritual and emotional needs of the people were the same whatever their background. 'We are in the midst of a perfect world of show and glitter', wrote Elizabeth. 'But how many empty hearts drive up and down in this gay procession of wealth and fashion.'

When visiting, George and Elizabeth were often plied with over abundant hospitality, which had to be received graciously. For example, one morning George had to take a funeral at 10 am, having been out at a large dinner party until midnight the preceding day. When the funeral was over, he and Elizabeth had to make a call. Their hostess told them she 'never' let people go away without lunch, and made them sit down to 'buns, three kinds of cake, doughnuts, cheese, lemonade, apples, oranges, pineapples, a soup tureen of strawberries, a quart of cream, two custard puddings, one hot and one cold, home-made wine, cold corned beef, cold roast beef, and for aught I know forty other things. We came away awfully tired.'

George and Elizabeth sought to bring comfort to the families of church members who had passed away. One young member of Elizabeth's prayer group was in church on a Sunday afternoon for the baptism of her baby. The next morning, at half-past two, she died. On another occasion, Elizabeth went to visit the beautiful new home of one young couple and admired the lovely decorations and furnishings. The next week the young wife was dead. She hesitated about whether to 'intrude' on the grief of the bereaved husband and mother, but decided to visit nonetheless. The warmth of her reception made her resolve never to hesitate to visit a bereaved family again. The husband, she told her daughter, 'said I seemed like a mother to him, which made me feel very old on the one hand and very happy on the other. If I were you, I wouldn't marry anybody but a minister; it gives one such lots [sic] of people to love and care for.' George and Elizabeth were particularly shaken by this woman's death. However, Elizabeth had cause to write wryly to her daughter: 'Mrs – told a friend of ours that Mr and Mrs Prentiss really enjoyed Mrs C–s death, and they seemed destitute of natural affection; and as for Mrs P[rentiss] it was plain she had never suffered in any way. Considering the tears we both shed over Mrs C, and some other items in our past history, we must set Mrs – down as wiser than the ancients.' Elizabeth knew what it was to be misunderstood. It was hurtful, but not worth getting overly upset about.

She counted it one of the joys of being a pastor's wife that she had the opportunity of being the first on the scene of human tragedy or need, bringing the consolation of Christ. She wrote to a friend: 'You can't think how sweet it is to be a pastor's wife; to feel the right to sympathize with those who mourn, to fly to them at once, and join them in their prayers and tears. It would be pleasant to spend one's whole time among sufferers, and to keep testifying to them what Christ can and will become to them if only they will let Him . . .' She wrote to her eldest daughter Annie: 'Papa says our house ought to have a sign put out, "Souls cured here"; because so many people come to tell their troubles. People used to do just so to my mother, and I suppose always do to parson's wives if they'll let 'em.'

Elizabeth didn't find talking about spiritual things easy, and confessed later in life that she never asked to pray with people; but despite that, her ministry of visitation was evidently helpful. Her visits to the sick were not just characterized by spiritual conversation: she managed to bring humour and life to any sick room. In a letter to Annie she explains how she called on one very ill woman 'and kept her and the girls screaming with laughter for an hour, which did me a lot of good and I hope did not hurt them'. She also looked for practical ways to relieve people's suffering. Since childhood she had been accustomed to taking gifts of food to sick people, and regularly made up batches of wine jelly and other goodies. But she looked for other ways to keep invalids occupied, often making gifts of writing materials, books, illustrated verses to hang beside the bed, and so forth. When she began visits to a hospital for people with spinal injuries, she hunted down supplies of blotting paper so that they could write more easily while lying on their backs.

There were plenty of lighter moments in the midst of their pastoral labours. In such a large and busy church Elizabeth sometimes found it difficult to remember everyone. 'Coming out [of church] I said to a gentleman who approached me, "How is little baby?" "Which little baby?" "Why, the youngest." "Oh, we haven't any baby." And lo! I had mistaken my man! Imagine how *he* felt and how *I* felt!'

In the summer of 1866, Annie took the three younger children down to Williamstown to stay with their uncle Albert, while Elizabeth and George had a holiday on their own. When they rejoined the family in Williamstown, they received news of a great fire, which had devastated large areas of Portland on 4 July. The home where Elizabeth was brought up had been destroyed, as had the Second Parish Church. Her father's unpublished manuscripts had gone up in flames. Many of Elizabeth's friends and relatives had lost their homes together with all their possessions. Elizabeth was distressed for all the suffering that had been caused and also upset that she had not taken the initiative sooner to retrieve her father's papers and distribute them among the family, as she had long intended to do.

From Williamstown, the family moved on to take summer lodgings in Dorset – a quiet country community about twenty-five miles south of Rutland. To the east lay the exquisite Green Mountains; to the west a succession of maple-covered hills. Here Jonathan and Anna Stearns joined them, with their family. It was a special time. Anna was ill, and this was their last holiday together.

It was the first time they had visited Dorset, and they loved it. 'We are enchanted with Dorset', wrote Elizabeth. 'We are so near the woods and mountains that we go every day and spend hours wandering among them . . . we are mean enough to want to keep it as quiet and secluded as it is now . . . a very few fashionably dressed people would just spoil it for us.' The family liked the area so much that George and Elizabeth decided to build a holiday home there. Planning and supervising its construction would absorb their attention through the next two summers.

In 1867 the large new parsonage on Thirty-Fifth Street was ready for occupation. Members of the Church of the Covenant had been more than generous in building and furnishing it. A special house-warming was held, attended by crowds of friends. The evening ended with everyone singing 'All hail the power of Jesus' name', before Dr Skinner and Henry Smith read the Scriptures and prayed. The six years spent in this home were very happy. It was ideal for offering hospitality, not only to the members of the church, but also to George's fellow ministers and seminary colleagues.

The family returned to Dorset for the summer of 1867, and for much of the time were absorbed with plans for their new home. Despite this and having to nurse Annie through a serious illness, Elizabeth managed to write no less than four children's books.

She had published six children's books between 1853 and 1856. Then, for a decade, ill health had conspired against further creativity. But those ten years had not been wasted. When she took up her pen again, she brought to her work a deeper understanding of human suffering and a stronger appreciation of the sufficiency of God's grace. She would continue to write for children, but was now ready to write for adults too.

Elizabeth's short novel, *The Little Preacher,* was published during this year, and it formed something of a bridge between her children's books and her longer adult novels which were to appear later. The setting was the Black Forest in Germany. She used the Astor Library in New York to research the customs and lifestyles of that area. Her fluency in the German language enabled Elizabeth to use primary source material for the book. It contained a vivid portrayal of a culture that was a world away from nineteenth-century New York City. One cultured German reader spoke of it as 'a perfect picture . . . a miracle of genius to be able thus to portray the life of a foreign people'.[2] It was enjoyed by older children and young people, as well as adults, and has been reprinted recently.

Elizabeth uses a simple story to carry the themes of the influence of praying women, the dangers of idolizing wealth, and the importance of understanding the individual needs of children. One of the subtexts in the work is a commentary on the appalling position of peasant women and children in the rural Europe of the time, offering an implicit contrast with middle-class American values. Max 'loves' his wife, but regards her very much as part of the labour force. Only when he sees her desperate grief at their son's disappearance does he perform his first ever act of gallantry, lifting a heavy burden from her head on to his own. After his conversion he begins to treat his family with tenderness and consideration. He is then able to contemplate spending some of his hard-earned money on further education for his sons. Up to that point such 'extravagance' was inconceivable to him. The message is plain: Christianity leads to a softening of chauvinistic attitudes towards women and a willingness to educate children, rather than regarding them simply as a source of unpaid labour.

Elizabeth drew upon some of her own observations of peasant life in Switzerland. During her stay in that country she was shocked to see the extreme poverty and the harsh way of life of so many, and commented: 'I grow more and more patriotic every day, and am astonished at what I see and hear of life in Europe.'[3]

The Little Preacher is easy to read and an appealing book. While didactic in character and purpose, it works well as a story. Its good reception encouraged Elizabeth to begin work on a full-length novel, which she initially simply called her 'Katy story'.

In October 1867, Nelly Payson (wife of Elizabeth's brother Edward), died after a lingering and painful illness. Nelly's friendship with Elizabeth dated back to their childhood in Portland. One of Elizabeth's last letters to Nelly illustrates her complete confidence that, for the Christian, 'to die is gain':

> I have been so engrossed with sympathy for Edward and your children, that I have just begun to realize that you are about entering on a state of felicity which ought, for the time, to make me forget them. Dear Nelly, I congratulate you with all my heart. Do not let the thought of what those who love you must suffer in your loss, diminish the peace and joy with which God now calls you to think only of Himself and the home He has prepared for you. Try to leave them to his kind, tender care. He loves them better than you do; He can be to them more than you have been; He will hear your prayers . . . All your tears will soon be wiped away; you will see the King in His beauty; you will see Christ your Redeemer and realize all He is and all He has done for you; and how many saints whom you have loved on earth will be standing ready to seize you by the hand and welcome you among them! As I think of these things my soul is in haste to be gone; I long to be set free from sin and self

... Dear Nelly, I pray that you will have as easy a journey homeward as your Father's love and compassion can
make for you; but these sufferings at the worst cannot
last long, and they are only the messengers sent to loosen
your last tie on earth, and conduct you to the sweetest
rest ... [4]

After Nelly died, her bereaved husband and their youngest
son Francis spent much of the winter in New York with the
Prentiss family. Elizabeth was devoted to her nephew, who
was himself very ill. She wrote much of her novel *Stepping
Heavenward* with him in her arms. 'My hands and my heart
are full', she said of this period in her life. Shortly afterwards
the little lad died too.

The family was to experience yet more grief when, during
the spring of 1868, it became clear that George's sister Anna
was terminally ill. She came to stay with Elizabeth and
George for some weeks, before returning to her home on the
Hudson River.

Even while looking after her family and their many visitors, Elizabeth grabbed a few moments to write. She was often
asked for short pieces for inclusion in magazines, and when
the National Temperance Society requested a story for their
magazine, she was happy to oblige. *The Old Brown Pitcher* (or
Little Rosa, the title of some later editions) was published in
1868. Like *The Story Lizzie Told, Gentleman Jim*, and *The Little
Preacher,* it is set in a poor working-class community (the
majority of her works depicted a middle-class environment).
The story depicts the appalling effects of alcohol abuse: little
Rosa's mother dies; her father is a violent alcoholic who beats
his children, forces them on to the streets to beg, and takes
away their warm clothes so that they will look even more
pitiful. When Rosa takes care of a dying neighbour, she is left
the old woman's life savings (hidden in the old brown
pitcher). After killing someone, the father is imprisoned, the

children are taken into the care of a kind woman, and the money used to set this woman up in business.

Back in Dorset for the summer, the family stayed in rented rooms, and spent much of the time working on the construction of their new home. This kept all of them busy, as Elizabeth explained to her friend Mary Shipman: 'Our [new] house is very pretty, and I suppose it will be done by next year . . . George is so happy in it, and in working in his woods, that I am perfectly delighted that he has undertaken this project. It may add years to his life.' She wrote to Elizabeth Smith in the same vein:

> . . . we are having the nicest time in the world. I have not seen George so like himself for many years; he lives out of doors, pulls down fences, picks up brushwood, and keeps happy and well. I feel it a real mercy that his thoughts are agreeably occupied this summer, as otherwise he would be incessantly worried about Anna. We work together a good deal; this morning I spoiled a new hatchet in cutting down milkweed where our kitchen garden is to be and we are literally raising our Ebenezer, which we mean to conceal with vines in due season. George is just as proud of our woods as if he created every tree himself. The minute breakfast is over the boys dart to the house like arrows from the bow, and there they are till dinner, after which there is another dart and it is as much as I can do to get them to bed; I wonder they don't sleep down there on the shavings. The fact is the whole Prentiss family has got house on the brain.[5]

It was during this summer of 1868 that Elizabeth first met Eliza Warner, a young writer, who was to become one of her closest friends. Eliza had come to Dorset for a holiday with her best friend, Hannah Lyman. George had known Hannah many years previously, when they were both teaching in

Gorham. Since then, Hannah had become well-known as the Principal of the prestigious Vassar Female Seminary. Eliza and Hannah took their meals at the same boarding house as the Prentisses, though their lodging rooms were elsewhere. Both were poorly: Hannah with a hacking cough, Eliza looking so frail that her friends wondered whether she would live through the next winter. She was unable to go out walking or driving, and every conversation exhausted her. Elizabeth was not sure what to make of her at first, writing at the end of July: 'Miss W. is in delicate health, takes no tea or coffee, and is full of humour. We have run at and run upon each other, each trying to take the measure of the other, and shall probably end in becoming very good friends.' The three ladies came to have riotous times together, with 'a vast amount of laughter'.

Having begun work on her 'Katy book' (which was to become *Stepping Heavenward*), Elizabeth became thoroughly discouraged and resolved to abandon it. George persuaded her to read the manuscript to Hannah and Eliza to see what they thought of it. They promised her their honest opinion. 'The next morning she came to our room with a little green box in her hand, saying with her merry laugh "Now you've got to do penance for your sins, you two wicked women!"', and proceeded to read the incomplete manuscript to them. Hannah and Eliza encouraged her to persevere with it, adding their own comments and suggestions. By the end of the stay at Dorset, Elizabeth had completed the manuscript and gone right through it, incorporating Hannah and Eliza's suggestions and corrections. She also found her title, as Eliza recalled: 'One morning she came to the breakfast table with her face all lighted up. "I've got a name for my book," she exclaimed; "it came to me while I was lying awake last night. You know Wordsworth's *Stepping Westward?* I am going to call it *Stepping Heavenward* – don't you like it? I do.'

Following Eliza's departure from Dorset, she and Elizabeth began what was to become a regular correspondence. Elizabeth was a prolific writer of letters. She and her female friends shared all the homely details of their lives. 'Everybody spoke for pies this year', she told Eliza, '(you know we almost never make such sinful things) and they all said ice-cream wouldn't do at all, so yesterday I made fourteen of these enormities, and mean to stuff them (the children, not the pies!) that they won't want any more for a year.' They would routinely enclose cuttings of plants, seeds, samples of material, and recipes. 'I opened your letter in the street, and was at once confronted by a worldly piece of silk!', wrote Elizabeth playfully to Eliza. 'How can you? Why don't you follow my example and dress in sackcloth and ashes? I think, however, if you will be worldly, you have done it very prettily, and on the whole don't know that it is any wickeder than I have been in translating a "dramatic poem" in five acts from the German.'[6] Or, to another friend: 'I enclose an extract I made for you from a work on the baptism of the Holy Spirit. This was all the paper I had at hand at the moment. The recipe for curry I have copied into my recipe book ... A queer mixture of the spiritual and the practical, but no stranger than life's mixtures always are.'

Before she married, Elizabeth corresponded at length with her cousin George. But afterwards, she corresponded almost exclusively with other women. Right through life, female friends were very important to her, especially those with whom she could communicate on a spiritual level, and fellow writers with whom she could discuss her manuscripts. Elizabeth found that letter writing was a great catharsis: 'As to letters, I scratch them off at odd moments, when too tired to do anything else. What a resource they are! They do instead of crying for me. And how many I get each week that are loving and pleasant!'

Sometimes letter-writing spilled over into pieces for publication, as when Elizabeth incorporated some of the accounts of the Civil War received in friends' letters into her short stories. But whether writing general letters, pastoral letters, poems, hymns, short stories, children's books, or novels, Elizabeth was never happier than when she had a pen in her hand. She confessed that without access to pen and paper, she was 'like a kitten without a tail to play with, a mariner without a compass, a bird without wings . . . '

Back in the City for the autumn, Elizabeth again threw herself into the round of visiting, hospitality, and meetings. She also reorganized her 'sewing circle', and visited Anna in Newark as regularly as possible. Visits were paid to her old friend Mrs Leonard, when her husband Charles died suddenly at their summer house in Rochester. After attending the funeral, Elizabeth wrote to her widowed friend:

This morning I am restless and cannot set about anything. It distresses me to think how little human friendship can do for such a sorrow as yours. When a sufferer is on the rack he cares little for what is *said* to him, though he may feel grateful for sympathy. I found it hard to tear myself away from you so soon, but all I could do for you there I could do all along the way home and since I have got here: love you, be sorry for you, and constantly pray for you. I am sure that He who has so sorely afflicted you accepts the patience with which you bear the rod, and that when this first terrible amazement and bewilderment are over, and you can enter into communion and fellowship with Him, you will find a joy in Him that, hard as it is to the flesh to say so, transcends all the sweetest and best joys of human life. You will have nothing to do but to fly to Him. I have seen the time when I could hide myself in Him as a little child hides itself in its mother's arms, and so have thousands of aching hearts. In all our afflictions He is afflicted. But I must not weary you with words. May God bless and keep you, and fully reveal himself unto you![7]

Elizabeth celebrated her fiftieth birthday on 26 October 1868: 'I begin to feel antiquated, dilapidated, and antediluvian, etc., etc.' In fact, she was in better form than she had been for many years. She had just completed what was to be her most successful book, *Stepping Heavenward,* and George noted that something of the 'cheery, loving spirit of the book seemed still to possess her whole being'. He said that from day to day his wife lived out the experience of her heroine Katy: 'Yes, I love everybody! That crowning joy has come to me at last. Christ is in my soul; He is mine.'

10

STEPPING HEAVENWARD
1869

'To love Christ, and to know that I love Him − this is all!'

THE YEAR 1869 saw the publication of Elizabeth's most successful novel: *Stepping Heavenward*. The *Chicago Advance* began publishing it in instalments from February. The book in its entirety was published in October. It attracted many favourable reviews, letters, and comments. But for Elizabeth the excitement of success was overshadowed by sadness over the illness and loss of family and friends.

By December 1868, her sister-in-law Anna Stearns was very near death. Elizabeth thought of her continually and wrote many letters and notes, such as the following, written on Anna's silver wedding anniversary:

My dearest Anna,
I have thought of you all day with tenderest sympathy, knowing how you had looked forward to it, and what a contrast it offers to your bridal day twenty-five years ago. But I hope it has not been wholly sad. You have a rich past that cannot be taken from you, and a richer future lies before you. For I can see, though through your tears you cannot, that the Son of God walks with you in this furnace of affliction, and that He is so sanctifying it to your soul, that ages hence you will look on this day as better, sweeter than the day of your espousals. It is hard now to suffer, but after all, the *light* affliction is nothing,

and the *weight* of glory is everything . . . Don't you see that in afflicting you He means to prove to you that He loves you, and that you love Him? Don't you remember that it is His son – not His enemy – that He scourgeth?

The greatest saint on earth has got to reach heaven on the same terms as the greatest sinner; unworthy, unfit, good-for-nothing, but saved through grace. Do cheer and comfort yourself with these thoughts, my dearest Anna, and your sick-room will be the happiest room in the house, as I constantly pray it may be!

Your ever affectionate Lizzy.[1]

Elizabeth made the journey to be with Anna until she died on 2 January 1869. This was a traumatic time for both Elizabeth and George. They missed Anna greatly and felt deeply for her grieving husband and children.

Then, in February 1869, one of George's nieces, Eva, aged just seventeen, was brought to their home to spend her last days on earth. Elizabeth had already regularly visited Eva's sister Jennie, who died from terrible convulsions. She felt that she could not possibly cope with another terminal case. But, she wrote, 'At last they came with the sick girl, and one look at the poor, half-fainting child, and her mother's "Nobody in the world but you would have let us come", made them welcome; and I have rejoiced ever since that God let them come.' Eva was with them for about a fortnight. She was able to come down to meals for a week, but then her breathing got so bad that six people were needed in shifts to support and help her. She died after four traumatic days and nights; her suffering had been agonizing to witness.

No sooner had the funeral taken place than another item of shocking news rocked the Prentisses: Henry Boynton Smith had fallen critically ill. He was one of George's oldest and closest friends, and a valued colleague at Union Theological Seminary. The two families spent a lot of time together. Henry and George regularly attended ministers' meetings on Saturday afternoons, while their wives enjoyed getting together for a chat and gave tea parties for the children. Just as George had left for Europe to recover his health back in 1858, so Henry and his wife Elizabeth were encouraged to do the same now. For the spring and summer of 1869 Elizabeth and George took care of the two young Smith children. For Henry Smith, the timing of the illness was especially poignant; the New-School General Assembly, which met in New York that June, resolved to pursue union with the Old-School Presbyterians. Smith had been one of the key players in the movement towards reunion.

Stepping Heavenward began to attract considerable notice as soon as the first instalments appeared. This was due mainly to the transparent sincerity of the author. Elizabeth later said: 'Every word of the book was a prayer, and seemed to come of itself.' The universal response of women readers was, 'It seems to be myself that I am reading about.' The central message of the novel was that God uses suffering to bring his people closer to himself, and that true happiness is found in submitting one's will to his. Having been through the 'school' of suffering herself, in terms both of losing her children and of severe bouts of ill-health, Elizabeth wanted to bring the comfort she herself had experienced to others, especially other women.

Marriage and childbearing were the inevitable destiny for the great majority of women in the nineteenth century. All too often the joy of having children was overshadowed. Many infants were still-born, childhood disease carried off others, and many mothers suffered the breakdown of their health, if not by the trauma of a mismanaged labour, then by the constant anxiety of nursing critically ill children.[2] Elizabeth had experienced this herself and, as a minister's wife, she was constantly called on to visit women whose babies had died, or whose children were critically ill. The number of funerals of infants she attended probably ran into hundreds.

As far as she could see, the biological destiny of the women around her was not going to change: they would go on having babies, they would continue to suffer ill health, and many of their babies would die. But she felt compelled to share the life-changing comfort which her experiential knowledge of Christ had brought to her. She regarded her own ill health as the means God used to make her depend more on him. The death of her children drew her heart closer to heaven; she believed her children to be with Christ in heaven and she longed to be there with them. Merely stating these truths to sick and grieving mothers seemed too crass, so she decided to write a novel that would entertain, grip, and move the reader, while at the same time communicating spiritual lessons which were vitally important.

At first reading *Stepping Heavenward* appears to be a fairly stereotypical Victorian novel. A plethora of female novelists churned out cartloads of romantic novels during those years, many of which were directed to teaching the virtues of true womanhood. We find in *Stepping Heavenward* the typical themes of an impetuous young woman falling in love with a good-looking but undesirable young man; the break-up of the romance; a premature proposal from the suitable but 'unromantic' hero which is, of course refused; the realization of the heroine that she really is in love with him; her jealousy when a misunderstanding leads her to think that he is attached to another; and finally, the resolution of the misunderstandings. Another typical feature is the rather unlikely 'coincidence', such as when Katy visits a dying woman and later finds that she is in fact the beneficiary of her will.

The story is written in the form of a journal. This begins when Katy is sixteen. Self-willed and impetuous, she cannot see any appeal in the godliness displayed by her mother. Gradually she realizes that real happiness is only found in knowing God. Marriage and motherhood pose real challenges: she struggles with exhaustion, irritability, sleeplessness, and the feeling that she is failing as a mother and a wife. There is the strain of difficult in-laws living with the family, and the trauma of bereavement, poverty and ill health. In the midst of constant family demands she has to fight to maintain any form of devotional life, and worries that she is failing spiritually. Despite all this, the truth is that she is 'stepping heavenward'. Much of the rich tapestry of Elizabeth's own experience is reflected in the book and it clearly proved to be a real source of encouragement to many.

Perhaps the commonest complaint of a young Christian mother is, 'I'm just too busy to pray!' Katy is no exception. But she learns:

> I have made prayer too much of a luxury, and have often inwardly chafed and fretted when the care of my children at times made it utterly impossible to leave them for private devotion – when they have been sick, for instance, or in other similar emergencies. I reasoned this way: 'Here is a special demand on my patience, and I am naturally impatient. I must have time to go away and entreat the Lord to equip me for this conflict.' But I see now that the simple act of cheerful acceptance of the duty imposed and the solace and support withdrawn would have united me more fully to Christ than the highest enjoyment of His presence in prayer could.[3]

The novel thus urged women to view every act of obedience, however humble, as an act of worship. This gave significance to all aspects of everyday life. Women with a sense of purpose and dignity were less likely to succumb to depression and all the associated physical problems.

The book is also realistic about the tensions found in many marriages. As a harassed mother, Katy often feels her husband is neglecting her and the children, and focusing too much on his work.[4] The prescribed antidote is for both husband and wife to become more Christlike and more willing to sacrifice their own interests. Certainly, it often seems at first sight as if the wife must make the greater sacrifices. At one point, Katy asks angrily: 'I should like to know if there is any reason on earth why a woman should learn self-forgetfulness which does not also apply to a man?' True Christian progress is regarded as the suppression of such rebellious feelings. But *Stepping Heavenward* is also an appeal directed at husbands, urging them to understand their wives and treat them in a more sensitive and unselfish way.

Elizabeth empathized with wives for whom another pregnancy was a burden rather than a delight. When Katy finds she is expecting a fifth baby, she writes in her journal:

I can see in my wisdom forty reasons for having four children and no more. The comfort of sleeping in peace, of having a little time to read, and to keep on with my music, strength with which to look after Ernest's poor people when they are sick; and, to tell the truth, to be bright and fresh and lovable to him – all these little joys have been growing precious to me, and now I must give them up. I want to do it cheerfully and without a frown. But I find I love to have my own way, and that at the very moment I was asking God to appoint my work for me, I was secretly marking it out for myself. It is mortifying to find my will less in harmony with His than I thought it was, and that I want to prescribe to Him how I shall spend the time, and the health and the strength which are His, not mine. But I will not rest until this struggle is over; till I can say with a smile, 'Not my will! But Thine!'[5]

'Not my will! But Thine!' This is really the motif which runs through the whole novel. There are allusions throughout to the teachings of François Fénelon (1616–1715), author of *Letters of Spiritual Counsel*, and Thomas à Kempis (1380–1471), author of *The Imitation of Christ*. Both writers place great emphasis on submission to God. Katy learns submission most particularly in being willing to 'give her children back to God'.

It is in the smaller details of life that Katy actually finds patient submission hardest.

> What grieves me is that I am constantly forgetting to recognize God's hand in the little everyday trials of life, and instead of receiving them as from Him, find fault with the instruments by which He sends them. I can give up my child, my only brother, my darling mother without a word; but to receive every tiresome visitor as sent directly and expressly to weary me by the Master Himself . . . all this I have not fully learned.[6]

At the close of the novel (the implication is that Katy is about to die), Katy looks back on a quickening in her spiritual life which took place seven years previously:

> If I die it will be to leave a wearied and worn body, and a sinful soul, to go joyfully to be with Christ, to be weary and sin no more. If I live, I shall find much blessed work to do for Him. So living or dying, I will be the Lord's. But I wish, oh, how earnestly, that whether I go or stay, I could inspire some lives with the joy that is now mine. For many years I have been rich in faith; rich in an unfaltering confidence that I was beloved of my God and Saviour. But something was missing; I was always groping for a mysterious grace the lack of which made me often sorrowful in the very midst of my most sacred

joy, imperfect when I longed most for perfection. It was that personal love of Christ of which my precious mother so often spoke to me, which she often urged me to seek upon my knees. If I had known then, as I know now, what this priceless treasure could be to a sinful human soul, I would have sold all that I had to buy the field in which it lay hidden. But not till I was shut up to prayer and the study of God's word by the loss of earthly joys, sickness destroying the flavour of them all, did I begin to penetrate the mystery that is learned under the cross. And wondrous as it is, how simple is that mystery! To love Christ, and to know that I love Him – this is all![7]

What was Elizabeth saying here? Recently it has been argued that this episode in the novel demonstrates at least an equivocation about the validity of the 'perfection' that the 'higher life' movement advocated at this time.[8] Elizabeth had rejected the claims of the 'perfectionists' earlier in her life. She had always believed that the battle against sin was a life-long reality and that there was no easy way to ascend to a higher plain of Christian experience.[9] She could sometimes write about the 'perfectionists' humorously: 'We called on her this afternoon. What a jolly old lady she is! Of course, anybody could believe in perfection who was as fat and well as she!' Or, 'It seems almost incredible that a wholly sanctified character could publish such a book, made up as it is of the author's own letters and journal and most sacred joys and sorrows; but perhaps when I get sanctified I shall go to printing mine – it really seems to be a way they have.'

Later in life, during the years 1871–2, Elizabeth began to reconsider the issue, and for a while became genuinely perplexed by perfectionist teaching.[10] But her settled conviction for *most* of her life (including the period when *Stepping Heavenward* was written) was that perfectionist claims were spurious and dangerous. Having said that, she was willing to concede that she respected their thirst for holiness, and that one could learn from some, if not all, of their teaching. She agreed with them that *sometimes* Christians do experience a 'sudden and extraordinary experience' which transforms their lives, but she argued that this is normally preceded by much prayer and obedience.[11]

Although *Stepping Heavenward* does not endorse the teaching of the perfectionists, it was published at a time when there was widespread interest in the quest for holiness. The transparent sincerity of Katy's pursuit of godliness thus struck a chord with Christians from different traditions, and this partly accounts for the success of the book.

Soon after serialization began, both publisher and author received numerous letters of praise. Letters also came in from wives who admitted that all too often their husbands behaved in the ways described so vividly in the novel. In a letter written in May to Elizabeth Smith, Elizabeth said: 'You who helped me fashion her [Katy], would be interested in the letters I get from wives, showing that the want of demonstration [of affection] in men is a wide-spread evil, under which women do groan, being burdened. *Entre nous*, Mrs Dr − is one, and I got a letter today from Michigan to the same effect.'

It was not only women who read the serialized novel; men took an interest in it too. In May 1869 about two hundred and fifty New-School ministers converged on Mercer Street Church for the General Assembly. Many of them found their way to the manse for a meal. Elizabeth plied them with coffee and her speciality, strawberry shortbread, and they plied her with compliments about her novel.

When the complete novel was published in October, Elizabeth was apprehensive about how it would be received and whether it would sell. Her anxieties were unfounded. It was an immediate success. By the time of her death, 60,000 copies had sold in America, and many more in Britain, Canada, Australia, and in Europe (in translated editions).

The other significant event of 1869 for Elizabeth was the completion of the house in Dorset. By the summer of that year it was ready for them to move in. For the first time they were able to have a house of their own for the summer rather than rented accommodation. Elizabeth and the children spent about four months of this and each subsequent year there. George reckoned that this added several years to her life, and that it thus 'paid for itself many times over'. Although George remained in New York working for much of the summer, he went over to the house at Dorset for short stays, and generally managed to take some weeks of rest with the family.

The Prentisses chose to name their house *Kauinfels*. Elizabeth explained: '*Kauinfels* is a word we invented, after spending no little time, by referring to a spot in a favourite brook as 'the place where the old cow fell in'; it looked so German and pleased us so much that we concluded to give our place that name. We are fond of odd names.'

The summers spent in the country continued to be a real joy. Elizabeth loved exploring the area with the children, and always came home with armfuls of flowers, branches, stones and mosses to decorate the house and garden. The Dorset house allowed her the scope to indulge her own creativity: she eagerly pounced on any cheques that came in through her writing and gleefully 'changed them into chairs and tables and beds and blankets.'

Her husband also enjoyed the new family home: 'Mr P. is unusually well. His house is the apple of his eye and he is renewing his youth. Thus far the project has done him the world of good',[12] wrote Elizabeth to a friend. He even made her a bookcase – 'the first thing "he" ever made for "her" in his life', she observed.

Elizabeth loved beautiful things; with great artistry and skill she collected flowers and pressed them to make pictures and dried-flower arrangements. The house was soon full of her artistic efforts. She also took painting lessons and it was not long before she proudly began to hang her pictures on the walls.

Women often asked her whether it was 'worldly' to devote time to making a home beautiful. Elizabeth was convinced that God made a beautiful world, and that he gifts people with creativity. He is glorified when human beings make their surroundings clean, attractive and pleasant. She would sometimes joke about her mosses and branches being her 'idols', but in reality she believed that enjoying the creation and giving God thanks for it brings glory to the Creator. She did not believe that costly extravagance was justified: the many decorations found in her house actually cost very little in monetary terms, though a good deal in time and effort. Moreover, much of her time was employed in making gifts for friends and relatives, and she believed that giving others pleasure in this way also brought glory to God. She loved to welcome visitors to Dorset and her hospitality was legendary. One grateful guest wrote:

What a delightful home she made! The 'good cheer' she furnished for the minds, hearts, and bodies of her guests was something remarkable. I shall never forget my visits; I was in a state of high entertainment from beginning to end. What entertaining stories she told! What practical wisdom she gave out in the most natural and incidental way! And what housekeeping! Common articles of food seemed to possess new virtues and new zest. I always went away full of the marvels of the visit, as well as loaded down with many little tokens of her kindness and thoughtfulness.[13]

The four months each summer were not a complete 'holiday' from church work. The family increasingly became involved with the church community at Dorset. Elizabeth taught at the mission school, taking a class of lads in their early teens. 'I find my mission-school a good deal of a tax on time and strength, and it is discouraging business too.' She also taught an adult Bible reading class. 'My Bible reading is thronged, and I can't but hope the Holy Spirit is helping my infirmities and blessing souls. My heart yearns after these women, many of whom have faces stamped with care. There is a class here that nobody has any idea how to get at.'

While enjoying the glorious scenery and fresh mountain air at Dorset, Elizabeth never could quite forget the discomfort suffered by those left behind in town. 'I have thought painfully of the narrow quarters and the hot nights endured by so many in New York, during this unusually warm weather – especially of Mrs G. with her three restless children in bed with her and her poor lonely heart.' She often invited people to stay whom she thought would benefit from the holiday, covering travelling expenses as and when necessary. But Dorset was the place where Elizabeth made her own family her priority.

Back in New York, George and Elizabeth were both often summoned out to all manner of pastoral crises. She often felt pulled in all directions at once. But in Dorset for several months each summer, she was 'there' for the children in a special way, and she could relax and unwind in a way not possible in the city.

Once the Prentisses began spending summers at Dorset, Elizabeth found that she had ideal time for writing. Away from the pastoral demands of the church in New York, free from the business of running a large house, refreshed by the country quiet, inspired by the wonderful scenery, she was better able to focus. It was not that she stopped writing during the winter months. But the summer months gave her the head start she needed for her various writing projects.

In October 1869 Annie left for an extended trip to Europe, accompanying the Smith children who were travelling to join their parents. The intention was that she should then stay on for a year. George and Elizabeth's eldest child had been responsible for schooling her younger siblings; now they would be going to day school. Elizabeth found it no easier to let her children 'leave the nest' than any other mother. Thus far she had been able to shield and shelter them, now they needed to be more independent. 'Her [Annie's] going plunges us into a new world of care and anxiety and tribulation; we have thrust our children out into, or onto, the great ocean, and are ready to sink with them.' In fact all three did well at their different schools.

Saying goodbye to Annie for the first time was heart-rending. The concerned mother wrote to her friend, Elizabeth Smith, urging her to keep a good eye on Annie, and lamented, 'Who is to keep me well snubbed? Who is to tell me what to wear? Who is to keep Darby and Joan from settling down into two fearful old pokes? . . . I miss you all ever so much, and George keeps up one constant howl for your husband.'

Once a week Elizabeth wrote to Annie keeping her up to date with the family comings and goings. The boys adopted a stray dog, which delighted them, though they knew their father would not be pleased. They grieved the loss of their cat when it committed suicide by knocking the ironing board over on to itself, 'H[enry] made a diagram of the position of the board that I might fully comprehend the situation, and then showed me how the corpse lay. They were not willing to part with the remains and buried them in the yard.' They missed Annie badly at Christmas, and wrote describing the stockings and presents.

A letter to her cousin, George Prentiss,[14] expressed something of Elizabeth's frame of mind at the close of 1869. It had been an exciting year. But her greatest happiness did not lie in the success of her novel, or the completion of her summer house. It lay in God: 'My heart sides with God in everything, and my conception of His character is such a beautiful one that I feel He can not err . . . The more time we spend upon our knees in real communion with God, the better we shall comprehend His wonderful nature . . . Every turn in life brings me back to this – *more prayer*.'

11

'I Have Lived, I Have Loved'
1870–73

'It is sweet to be in the sunshine of the Master's smile, but I believe our souls need winter as well as summer, night as well as day.'

THE SUCCESS OF *STEPPING HEAVENWARD* gave Elizabeth the confidence to continue writing, and her output was prolific throughout the next few years. The following year, 1870, saw the publication of two new books. *The Percys* was a treatise on child rearing in the form of a story. It deals with nurturing faith in young children and how to encourage them to maintain a Christian testimony at school (which reflected Elizabeth's own anxieties about sending her children to school for the first time). Their struggles, temptations, experiences of unkindness from other children and unfairness from teachers, are all vividly conveyed.

The Story Lizzie Told is probably her best short story. Set in the slums of London, it is a beautifully drawn portrait of a young girl coming to faith. She wrote it swiftly, while at Dorset, probably in a single sitting. The characters were so real to her that while reading the story aloud to her husband, she couldn't stop crying. "'What a little fool I am!" she would say after a fresh burst of tears.'

Her husband looked back at this year as one of the high points in Elizabeth's spiritual life. A letter written to a friend in March reveals something of her experience at this time. Her younger son, ten-year-old Henry, had been seriously ill and Elizabeth had dropped all her other responsibilities in order to nurse him. When he had pulled through the worst, she wrote:

I have had some really sweet days, shut up with my dear little boy. He is better, and I am comparatively at leisure again, and so happy in meditating on the character of my Saviour, and in the sense of His nearness, that I ache, and have had to beg Him to give me no more, but to carry this joy to you and to Miss K and to two friends, who, languishing on dying beds, need it so much . . . I wish I could put into words all the blessed thoughts I had last week about God's dear will: it was a week of such sweet content with the work He gave me to do; naturally I hate nursing, and losing the air makes me feel unwell; but what can't God do with us? I love, dearly, to have a Master. I fancy that those who have strong wills, are the ones to enjoy God's sovereignty most. I wonder if you realize what a very happy creature I am and how much too good God is to me? I don't see how He can heap such mercies on a poor sinner; but that only shows how little I know Him. But then, I am learning to know Him, and shall go on doing it forever and ever; and so will you. I am not sure that it is best for us, once safe and secure on the Rock of Ages, to ask ourselves too closely what this and that experience may signify. Is it not better to be thinking of the Rock, not of the feet that stand upon it? It seems to me that we ought to be unconscious of ourselves, and that the nearer we get to Christ, the more we shall be taken up with Him. We shall be like a sick man who, after he gets well, forgets all the old symptoms he used to think so much of, and stops feeling his pulse, and just enjoys his health, only pointing out his physician to all who are diseased . . . You can't think what a sweet, peaceful winter this has been, nor how good the children are. My cup has just run over, and at times I am too happy to be comfortable, if you know what that means.[1]

Elizabeth and George celebrated their Silver Wedding anniversary on Saturday 16 April 1870. Despite Annie's absence, this was a very joyful day, celebrated with their family and a few close friends. Elizabeth wrote: 'I have a very curious feeling about life; a satisfied one, and as if it could not possibly give me much more than I now have. *"I have lived, I have loved."*'[2]

A letter to Annie, then travelling in Europe, gives a description of a typical day for Elizabeth in 1870:

Now let me give you the history of this busy day. We got up early and Miss F. called with M.'s two dresses. After prayers and breakfast I wrote to papa, went to school with H., and marketed. Came home and found a letter from Cincinnati, urging for two hymns right away for a new hymn-book. They had several of mine already. I said, 'Go to, let us make a hymn' and made and sent them. Then I wrote to Mr S. and to Mrs Charles W. Then Mrs C. came and stayed till nearly four, when she left and I went down to Twenty-second street to call on a lady at the Water Cure.[3] Then I went to see Mrs C. (the wife of the Rev. Mr C.). I think I told you she had lost her little Florence. I do not remember ever seeing a person so broken down by grief; she seemed absolutely heart-broken. I could not get away till five, and then I took two stages and got home as soon as I could, knowing the children would be famishing. So now count up my various professions, chaplain, marketer, hymnist, consoler of Mr S., Mrs W., Mrs C., and let me add, of Dr B., who came and made a long call. I am now going to lie down and read till I get rested, for my brain has been on the steady stretch for thirteen hours, one thing stepping on the heels of another.[4]

That 'busy day' (20 May 1870) was the eighteenth anniversary of Bessie's death. Elizabeth explained to George: 'She had been in heaven eighteen years; think what she has already gained by my one year of suffering! and I wanted to spend it [the day] for others, not for myself.'[5]

Another typical day was described in a letter to her friend Eliza Warner. Elizabeth was up at seven for prayers and breakfast, then walked Minnie to school, returning home for her quiet time and reading. At eleven o'clock she attended a ladies' prayer meeting, going straight afterwards to the funeral of one of their members. When she got home she found a message to say that a family were coming to stay that afternoon. Having given one of her servants the day off to visit a sick sister, Elizabeth had to 'turn chamber-maid' and clear out the guest room. When the visitors arrived, they kept her occupied until seven. She then went out to a prayer meeting. When she got home, she found a young man there to see her who had been converted through reading *Stepping Heavenward*. She just sat down to speak with him, when the family doctor arrived: he had just heard of the death of his only grandchild and wanted to talk. Elizabeth spoke to the doctor until 9.30 pm, then returned to the young man and spoke to him until 10.30 pm. The next morning, there were more visitors, Elizabeth went to a fair, visited a sick girl, had more visitors, and eventually, having had hardly time to eat that day, got to bed at eleven o'clock.

During the summer of 1870, the Presbyterian General Assembly voted that George should take up a professorship at the Seminary in far-off Chicago. This came as a thunderbolt to Elizabeth. She could only see the drawbacks: it would mean leaving all her friends in New York, George leaving pastoral ministry, her giving up the role of pastor's wife, and the family leaving behind their Dorset summer house. George felt more equivocal about it. On the one hand, he did not want to leave the church, or uproot his wife. He feared that her chronic insomnia would be worsened by the stress of the move. Nor did he want to give up the house in Dorset, believing it to be hugely beneficial to Elizabeth's health and emotional well-being. But on the other hand, he knew the pressure placed on her by the ministry. The life of a seminary professor's wife would inevitably be less burdensome than that of a pastor's wife. Much of the summer was spent wrestling through the issues. Elizabeth wrote to one friend:

> Do you know about Mr Prentiss' appointment by General Assembly to a professorship at Chicago? His going would involve not only our tearing ourselves out of the heart of our beloved church, but of my losing you and Miss K., and of our all losing this dear little home. Of course, he does not want to go, and I am shocked at the idea of him leaving the ministry; but on the other hand there is a right and a wrong to the question and we ought to do whatever God chooses. The thought of giving up this home makes me know better how to sympathize with you if you have to part with yours. I do think it is good for us to be emptied from vessel to vessel, and there is something awful in the thought of having our own way with leanness in the soul.[6]

It seems that they decided not to move to Chicago that year, but the invitation was extended again the following year, and they were once again plunged into uncertainty as to how to respond to it.

Despite these questions hanging over their future, the summer of 1870 at Dorset proved to be a wonderful time.

Elizabeth wrote to Annie most days, describing what was going on with the various members of the family.

Dorset, June 10, 1870. Here we are again in dear old Dorset. We got here about ten on Wednesday evening, expecting to find the house dark and forlorn, but Mrs F. had been down and lighted it up, and put on the dining-table bread, biscuits, butter, cakes, eggs, etc., enough to last for days. Thursday was hotter than any day we had had in New York, and not very good, therefore, for the hard work of unpacking, and the yet harder work of sowing our flower-seeds in a huge bed shaped like a palm-leaf. But, with M.'s help, it was done before one o'clock to-day – a Herculean task, as the ground had to be thoroughly dug up with a trowel; stones, sticks, and roots got out, and the earth sifted in our hands. The back of my neck and my ears are nearly blistered. M. is standing behind me now anointing me with cocoa butter. Our place looks beautifully [sic]. Some of the trees set out are twelve or fifteen feet high, and when fully leaved will make quite a show. Papa is to be here about ten days, as he greatly needs the rest; he will then go home till July 1 . . . The boys have a little black and tan dog which Culyer gave them, and M.'s bird is a fine singer. Our family circle now consists of Pa, Ma, Minnie, George, Henry, Maria [their servant], Coco (horse), Sukey (cow), Nep (dog), Cherry (bird).

Wednesday—Your letter reached us on Monday, and we all went out and sat in a row on the upper step, like birds on a telegraph wire, and papa read it aloud. I am lying by to-day – writing, reading, lounging, and enjoying the scenery. You ought to see papa eat strawberries!!! They are very plentiful on our hill. The grass on the lawn is pricking up like needles; easy to see if you kneel down and stare hard, but absolutely invisible otherwise; yet papa keeps calling me to look out of the window and admire it, and shouts to people driving by to do the same ... M[innie, then aged 15] follows me round like a little dog; if I go down cellar she goes down; if I pick a strawberry she picks one; if I stop picking she stops. She is the sweetest lamb that ever was, and I am the Mary that's got her. I don't believe anybody else in the world loves me so well, unless it possibly is papa, and he doesn't follow me down cellar, and goes off and picks strawberries all by himself, and that on Sunday, too, when I had forbidden berry-picking! We are rioting in strawberries, just as we did last summer. We live a good deal at sixes and sevens, but nobody cares. This afternoon I have been arranging a basket for the hall table, with mosses, ferns, shells and white coral; ever so pretty ...

Tuesday— We all set out to climb the mountain near Deacon Kellogg's. We snatched what we could for our dinner, and when we were ready to eat it, it proved to be eggs, bread and meat, cake, guava jelly, cider and water. We enjoyed the splendid view and the dinner, and then papa and the boys went home, and M., Nep and myself proceeded to climb higher, Nep so affectionate that he tired me out hugging me with his 'arms', as H. calls them, and nearly eating me up, while M. was shaking with laughter at his silly ways. We were gone from 10 am to nearly 6 pm, and brought home in baskets, bags, pockets and bosom, about thirty natural brackets, some very large and fearfully heavy. One was so heavy that I brought it home by kicking it down the mountain. I have just got some flower seeds for fall planting, and the children are looking them over as some would gems from the mine ...[7]

October saw the return of Annie and the Smiths from Europe; 'It is years since I got so excited and wrought up', noted Elizabeth. However, there was a deeper underlying certainty in her life through this winter: a deep assurance of the love of Christ.

In a December letter to 'a young friend' Elizabeth revealed a new appreciation of the work of the Spirit:

I have been led, during the last month or two, to a new love of the Holy Spirit, or perhaps to more conscious-ness of the silent, blessed work He is doing in and for us, and for those whose souls lie as a heavy and yet a sweet burden upon our own. And joining with you in your prayers, seeking also for myself what I sought for you, I found myself almost startled by such a response as I can not describe. It was not joy, but a deep solemnity which enfolded me as with a garment, and if I ever pass out of it, which I never want to do, I hope it will be with a heart more than ever consecrated and set apart for Christ's service. The more I reflect and the more I pray, the more life narrows down to one point – What am I being for Christ, what am I doing for Him? Why do I tell you this? Because the voice of a fellow-traveller always stimulates his brother-pilgrim; what one finds and speaks of and rejoices over, sets the other upon deter-mining to find too. God has been very good to you, as well as to me, but we ought to whisper to each other now and then, 'Go on, step faster, step surer, lay hold on the Rock of Ages with both hands.' You never need be afraid to speak such words to me. I want to be pushed on, and pulled on, and coaxed on.[8]

As Elizabeth reflected on 'What am I doing for Him?', she was always grounded in the daily reality of family and church life. 'Holiness is not a mere abstraction: it is praying and loving and being consecrate [sic], but it is also the doing [of] kind deeds, speaking friendly words, being in a crowd when we long to be alone.' Being spiritual, for her, was not some esoteric experience. It was being patient with a tired and grumpy child; serving the needs of her husband when exhausted herself; listening patiently to the complaints of a discontented church member. Her ability to convey the down-to-earth reality of holiness in a way that other women could understand helps to explain the success of her writing ministry during this period of her life.

Elizabeth firmly believed that a Christian could know 'peace' whatever the circumstances through submitting to the will of God. This was her own experience and she longed to help others come to know this peace too. Little did she know but she was about to be plunged into a 'dark night' experience in which her sense of peace would vanish. If 1870 had been a 'mountain top' year, the following two years would feel more like a journey through a deep and dark valley.

Throughout church history, many exemplary Christians have testified to passing through some kind of 'dark-night-of the-soul' experience in which they possess no conscious sense of the presence of God. This sense of desertion can serve to wean a Christian away from an excessive reliance on feeling. During 1871 and 1872 Elizabeth went through just such a period.

At the time, only George seemed to be aware of Elizabeth's inner conflict. She kept as busy as ever, with family, writing, and pastoral visitation. But as she began to emerge from this 'dark tunnel', she wrote about it to a few close friends. 'Sometimes I think that the dreadful experience I have been passing through is God's way of baptizing me; some have to be baptized with suffering', she wrote to Mrs Condict. 'Certainly He has been sitting as the Refiner, bringing down my pride . . . If it all ends in sanctification I don't care what I suffer.'

In a letter of March 1872 Elizabeth told her cousin George Prentiss that she had been 'buffeted by a messenger of Satan' for more than a year in a way she had never before known. This was giving her a new sympathy for those afflicted with doubt and despair. She refrained from speaking much about this loss of the sense of God's presence for fear of discouraging others, but believed that this 'baptism of fire' was necessary to consume remaining selfishness.[9]

Then, in May, she explained to her cousin something of the desolation caused by the loss of the felt sense of the presence of God:

> I knew, for years, the sweetest peace and rest, with periods of joy that was [sic] almost insupportable. At the same time I never thought myself sinless. I only knew that I had a perfect Saviour, and the instant I fell into inadvertent sin, I asked Him to forgive me, and He did ... But whether I was exalted by the abundance of revelations, or whatever else might be the reason, I was suddenly cast down from heaven to hell – yes, to hell; for the loss of the Presence, in which I had lived so long, is nothing less; and I have been in this valley of humiliation eighteen months, or somewhere near that, and it has been precisely like that described by Bunyan. I used to preach, in season and out of season, the doctrine that anybody could live in perfect peace; but now I have come to an *experience* wholly new, and I know other Christians in the same condition ... Now you may never need and so never have such an awful affliction, but as I have learned it through personal experience, I cannot doubt that God has permitted it for some wise, some kind reason, for which I shall bless Him in the next life, if I never know enough to do it in this. As He could not severely hurt me by taking away any beloved earthly

object, since if He were left, enough would be left to make life perfectly sweet, He has come nearer, and inflicted blows of tenfold severity. Madame Guyon[10] had nearly seven years of such desolation, and it completed the work God was resolved to do in her . . . Certainly I could not have endured, in my youth, the anguish of the last months.

May 3, 1873 – The fact that our Saviour was deserted, or thought Himself deserted, seems to me to imply that we too are liable to the same discipline. And it may be that I shall yet come to see that this period of new and most painful conflict, has been one of sharp temptation, rather than of sin. At any rate we both know and love the Lord Jesus better than any earthly friend, and He will keep us, blessed be His name! . . . [11]

The allusion to Madame Guyon is telling. During the first part of 1870, Elizabeth had spent a considerable amount of time studying the writings of this French mystic. The two central emphases in Guyon's writings are the need to accept the will of God in all the sufferings of life, and the need to die to self. These were the very themes that had become so central to Elizabeth's spiritual life. Her husband wrote: 'Madam Guyon for several years exerted a decided influence on her views of the Christian life; nor is there reason to think that this influence was not, on the whole, salutary.'[12] However, it is arguable that the introspective element of Guyon's thought can be unhealthy, if not dangerous, and it is possible that this may have exacerbated Elizabeth's difficult experience.[13]

On further reflection, her husband later came to the conclusion that part of Elizabeth's problem was due to confusion arising from her renewed study of perfectionist claims. The controversy about 'Christian perfection' resurfaced at this time with the publication of Robert Pearsall Smith's popular book, *Holiness through Faith* (Boston, 1870). Elizabeth was thrown into turmoil for a season. Were the perfectionists right? Maybe holiness is something that can be achieved 'by faith'. In August 1871 she wrote to a close friend:

> I have *Holiness through Faith;* the first time I read it at Mr R— 's request, I said I believed every word of it, but this summer, reading it in a different mood, it puzzles me. The idea is plausible; if God tells us to be holy, as He certainly does, is it not for Him to provide the way for our being so, and is it likely He needs our whole lives before He can accomplish His own design? I talked with Mr Prentiss about it, and at first he rejected the thought of holiness through faith, but last night we got upon the subject again and he was interested in some sentences I read to him and said he must examine the book.[14]

In the end, Elizabeth again found herself compelled to reject the notion of 'holiness through faith'. Her difficult experience caused her to become, if anything, clearer and stronger in her own arguments against perfectionism. In a letter to a friend in October 1871, she delivered a devastating critique of perfectionist thinking. Perfectionists, she observed, pour scorn on the vast majority of Christians as 'ordinary' and 'miserable doubters'. They deny the truth that God chastises those he loves. They say that true religion is rapture, not conflict. They claim exclusive knowledge of truth, and accuse anyone who doubts perfectionist claims of doubting God himself. Such positions angered Elizabeth. 'Imagine soldiers getting ready for warfare, being told by their commander that they had no need to drill, and had nothing to do but drink nectar!'[15]

Writing to cousin George in 1872 she said: 'I have read and re-read the books that treat on this subject, and cannot believe in that instantaneous sanctification that looks so plausible, but which thus far I have vainly sought on my knees and in my Bible.'[16] And later still, in 1877, to another friend:

I am glad you found anything to like in *Urbane* . . . My friend Miss — , reproached me for not having preached perfection in it; but I told her I could not find perfection in the Bible, had never seen it in my life, and had observed that those who claimed that they attained it, usually ended by running into spiritualism or antinomianism, and made shipwreck of their faith. One, who assured me he had not sinned for twenty-five years, talked and behaved (in the one interview I had with him) in such a manner that for days I was so staggered I could not pray . . . If this had been a common man I should not have been so upset; but he was a leader in the church and had been a great light . . . I had a perfection-ist in my house a month, during which, though she rose hours before breakfast, she never once came to prayers, thereby bidding defiance to our habits as a family. The idea appeared to be that she could not join in confession of sins. But that we may be kept from wilful sin I do not doubt.[17]

Another factor in Elizabeth's spiritual struggles during these two years may well have been due to her anxiety over the possible move to Chicago. In the early summer of 1871, the General Assembly again unanimously elected George to the professorship at Chicago. Once more George and Eliz-abeth spent the summer wrestling over the decision:

We are perplexed beyond measure what to do, the thought of losing my minister and having him turn into a professor, agonizes me; on the other hand, who knows but he needs the rest that change of labour and the five months' vacation would give him? His chief worry is the effect the attending funerals all the time has already had on my health. One day I part with and bury (in imagination!) now this friend, now that, and this mournful work does not sharpen one's appetite or invigorate one's frame. I don't know how we've stood the conflict; and it seems rather selfish to allude to my part of it; but women live more in their friendships than men do, and the thought of tearing up all our roots is more painful to me than to my husband, and he will not lose what I must lose in addition, and as I have said before, my minister, which is the hardest part of it.[18]

And yet, as always, Elizabeth found herself able to laugh about the situation. One evening in Dorset she quickly composed a humorous impromptu song about the move to Chicago, with verses for each member of the family. That about Annie went as follows:

> Next comes Miss P.; how she will make
> The hearts of all the students quake!
> She'll wind them round her fingers' ends,
> And find in them one hundred friends.
> They'll sit on benches in a row
> And watch her come, and watch her go;
> But they'll be safe, the precious rogues,
> Since she don't care for theologues.[19]

Eventually, in early September, George accepted the invitation to lecture at Chicago. He sent his resignation to the Church. On that day, Elizabeth wrote as follows:

I have had many letters to write to-day, for to-day our fate is sealed, and we are to go . . . This has not been a sorrowful day to me. I hope I am offering to a 'patient God a patient heart.' I do not want to make the worst of the sacrifice He requires, or to fancy I am only to be happy on my own conditions. He has been most of the time for years 'the spring of all my joys, the life of my delights'. Where He is, I want to be; where He bids me go, I want to go, and to go in courage and faith. Anything is better than too strong cleaving to this world. As I was situated in New York, I lacked not a single earthly blessing. I had a delightful home, freedom from care, and a circle of friends whom I loved with all my heart, and who loved me in a way to satisfy even my rapacity. Only one thing was wanting to my perfect felicity – a heart absolutely holy; and was I likely to get that when my earthly cup was so full? At any rate I am content. Now and then, as the reality of this coming separation overwhelms me, I feel a spasm of pain at my heart (I don't suppose we are expected to cease to be human beings or to lose our sensibilities), but if my Lord and Master will go with me, and keeps on making me more and more like Himself, I can be happy anywhere and under any conditions, or be made content not to be happy. All this is of little consequence in itself, but perhaps it may make me more of a blessing to others, which, next to personal holiness, is the only thing to be sought very earnestly.[20]

Elizabeth spent most of September and October reconciling herself to the prospect of the move. But on 20 October 1871, the Church of the Covenant met, and unanimously decided not to release George to the Seminary in Chicago. Earlier that month much of Chicago had been devastated in a great fire, which cut a swathe through the city, four miles long and three quarters of a mile wide. The destruction was so extensive because the buildings, bridges, streets, and sidewalks had all been made of wood. Eighteen thousand buildings were gutted and about thirty percent of the city's value was lost. Tens of thousands of people lost their homes and in the confusion many families were separated. One of Elizabeth's brothers lived in Chicago. His home was burned down, and in the chaos he and his wife lost their five-month-old baby for two days and a night. Eventually reunited with their child, they found refuge with a cousin, who ran an orphanage which was unscathed by the fire. It is unclear whether the fire was a factor in the Church's decision not to let the Prentisses go to Chicago: Elizabeth wrote of having been 'providentially burned out', but that may have been a touch of understandable hyperbole. Whatever the reasons for the change of plan, the whole family were overjoyed to be staying in New York with their church.

In 1871, *Aunt Jane's Hero*, an 'advice' manual on courtship and marriage cast in the form of a novel, was published. It has recently been reprinted. [21] It was written in the context of a society mesmerized by a bewildering new array of consumer goods. Elizabeth challenged the reticence of young people to commit to marriage and family life who could not attain to expensive homes and up-to-date furnishings. The novel, which set out to promote the dignity of hard work and the virtues of thrift and contentment, was a direct attack on materialism.

Of all Elizabeth Prentiss' works, *Aunt Jane's Hero* most clearly represents the nineteenth-century attitude towards 'true womanhood'. The heroine, Maggie, is godly, prayerful, patriotic, hardworking, thrifty, domesticated, contented, un-selfconscious, modest, and chaste, and she loves babies. When she falls in love with Horace, she conceals her feelings perfectly until she is absolutely sure of his. She never flirts. When they marry, she does not nag him about their poverty, but makes the best of their situation, working hard to make every penny count. She is content within her sphere (homemaking and good works).

The 'separate-sphere' teaching, so clearly articulated in nineteenth-century America, led to the notion that women are superior to men 'in their sphere' of the home. Increasingly, religion was seen as part of that domestic sphere, over which women were to exercise their feminine influence. It is notable in this novel that the spiritual initiative is always taken by a woman. Horace is a hero because he has been so totally influenced by Aunt Jane and Maggie (and the prayers of his late mother). His father is a feeble, passive figure. Aunt Jane is the force to be reckoned with in this book: both her prayers and her money achieve much. She constantly takes the initiative, even to advising Horace of the best way to pray aloud in church prayer meetings ('Don't use the name of God too much.').

Aunt Jane believes that it is a 'true woman'[22] who will be the making of Horace. 'True', here, of course, has a double meaning. A 'true' woman will be faithful to her husband ('true' as in steadfast). But a 'true' woman is 'genuinely feminine' (a 'real' woman).

When Horace and Maggie marry, it is Maggie who takes the initiative to begin family prayers, who points out that they also need to set time aside for individual devotions, who suggests giving hospitality to poor students, and who pushes her husband into challenging her sister about her spiritual state.

In other words, the 'true woman' may have to take the initiative spiritually, but she will manage it in such a subtle way that she herself will hardly realize what she is doing.[23] The conservative doctrine of male headship is only notionally upheld; it is really the wife who is giving spiritual leadership. Given the reality that there were many more women than men in the churches at that time, Prentiss was probably responding pastorally to the many young wives who asked her for advice: 'What should I do when my husband does not give a lead spiritually?' She urged such women to take the initiative, but in a gentle and subtle way, in the hope that their husband will be won over and become more spiritually active. [24]

This novel never achieved the popularity of *Stepping Heavenward*, perhaps because the characters are too stereotyped. Aunt Jane and Maggie are simply 'too good to be true', unlike Katy in *Stepping Heavenward* whose struggles are recorded with more realism. *Aunt Jane's Hero* worked within its context as a marriage manual, and also as an exhortation to greater godliness. It stood alongside many other nineteenth-century novels by female authors: sentimental, didactic, and with the recurring motifs of critical illness and death. Novels of this type struck a chord with contemporary readers, living as they did in an age of infectious diseases, Civil War, and low life expectancy.

In the year after the publication of *Aunt Jane's Hero*, Elizabeth had to cope with yet another family bereavement. Her brother-in-law, Albert Hopkins, died aged sixty-four in May 1872. The Professor of Mathematics, Natural Science and Astronomy at Williamstown had had a long and distinguished teaching career. He had also worked tirelessly in the cause of the gospel. During the later years of his life he devoted himself to a very deprived area of Williamstown. For Elizabeth, winding up the affairs proved to be emotionally draining. In the Hopkins' house she continually found reminders of her own mother (who had spent her last months there), her sister Louisa, and her nephew Eddy, all of whom had died earlier. Elizabeth had particularly wanted to be at the committal, which followed the church service, so that she could see the graves of her sister and nephew. However, her disappointment was great when the decision had to be taken not to allow the women to proceed to the cemetery due to torrential rain.

The next month was marked by a more joyful event. The three younger Prentiss children, Minnie (17), George (15), and Henry (13) made a public profession of faith and joined the church in June 1872. The service was very moving for all in attendance. 'It was a touching sight to our people', Elizabeth recorded.

> Mr P. looked down on his children so lovingly, and kissed them when the covenant had been read. . . . Someone said there was not a dry eye in the house. I felt not elated, not cast down, but at peace. I think it plain that Christian parents are to expect piety in their children, and expect it early.[25]

That summer, like every past summer, brought the inevitable death toll of children, carried away by infectious disease. Wherever possible, Elizabeth endeavoured to comfort the bereaved parents. The death of her own children filled her with an instinctive empathy, which greatly comforted those she visited. In a letter to a friend, written in this period, she described this ministry:

> People who set themselves up to be pastors and teachers must 'learn in suffering' what they teach in sermon and book . . . The little boy died early on the next day, and before his funeral, his poor mother, neglected by everyone else, found it some comfort to get into my arms and cry there. It made no difference that twenty years had passed since I had sorrow akin to hers; we mothers may cease to grieve, outwardly, but we never forget what has gone out of our sight, or ever grow unsympathetic because time has soothed and quieted us. But I need not say this to *you*. This was on Saturday; all day Monday I was there watching a most lovely little girl, about six years old, writhing in agony; she died early next morning. The next eldest has been in a critical state, but will

probably recover a certain degree of health, but as a
helpless cripple . . . The tax on my sympathies in the case
of these half-distracted parents has been terrible, and yet
I wouldn't accept a cold heart if I had the offer of it.[26]

Writing to another friend at this time:

Just as I was going out to church this morning Mr
Prentiss told me of the death of a charming baby boy,
one of our lambs, and I could scarcely help bursting into
tears, though I had only seen him once. You can hardly
understand how I feel, as a pastor's wife, toward our
people. Their sorrows come right home. I have a friend
also hanging in suspense over a little one who has been
injured by a fall; she is sweetly submissive, but you know
what a mother's heart is. I have yet another friend, who
has had to give up her baby. She is a young mother, and
far from her family, but says she has 'perfect peace'. So
from all sides I hear sorrowful sounds, but so much faith
and obedience mingled with the sighs, that I can only
wonder what God will do.[27]

She well remembered just how enervating and exhausting
bereavement is. 'One of the hard things about bereavement is
the physical prostration and listlessness which make it next to
impossible to pray, and quite impossible to feel the least interest in anything', she wrote. 'We must bear this as part of the
pain, believing that it will not last for ever.'[28]

Elizabeth also continued to visit the sick and dying. Her
own experience of acute sickness, and her memory of drawing close to death, prevented her from insensitive and crass
words. She had learned from bitter experience that weakness
was not a sign of spiritual laziness, and could gently reassure
sick people who reproached themselves for not being able to
pray as they wished:

I used to reproach myself for religious stupidity when not well, but see now that God is my kind Father – not my hard task master, expecting me to be full of life and zeal when physically exhausted. It takes long to learn such lessons. One has to penetrate deeply into the heart of Christ to begin to know its tenderness and sympathy and forbearance.[29]

The following year, Elizabeth suffered a different kind of 'bereavement' when her husband resigned his pastorate at the Church of the Covenant in order to take up a full time position at Union Theological Seminary, New York. This brought an end to her role as pastor's wife. No more would she and George feel that they were right at the heart of the life of their church fellowship. After their removal from the large manse Elizabeth found herself with a lot more time. This allowed her to continue with her prayer circle and Bible study group, and of course, to continue writing (books and letters). Each summer in Dorset she took a leading role in a ladies' Bible study group which met regularly, and continued writing and painting, all the while developing real skill with water colours and oils.

While in Dorset for the summer of 1873, Elizabeth fell critically ill. All the children were called to her bedside, where she gave them her last words of counsel and kissed each of them good-bye. Mercifully for George she recovered. 'You don't get away this time', he said, half playfully, half exultingly. However, it was obvious to all that she was eager to depart and be with Christ. Writing later, George noted:

Her feeling about dying seemed to me to be almost unique. In all my pastoral experience, at least, I do not recall another case quite like it. Her faith in a better world, that is a heavenly, was quite as strong as her faith in God and in Christ; she regarded it as the true home of the soul, and the tendency of a good deal of modern culture to put *this* world in its place as man's highest sphere and end, struck her as a mockery of the holiest instincts at once of humanity and religion ... She viewed it [death] as an invitation from the King of Glory to come and be with Him. During the more than three-and-thirty years of our married life I doubt if there was ever a time when the summons would have found her unwilling to go; rarely, if ever, a time when she would not have welcomed it with great joy. On putting to her the question, 'Would you be ready to go now?' she would answer 'Why, yes' in a tone of calm assurance ... And during all her later years her answer to such a question would imply a sort of astonishment, that anyone could ask it ... not merely was there an absence of all apparent dread of death, but an exulting joy in the thought of it.[30]

This was the second time that Elizabeth had rallied from what seemed to be certain death. On both occasions she was ready to meet it, believing that a Christian should always be ready to 'go home' when called. Yet she also believed that a Christian should be ready to go on living in this present world, in spite of severe suffering, giving testimony to 'God's strength in weakness'.

Her unexpected recovery naturally brought great joy to all the family. Elizabeth herself was grateful for the extended opportunity to serve family and church, but for the remainder of her life she was aware of living just one day at a time – as if each day was to be her last.

12

'YEARNING FOR HOME'
1873–78

'She was an exile yearning for her home, "stepping heavenward",
and knowing better than the rest of us what it meant.'

'To love Christ more – this is the deepest need,
the constant cry of my soul.'

ON THEIR RETURN to New York City in September 1873, Elizabeth started the process of making their new house on Sixty-First Street into a family home. This was a time for major adjustments; not only in terms of the move into a new house, but the changing of roles. She was no longer the pastor's wife, at the heart of church life, with a demanding ministry of visitation and counselling. However, the adjustments involved were not so great as those connected with their proposed move to Chicago: Elizabeth was able to maintain her friendships, and the Prentisses kept their Dorset home.

The first project was the compilation of a book of religious verse, published in 1873 under the title *Golden Hours: Hymns and Songs of the Christian Life*. This was followed by a full-length book (*Urbane and His Friends*, 1874), the publication of her translation of a long German poem (*Griselda*, 1876), a novel for adults (*The Home at Greylock*, 1876), a serial story (*Pemaquid*, 1877) and a short story (*Gentleman Jim*, 1878).

ELIZABETH PRENTISS

GOLDEN HOURS
Elizabeth remained a deeply reserved person, and found it
hard to speak of her feelings or of the things that mattered
most to her. It was easier to express herself in writing. She
often put down her feelings in verse, creating a kind of spiritual journal, for her own benefit. From the time of the death
of her two children in 1852, her poems became a means of
emotional catharsis; they were not originally intended for
publication. Indeed, only her husband and two or three close
friends even knew she had composed them. In 1870, writing
to one such friend, she said: 'Most of my verses are too much
my personal experience to be put in print now. After I am
dead I hope they may serve as language for some other
hearts.'[1]

In 1873, however, she was persuaded to let her publisher,
Mr Randolph, look at her poems. He was adamant that they
should be published, and sure that they would prove to be an
encouragement to many. A collection of verses soon appeared
under the title *Religious Poems.* The title was later changed to
Golden Hours: Hymns and Songs of the Christian Life.[2] Elizabeth
was hesitant about 'baring her heart' to the world, and anticipated a poor reception for the anthology. The pieces had not
been written for literary appreciation, but as a simple expression of her own faith. She wrote to a friend:

> I am glad you find anything to like in my poor little
> book. I hear very little about it, but its publication has
> brought a blessing to my own soul, which shows that I
> did right in thus making known my testimony for
> Christ. My will in the matter was quite overturned.[3]

The book received a mixed reception. Some critics and
reviewers found it too morbid, with the emphasis on suffering too intense. But many readers, who had been through
similar experiences to Elizabeth, found it a great comfort. For

example, a Swiss woman wrote from Geneva: 'What a precious, precious book! And what mercy in God to enable us to understand, and say "Amen" from the heart to every line! It was He who caused you to send me a book I so much needed; and I thank Him as much as I do you.'

Most of the verses are in the form of personal prayers, many of which are addressed to Christ. Response to suffering is the major theme; but contained in the book are also prayers of thanksgiving and consecration. Some verses deal directly with the death of a child. Elizabeth did not set out to write a book of doctrine, so it is perhaps unfair to point out that only one or two of the verses are clearly Trinitarian.[4] About a quarter are addressed to God (not expressly the Father); the rest are addressed to Christ. Perhaps this is merely an indication that nineteenth-evangelicalism was becoming less robust in its theology. The emphasis in the New Testament is that Christ came into the world as the Mediator to bring all who believe in him to the Father. He taught his disciples to pray 'Our Father'.

The hymns and poems emphasize Christ as the believer's loving friend, against whose breast the suffering Christian may lean for comfort. Consider these examples:

> Go and tell Jesus; never yet,
> Did He a breaking heart forget;
> Press closely to His bleeding side,
> There, there thou shalt be satisfied.[5]

> Jesus, I turn to Thee! oh, let me hide
> Within Thy breast,
> Refuge and shelter, peace and grace provide,
> And needed rest.[6]

> What can earth give
> That will untarnished live?

Hast thou found any rest
Save on Christ's breast?[7]

A missing perspective is that of Christ as King of kings and
Lord of lords, reigning until his enemies are made his foot-
stool. He is a warrior as well as a friend, the victor over all
evil.

Perhaps this is indicative of the purpose for which the
verses were written: personal encouragement. However, individual reassurance in time of suffering ought also to be drawn
from the 'big picture', that Christ came to destroy the works
of the evil one, and that his kingdom is spreading all over the
world. It is this bigger picture which is lacking in Elizabeth's
poems.

URBANE AND HIS FRIENDS

Elizabeth's next book, *Urbane and His Friends* (published in
1874; recently reprinted)[8], was of a very different stamp: a
doctrinal work in the form of a series of dialogues. We have
seen that by this time she had decisively rejected the ideas of
the perfectionists. But that did not mean that she minimized
the need for holiness. Much of this book focuses on the
theme of greater holiness of life and its practical outworking
in the lives of real people. Several of the characters suffer great
trials. Pastor Urbane's ministry helps them to see that their
exercise of patience in these trials is an essential preparation
for heaven.

Elizabeth's forte was story telling, not theological discussion. At several points in this work she seems to put Christians
into two categories: ordinary Christians who have merely
accepted Christ as a Saviour from judgment, and those
Christians who have progressed to sanctification.[9] 'You have
accepted Christ as your Saviour from eternal death, but not
as your Saviour from present sin.'[10] The latter she describes as
those who have been 'baptized in the Holy Spirit'[11] (whereas

the New Testament teaches that all true believers have been baptized in the Spirit, see *Rom.* 6:3; *1 Cor.* 12:13).

Many Christians struggle through life without a clear sense of victory over sin and self. When Urbane is asked how such a Christian is to move beyond this sad condition, he answers: 'By receiving Christ, by faith into his soul. The union is mystical and indescribable . . . Just in proportion as Christ lives in the soul, self goes out, and with it, sin.'[12] Yes, 'Christ lives in every renewed soul, but . . . more completely in some souls than others.'[13] Again, Elizabeth's words are confusing, since the New Testament teaches that every true believer is united with Christ (*Rom.* 6:5). It may be true to say that Elizabeth's reading of Madame Guyon and the mystics influenced the writing of this book, perhaps more than any other.

Nevertheless, *Urbane and His Friends* clearly communicates Elizabeth's passion for holiness of life. Through the lives of its characters she extols the joy of fellowship with God in prayer, union with Christ, and the indwelling of the Holy Spirit.

In the year *Urbane* was published, Elizabeth was confronted by the possibility of widowhood. George fell suddenly and dangerously ill in 1874, and had to undergo immediate surgery. His survival was due in part to Elizabeth's quick thinking, as she described in a letter to her New Bedford friend Mrs Leonard on 21 May:

On Monday evening of last week Mr Prentiss delivered his inaugural address in a very animated manner, but on the way home told me he was in pain. I treated him for colic, which he supposed it to be, but he had a restless, suffering night, and in the morning called my attention to a swelling near the groin. I saw the whole story at a glance and leaped out of bed in an agony of terror. *How* I knew it to be a case *strangulated hernia* of a most alarming character I do not know, but believe I was taught of God. Ignorance on my part, and consequent delay, would have been fatal. I succeeded in getting a doctor in eight or ten minutes, but he said it was not a medical case, but a surgical one and I finally got Drs Buck and Post, and the operation was successfully performed [at home]. But Dr Buck did not conceal from me that the danger was not over, and it was not till Friday, that he gave us assurance of safety. Meanwhile Mr Prentiss has suffered great discomfort from various causes, and had one day of terrible pain, so that Dr Buck called in Dr Post again, and we were much distressed. But they say he is doing as well now as can be expected, and I am to be entrusted to dress the wound myself tomorrow. Most of the nursing has been done by M[innie], though we have all had our hands full. We have had crowds coming to ask about him. I tried to issue bulletins, but people *would* come in. If this thing had occurred in Dorset he must have inevitably died. It all came upon me so suddenly that it was a great shock. It was not till yesterday that Mr Prentiss began to ask questions about what has passed. Of course we have watchers at night, and shall have to do so for some time to come.

The reason that M[innie]. has been head nurse is that she is not nervous; worry does not excite her as it does Annie and myself, and she can drop to sleep at any spare moment, whereas the more tired we are, the more we can't sleep. I get up every morning feeling as if body and soul could drop to pieces, but brighten up after my breakfast. I am saving my strength against the time, sure to come, when apprehensions about their father being over, the children will be less assiduous nurses.[14]

Although George recovered, Elizabeth took months to get over the shock. That summer in Dorset he still struggled with 'nervousness and troubled sleep' owing to the inability to take exercise. When one lady wrote to Elizabeth, inquiring whether the illness of her husband had been a time of 'great religious enjoyment', Elizabeth humorously said of her, 'Of course *she* never had a husband! Peaceable fruits are not to be expected till "afterward".' Thankfully, though, the children were all happy and well. Elizabeth told a friend that Minnie was 'the sunshine of the house, authority as to time, assistant-surgeon, assistant-gardener, assistant-laugher'.[15]

The following summer, 1875, Minnie was taken sick with typhoid fever. She hung between life and death for some weeks. Her parents took care of her in their Dorset home with the help of a professional nurse. Elizabeth grabbed a few moments on 3 September to write to her Mrs Condict:

My dear M. lies here with typhoid fever, and my heart and soul and body are in less than a fortnight of it pretty well used up, and my husband is in almost as bad a case with double anxiety, he and A. expecting every hour to see me break down. It has been an awful pull for us all, for not one of us has an atom of health to spare . . . Dr Buck has sent us an excellent English nurse; she came yesterday and insisted on sitting up with M. all night and we all *dropped* into our beds like so many shot birds. I heard her go down for ice three times, so I knew my precious lamb was not neglected, and slept in peace. We are encompassed with mercies; the physician who drives over from Manchester is as skilful as he is conscientious; this house is admirably adapted to sickness, the stairway only nine feet high, plenty of water, and my room, which I have given her, admits of her lying in a draught as the doctor wishes her to do. While the nurse is sleeping, as she is now, A. and I take turns sitting out on the piazza, where there is a delicious breeze almost always blowing.

The ladies here are disappointed that I can no longer hold the Bible-readings, but it is not so much matter that I am put off work if you are put on it; the field is one, and the Master knows whom to use and when and where . . . I won't plague you with any more of this, nor must I forget how often I have said, 'Thy will be done.' You need not doubt that God's will looks so much better to us than our own that nothing would tempt us to decide our child's future.[16]

Elizabeth's older son George left for Princeton with the outcome of his sister's health still uncertain. Elizabeth wrote to him after his arrival at college:

September 19, 1875. On Friday . . . her pulse was 120 and her temperature 105 – bad, bad, bad. She is very, very weak. We have sent away Pharaoh and the kitten; Pha. *would* bark, and Kit *would* come in and stare at her, and both made her cry. The doctor has the house kept still as the grave; he even brought over his slippers lest his step should disturb her.

September 21 1875. It cuts me to the heart, my precious boy, that your college life begins under such a shadow. But I hope you know where to go in both loneliness and trouble. You may get a telegram before this reaches you; if you do not you had better pack your valise and have it ready for you to come at a minute's warning. The doctor gives us hardly a hope that M. will live; she may drop away at any moment. While she does live you are better off at Princeton; but when she is gone we shall all want to be together. We shall have her buried here in Dorset; otherwise I never should want to come here again. A. said this was her day to write you, but she had no heart to do it. The only thing I can do while M. is asleep, is to write letters about her. Good-night, dear boy.

September 22 1875. The doctor was here from eight to nine last night and said she would suffer little more and sleep her life away. *She* says she is nicely and the nurse says so. Your father and I have had a good cry this morning, which has done us no little service. Dear boy, this is a bad letter for you, but I have done the best I can.[17]

To everyone's amazement and joy Minnie pulled through. They brought her back to New York on 27 October 1875, by which time she had lost 36 pounds in weight. In the event, she made a remarkably rapid recovery, even to the extent of being able to take over some of Elizabeth's domestic responsibilities. Minnie loved practical activities, and insisted on going over the laundry of the whole family each week, picking out anything that needed mending or darning, and setting to work. Elizabeth wrote that she was 'one of the sunniest things in the house', and daily gave thanks that she was still with them.

George's departure for college had been a huge wrench for his mother. Now that Minnie was getting better, Elizabeth was able to spend time fitting out George's college room. Every homecoming was a cause for celebration. Like many mothers she was 'dancing mad' with her son when he didn't write home, but when she went into his room and saw the many and various 'ingenious devices' (he was a natural engineer), she confessed that her heart was filled with 'unholy pride'.[18]

Through all these years Elizabeth continued to offer hospitality in her new home. She also managed to keep her sense of humour. A dinner party for their new minister and his wife turned out to be a catalogue of disasters. Elizabeth described the evening, to the great amusement of her daughters who were visiting Portland at the time:

I undertook to get up a nice dinner for Dr and Mrs V[incent] about which I must now tell you. First I was to have raw oysters on the shell. *Blunder 1st*, small tea plates laid for them. Ordered off, and big ones laid. *Blunder 2nd*, five oysters to be laid on each plate, instead of which five were placed on platters at each end, making ten in all for the whole party! Ordered a change to the original order. Result, a terrific sound in the parlour of rushing feet and bombardment of oyster shells. Dinner was announced. *Blunder 3rd* from Dr P. [George] who asked helplessly where he should place Mrs V. *Blunder 4th* by Mrs P. [Elizabeth], who remarked that she had got fifty pieces of shell in her mouth. *Blunder 5th* by Dr P. who failed to perceive that the boiled chickens were garnished with a stunning wine-jelly and regarding it as gizzards, presented it only to the boys! *Blunder 6th*. Cranberry jelly ordered. Cranberry as a dark, inky fluid instead, gazed upon suspiciously by the guests and tasted sparingly by the family. And now prepare for *blunder no. 7*, bearing in mind that it is the third course! Four prairie hens instead of two! The effect on the Rev. Mrs E. Prentiss was a resort to her handkerchief and suppression of tears on finding none in her pocket. *Blunder 8th*. Iauch's biscuit glacé stuffed with hideous orange peel. *Delight 1st*, delicious dessert of farina smothered in custard and dear to the heart of Dr V. *Blunder 9th*. No hot milk for the coffee, delay in scalding it, and at last serving it in cracked pitcher. *Blunder 10th*. Bananas, grapes, apples and oranges forgotten at the right moment and passed after the coffee and of course declined. But hearing that Miss H.V. was fond of bananas, I seized the fruit basket and poured its contents into one napkin, and a lot of chocolate-cake into another, and sent them to the young princesses in the parsonage, who are, no doubt, dying of indigestion this morning.[19]

During December 1875 Elizabeth began a series of addresses to young women at the Collegiate Reformed Church. The youngsters loved her visits because she was able to open up biblical truth in a clear and compelling way. She also continued her ladies' prayer circle, and led a weekly Bible reading for between eight and fifteen women. One regular attendée appreciated Elizabeth's 'keen intellect, her warm heart, the rich stores of her experience, and her "sanctified common sense"'. Always allowing sufficient time for questions and discussion, Elizabeth made her own contributions with enthusiasm and energy, 'her eyes sparkling and her whole manner intensely earnest'. Elizabeth confessed that 'Since I began to *study* the Bible, it often seems like a new book.'

Elizabeth was one of several hundred Christian workers who took part in the massive crusade at the New York Hippodrome during the winter of 1875–6. D. L. Moody, the popular evangelist, preached to vast crowds. The hall, which could accommodate 7,000 people, was packed to capacity for the afternoon and evening meetings, prompting Moody to urge the Christians present to move into the alternative hall in order to make their seats available for non-Christians. Elizabeth wrote to a friend on 22 February 1876:

> You ask if I have been to hear Moody; yes I have and am deeply interested in him and his work. Yesterday afternoon they had a meeting for Christian workers, in which his sound common-sense created great merriment. Some objected to this, but I liked it because it was so genuine, and, to my mind, not un-Christlike. So many fancy religion and a long face synonymous. How stupid it is! I wonder they don't object to the sun for shining.[20]

She helped with the inquirers at some of the meetings, taking one convert under her wing, and inviting him to accompany the Prentiss family on their next summer trip to Dorset:

> One of the last things I did before leaving home was to decide to bring here one of the Hippodrome converts, about whom I presume I wrote you. We knew next to nothing about him, and I could ill afford to support him; but I was his only earthly friend. He had no home, no work, and I felt I ought to look after him. We gave him a little room in the old mill, and he is perfectly happy; calls his room his castle, does not feel the heat, takes care of my garden, enjoys haying, has put everything in order, is as strong as a horse, and a comfort to us all; being willing to turn his hand to anything.[21]

After the busy winter, George and Elizabeth received an invitation to visit friends in Philadelphia. The visit was timed by their friends to coincide with the Centennial Exhibition. Initially not especially enthusiastic ('If I go to the Centennial it will be to please some of the family, not myself'), Elizabeth was to be enthralled by the sheer scale of the grounds and the variety of the exhibits. The Exhibition was held to celebrate the one hundredth anniversary of the Declaration of Independence. Philadelphia was the obvious choice of site: the city where independence had been proclaimed and the Constitution written. It is estimated that nearly ten million people attended the Exhibition between May and November 1876 (at this time the population of the United States was around forty million). Nothing on this scale had been seen before: there were 236 acres of exhibits and exhibition grounds. 'The extent of this exhibition is simply beyond description', wrote Elizabeth. 'The only way to get any conception of it is to make a railroad circuit around the grounds.' Visitors could hire a wheelchair for $4.50: 'I only took a chair twice', wrote Elizabeth.

She and the girls loved the national exhibits which offered an insight into life in different cultures, while the boys enjoyed the machinery (the machinery hall displayed thirteen acres of new devices, and was dominated by the huge Corliss Steam Engine). A week proved insufficient to appreciate the wide variety of exhibits: the Prentisses were 'bewildered and amazed at the host of things we saw, and the host we didn't see'. Elizabeth's conclusion was that 'everyone should go who can afford it'.

THE HOME AT GREYLOCK

The Home at Greylock (published in 1876, but recently reprinted)[22] was the third in the trilogy of novels directed at young women. *Stepping Heavenward* (1869) focused on how to become a godly woman; *Aunt Jane's Hero* (1871) was an advice book on marriage; *The Home at Greylock* was a parenting manual. Elizabeth was fifty-eight when she wrote it, and she explained her purpose in a letter to a young friend:

> Your little boy must take a world of time, and open a new world of thought and feeling. But don't spoil him; the best child can be made hateful by mismanagement. I am trying to write a book for mothers and find it a discouraging work, because I find, on scrutiny, such awfully radical defects among them. And yet such a book would have helped me in my youthful days.[23]

Her aim was to provide a book that she herself would have appreciated having as a young mother. It was written in the form of a novel, simply because, in her opinion, that was the best way to get people to read it.[24]

Living out Christianity is the key to good parenting and child-rearing, according to Elizabeth. Parents need to acknowledge that the task of raising children is beyond their own ability to perform and that they stand in need of divine help. They are advised to engage in continued and detailed prayer about every aspect of family life.[25] Emphasis is placed on the importance of regularly giving encouragement and praise to children. She also shows how easy it is for parents to give unclear directions to their children and then to rebuke them for failing to carry them out. Examples are given of parents failing to read the signs of exhaustion, or illness, or lack of exercise and healthy food, and then inappropriately punishing children for their naughtiness.[26] She urges fathers to be careful not to adopt a domineering tone when talking to their children, but always to be courteous. 'Some men, even good men, as the saying goes, seem to think an imperious, harsh tone to their children perfectly becoming.'[27]

Children suffer when they do not have any boundaries. The ineffective parents portrayed in this novel try to get children to do what they want by coaxing, persuading, whining, bargaining, and bribing, when firm instruction is all that is required. At times, the novel veers uncomfortably close to the 'no-fault parenting' idea, which holds that if parents do their job properly then children will always turn out well. 'Dear Hatty, the children of *believing* parents never form habits of disobedience', says Mrs Grey.[28] But at other points, the author does accept the truth that ultimately each individual is responsible for his or her own actions, and that there are some individuals who, however good their parents were, make wrong choices.

As a child-rearing manual, *The Home at Greylock* was well received. Typical of the response was a letter Elizabeth received from the minister of a church with 1,300 members, who praised the book highly and said that, if he could afford it, he would supply every parent in his congregation with a copy of his own. Whether it worked well as a novel is open to question.[29] And yet, as with Elizabeth Prentiss' other books, the sheer force of her personality, sincerity, integrity, and honesty, go a long way to atone for its deficiencies.

After a long and difficult illness, Henry Boynton Smith, the Prentisses' close friend and colleague, died in February 1877. He had been with Elizabeth at the saddest and happiest moments of her life: conducting the burial of Bessie and the baptism of Henry. She grieved as if she had lost a brother.

Following the painting lessons she received during the winter of 1874-5, Elizabeth was growing in competence and found that painting was a great way to relax. She spent many enjoyable hours painting pictures for friends and family, especially during the winter of 1877 to 1878. Moreover, her boundless creativity led her to take lessons in drawing with charcoal too. She wrote to a friend: 'I sympathize with your fear of spending too much time adorning your home, etc. etc. It is a nice question how far to go and how far to stay. But I honestly believe that a bare, blank, prosaic home makes religion appear dreadfully homely [unattractive]. We enjoy seeing our children enjoy their work and their play; is our Father unwilling to let us enjoy ours? . . . It seems to me that we are meant to use all the faculties God gives us . . . I do not know how I should have stood the tremendous change in my life, through my husband's change of profession, if I had not had this resource of painting. O, how I do miss his preaching! How I miss my pastoral work!'

Through 1877, *The Christian at Work* ran a serial story: *Pemaquid: or, a Story of Old Times in New England*. Elizabeth had thoroughly enjoyed writing this, aiming to 'bring out the New England peculiarities as they would appear to a worldly stranger'. It was very popular. The way in which the reading audience eagerly followed, and even tried to influence serial stories, comes across in this letter Elizabeth received from the publisher:

Let me express to you my personal thanks for your most excellent serial. I feel that it has done a real good to thousands. You need to be in my position, receiving hundreds of letters daily from your readers, to be able to fully appreciate how intensely interested they are in the story. It does not seem to satisfy them to feel assured of Ruth's marriage, but they want *to be there* and see it. Juliet, too, is not with them, as with you, a mere impersonation, but a living reality, and they will never rest till they hear from her. If I was a betting man I would bet five to one that what your husband struck out, is just exactly what is wanted. What do we men know about such things anyway?[30]

This letter also hints at the way Elizabeth offered her work to George, for him to check; for better or worse, she usually submitted to his points of criticism. She confided in a friend that 'what I thought the best part of her [Juliet], George made me cut out'; 'my good man *loathes* so to read about bad people.'

During the spring of 1878, George became seriously worried about Elizabeth again. It seemed that her ever restless and sensitive spirit was literally consuming her physical energy. She persisted in continuing to visit the sick and bereaved whenever she could; she worked hard at her painting; she kept up teaching the Bible to her ladies' group; and, of course, continued managing the affairs of the home.

The last book to come from her pen was *Gentleman Jim*. It was a novel set in a rough mining community and its story told of how the love of a pure and modest woman 'saved' a man. Elizabeth clearly possessed a sympathetic understanding of the very real vulnerability of women in lawless communities.

The flurry of all this activity gradually drained Elizabeth and left her in a weakened state. She had so given herself to church, family, and friends that she had lost all her reserves of strength. However, when she left for Dorset in May 1878, it seemed that a summer in the country would renew her energy, as had been the case so often in the past. For a couple of months, she was able to continue working in the home, as well as in the garden. Minnie invited a friend, Hattie, to spend the summer with the family, and Elizabeth loved going on outings into the countryside with 'the girls'. She also resumed her Bible class for women.

On Thursday, 8 August, George was uneasy about her going out to lead this meeting, as she had been weak and poorly on the Monday of that week. But Elizabeth insisted. She had the energy to paint some tiles and a chair on Thursday morning, and, as usual, watered her flowers. When she got to the Bible class that afternoon, it was obvious to the women present that she was not well. She asked Annie to read the passage and related texts (the subject was John 15:27: 'And ye also shall bear witness, because you have been with me from the beginning'). Elizabeth then led the main part of the study, outlining for the women the ways they could witness for Christ. She emphasized the vital role of a woman's testimony within the family and home, by her manner and attitude as well as by her words. She encouraged the young women by showing them that God is pleased with even seemingly trivial acts of service. She talked about witness at the time of death and about prayer. By the end of the class she was visibly exhausted. Nevertheless, later that day, Elizabeth was able to welcome Dr Vincent (George's successor as minister of the Church of the Covenant) who had arrived for a short stay, and she 'appeared in excellent spirits all the rest of the day'.

A couple of days later, on Saturday, 10 August, George, Elizabeth and the girls took Dr Vincent on a drive to see some of the local views. On their return, their medical doctor happened to pass by the house and Elizabeth requested to see him. She felt dizzy and ill; and was evidently in some distress. She revealed to the doctor that she had been experiencing mental confusion all week. Bed rest was prescribed. When a friend called on the family and was ushered into Elizabeth's room. 'Her greeting was warm, her eyes bright, she was very cheerful', and simply said that she had suffered from what seemed to be sunstroke.

By Sunday morning, however, it was clear that Elizabeth was in the grip of severe gastro-enteritis. George remained by her side, while Dr Vincent and the others attended the church service. Between the paroxysms of pain, Elizabeth appealed to her husband to 'let her go'. He wrote:

> Soon after M. had left, during an interval of comparative ease, she fixed her eyes upon me with a most tender, loving expression, and in a sort of beseeching tone, said, 'Darling, don't you think you could ask the Lord to let me go?' Perceiving, no doubt, how the question affected me, she went on to give some reasons for wishing to go. She spoke very slowly, in the most natural, simple way, and yet with an indescribable earnestness of look and voice, as if aware that she was uttering her dying words. I can not recall all that she said, but its substance, and some of the exact expressions are indelibly impressed upon my memory. For my and the children's sake she had been willing and even desired to live; and for several years had made extraordinary efforts to keep up, although much of the time the burden of ill-health, as I well knew, had been well-nigh insupportable. So far as this world was concerned, few persons in it had such reasons for wishing to live, or so much to render life attractive. But the feeling in her heart had become overpowering that no earthly happiness, no interest, no distraction, could any longer satisfy her, or give her content, away from Christ; and she longed to be with Him,

where He is. During the past three months especially, she had passed through very unusual exercise of mind with reference to this subject; and it seemed to her as if she had now reached a point beyond which she could not go. She evidently had in view the dreadful *sleeplessness,* to which she had been so in bondage for a quarter of a century, whose grasp had become more and more relentless, and the effects of which upon her nervous system were such as words can hardly describe. No human being but myself had any conception of her suffering, both physical and mental, from this cause. . . . In answer to a question she replied that to her view heaven is being with Christ and to be with Christ is heaven. She did not mean to imply any doubt about individual affections surviving the grave . . . often she had delighted in the thought of reunion with her parents and children, only her mind was so absorbed in the thought of the presence and beatific vision of Christ in his glory that for the moment it was lost to anything else.[31]

Elizabeth continued unwell, but George felt sure that she would recover. Early on Monday evening he wrote to Annie, then staying in Maine, that her mother was weak, but that he hoped she would recover in a couple of days. No sooner was the letter written, than Elizabeth's symptoms worsened. She suffered acutely. The doctor was summoned, and later wrote of 'the patient and uncomplaining manner in which the most agonizing pains which it has ever been my lot to witness were borne – with no repining, no murmur, no fretfulness, but quiet peaceful submission to endure and suffer'. He administered morphine, which gave some relief. By dawn on Tuesday, Elizabeth was unconscious, and her life was slipping away. The family gathered round, weeping silently, and waited for more than four hours. 'Although the chamber of death, it was the chamber of peace', wrote George. She died on Tuesday morning, 13 August 1878, aged fifty-nine.

The next day, on Wednesday 14 August, a simple service took place at the family home, before the casket was borne to the cemetery, about a quarter of a mile away. Dr Vincent gave an address at the graveside, and the assembled family, friends, and neighbours sang Elizabeth's own hymn, 'More love to Thee'.

Her family, friends, the Dorset neighbours, the Church and Seminary in New York, all mourned her passing. But her legacy continued to live on in her writings. Her life and works pointed to her conviction that, for Christians, this life is but a preparation for heaven. Elizabeth herself summed up the deepest longing of her whole life:

> To love Christ more – this is the deepest need, the constant cry of my soul. Down in the bowling alley, and out in the woods, and on my bed, and out driving, when I am happy and busy, and when I am sad and idle, the whisper keeps going up for more love, more love, more love![32]

EPILOGUE

GEORGE AND THE FAMILY were inundated with messages of condolence from all over America and even from further afield. George commissioned a beautiful gravestone for his wife and brought the remains of Eddy and Bessie to lie beside her in the Dorset cemetery. He missed Elizabeth terribly and for some years was himself plagued with insomnia and depression. A brief diary entry for 11 September 1888 sums up his sense of loss: 'Forty-fourth anniversary of our engagement. Terribly lonesome.'

The gathering of his wife's letters in preparation of a memoir proved to be something of a catharsis for him. 'On looking over her papers, I have found such treasures of love and tenderness as no words can express. They have soothed and comforted me beyond expression, and will continue to do so while I live.'[1] Reflecting, at the grand old age of eighty-five, on his marriage to Elizabeth, he wrote to his daughter Minnie:

In her deep humility and self-depreciation she often misjudged herself. She used to say she was '*awfully human*', meaning that she was full of faults and imperfections. Certainly, she had her faults and imperfections; and sometimes they tried her exceedingly. Faults and imperfections are everybody's portion. But hers grew largely out of physical causes and were mostly on the surface; while her virtues and perfections were transcendent alike in quality and degree. They seasoned and beautified her whole being. She gave me a new and higher conception both of love and of womanhood. From the hour of our engagement to the day of her departure from earth, I honoured and revered as much as I delighted in her. Had she not been so 'awfully *human*' I do not think she would have been so dear to me . . .[2]

In much trepidation he published the *Life and Letters of Elizabeth Prentiss* in 1882. The book was a great success, attracting favourable reviews and many letters of appreciation. One of George's endearing features was how transparently proud he was of Elizabeth's writing. He continued to administer her publications and compiled a small anthology of extracts from her writings entitled *Thoughts concerning the King.*

George Prentiss remained in his professorship at Union Theological Seminary. He was one of those behind the move to secure the Seminary's full independence from the Presbyterian Church.[3] He compiled a *History of the Union Theological Seminary,* and continued lecturing at the Seminary until his retirement in 1897 when he was eighty-one years of age. He had served that institution for twenty-four years. George Prentiss always retained a keen interest in foreign missions and particularly enjoyed lecturing on the study of missions. He died in 1903.

Soon after Elizabeth's death, Annie, aged thirty-one, became engaged to Douglas Henry. The son of a Presbyterian minister, he was godly, if impecunious. 'A fine fellow, poor in this world's goods, but in a good position, and true of heart . . . he is a thoroughly Christian man', her father observed. The couple were dogged by financial difficulties for some years. But once these were resolved, they were able to make the obligatory European tour and Annie was able to revisit some of the places she had seen as a child. The family lived in an apartment in New York, near enough to George and Minnie to be able to take tea together every Sunday evening. Annie and Douglas had three daughters.

Epilogue

Minnie, who was twenty-four years old when her mother died, did not marry. For the next twenty-five years she devoted herself to the care of her father. She stepped into her mother's shoes, offering hospitality to visitors to the home, hosting the Chi Alpha meetings, and accompanying her father on social visits and official functions. Practical, kind-hearted, competent, and cheerful, she was an ideal companion. In 1889 her father wrote, 'M., dear child! What should I do without her? Always bright and cheerful, always on the watch to help and comfort me; always unworldly and full of faith.' Six years later he could add, 'M. is bright and well, takes the best possible care of me . . . She is all absorbed in her round of charity and visits, or letters of friendship and sympathy. I never knew a human being who seemed to take greater delight in trying to make others happy.'[4] In his eighty-fifth year her father compiled a personal memoir for her, and the dedication expressed something of his gratitude: 'This family story is dedicated to MWP, and if all the pages were so many diamonds they would but fairly reflect the beauty of her filial devotion and loveliness.' He ensured that she was well provided for after his death.

George, twenty-one years of age at his mother's death in 1878, completed his studies at Princeton, and settled down to become a lawyer after a period travelling around Europe. Henry, the youngest at nineteen when Elizabeth died, also completed his studies at Princeton, but academic work had never been his forte. He had always loved making things and tinkering with his inventions and soon discovered his niche when he established a clock-making company. 'The Prentiss Clock Improvement Company' grew from strength to strength, eventually issuing an eighty-five-page catalogue. Henry married Lila in 1889 and they had two daughters.

The whole family often gathered in the Dorset home during the summer months, and George was never happier than when his four children and five grand-daughters were all around him. He wrote on Thanksgiving Day 1901:

> My children and grandchildren were with me at table. It was a quiet, simple, lovely family scene, worth waiting for five and eighty years. And I enjoyed it to the full, in my heart giving thanks unto God in the name of our Lord Jesus Christ. To him be ascribed, as is most due, all glory and honour and might and dominion, world without end.[5]

CONCLUSION

ELIZABETH PRENTISS did not regard herself as a professional writer. First and foremost, she saw herself as a Christian, then a wife and mother.

ELIZABETH AS A CHRISTIAN

Although Elizabeth may have been converted at an early age, she had a profound experience of conviction followed by assurance in 1840 at the age of twenty-two. Throughout the following thirty-eight years a definite deepening of her spiritual life can be observed. One of the appealing things about her in her later years was her desire to see younger Christians grow in grace, and the candid way in which she spoke about her own spiritual struggles and failings. She readily admitted to the fitful nature of her own growth in grace in her earlier years:

> You can't complain of any folly to which I could not plead guilty. I have put my Saviour's patience to every possible test, and how I love Him when I think what he will put up with . . . As to my own sinfulness, that would certainly overwhelm me if I spent much time in looking at it. But it is a monster whose face I do not love to see; I turn from its hideousness to the beauty of His face who sins not, and the sight of 'yon lovely Man' ravishes me. But at your age I did this only by fits and starts and suffered as you do. So I know how to feel for you, and what to ask for you.[1]

Her temperament was volatile and passionate. When her mood swing was high, she could be enormously energetic and productive: she would throw herself furiously into whatever project was occupying her at the time. This would be followed by total exhaustion and corresponding depression. As she grew older, these extremes were moderated and she increased in calmness of spirit and self-control. She was acutely aware of her own faults:

> My husband has just come in and described the scene at Mrs De Witt's funeral, when her husband said, *Good-bye, dear wife, you have been my greatest blessing next to Christ;* and he added, 'And that I can say of you.' This was very sweet to me, for I have faults of manner that often annoy him − I am so vehement, so positive, and lay down the law so! But I believe the grace of God can cure faults of all sorts, be they deep-seated or external.[2]

Looking back on the year 1873, her husband wrote: 'Her religious life was all the time growing deeper and more fruitful, was centering itself more entirely in Christ and rising faster heavenward. Its sympathies became, if possible, still more tender and loving. Her whole being, indeed seemed to gather new light and sweetness from the sharp discipline she had been passing through.' During the same year Elizabeth herself wrote: 'The best I can say of myself is, that I see the need of *immense* advances in the divine life. I find it hard to be patient with myself when I see how far I am from reaching even my own poor standard; but if I do not love Christ and long to please him, I do not love anybody or anything.' In other words, while others saw how she was increasing in holiness, she herself remained humble and self-deprecating.

Her conviction that obedience meant surrender to God's will whatever the circumstances was worked out in her own experience. Through the most difficult of trials, she trusted

that the purpose of God for his children in this life is to prepare them for heaven. She believed that sufferings drive the
Christian closer to God because they force the Christian to
be more dependent on him. She also believed that surrender-
ing to the will of God was the path to holiness, in that it leads
to the death of self.

> God never places us in any position in which we can not
> grow. We may fancy that He does. We may fear we are so
> impeded by fretting, petty cares that we are gaining no-
> thing; but when we are not sending any branches upward,
> we may be sending roots downward. Perhaps in the time
> of our humiliation, when everything seems a failure, we
> are making the best kind of progress. God delights to try
> our faith by the conditions in which He places us. A plant
> set in the shade shows where its heart is by turning *towards*
> the sun, even when unable to reach it. We have so much
> to distract us in this world that we do not realize how
> truly and deeply, if not always warmly and consciously, we
> love Christ. But I believe that this love is the strongest
> principle in every regenerate soul. It may slumber for a
> time, it may falter, it may freeze nearly to death; but sooner
> or later it will declare itself as the ruling passion.[3]

While Elizabeth Prentiss learned many valuable lessons
from the writings of the mystics, her devotion was not
focused on her own soul at the expense of a ministry to
others. She maintained a balance between inner devotion and
outward service. Within her family she was loved for her
cheerfulness, her desire to make others happy, her energy, and
her gifts of home-making. She threw herself into gardening,
baking, painting, and decorating, with the same zeal that she
gave to hymn writing, prayer, and Bible reading. Within the
church she was known for her ceaseless visitation of the ill
and bereaved, her skilful nursing of the sick, and her hospital-

ity, as much as for her leadership of women's prayer meetings and Bible readings.

ELIZABETH AS A WIFE AND MOTHER

Elizabeth saw her role primarily as a wife: her aim was to be a help and support to George in his ministry. For thirty-three years they enjoyed a happy marriage which was full of companionship. Later George could reflect:

> Her own Christian life was to me a study from the beginning. It had heights and depths of its own, which awed me, and which I could not fully penetrate . . . If my pastoral ministrations gave any aid and comfort to other souls, I can truly say it was all largely due to her. And as for myself my debt of gratitude to her as a spiritual helper and friend in Christ was, and is, and ever will be unspeakable.[4]

Elizabeth served alongside George, first in New Bedford (1845–50) and then in New York (1851–73). When George became a professor at Union Theological Seminary in 1873, Elizabeth sorely missed the pastoral work that had been so much part of their lives: she had found her special role in visitation of the sick and bereaved, and in ministry among women. (For his part, George fully supported Elizabeth in her writing ministry, encouraging her to persevere when she wanted to give up, taking the time to read and comment on all her manuscripts).

Elizabeth regarded motherhood as her other primary calling. As a girl, she had dreamed of having a large family, and she was always so very fond of children. The tragic deaths of Eddy and Bessie were the greatest griefs she had to bear. Then Minnie suffered years of ill health, and on several occasions Elizabeth had to prepare herself for the loss of her too. But she saw these painful trials as necessary, lest she succumbed to the temptation of making 'idols' of her children. That, in the opinion of some, may make her appear super-spiritual and too-good-to-be-true. But the attractive thing about Elizabeth's life was the way she managed to create an atmosphere of fun and laughter for her family, even in the middle of otherwise dark times. Even when writing to her son about his sister's critical illness, her letter is not gloomy:

> September 19, 1875. M's fever ran twenty-one days, as the doctor said it would, and began to break yesterday . . . she is not yet out of danger; so you must not be too elated. We four are sitting in the dining-room with a hot fire; papa is reading aloud to A. and H.; it is evening, and M. has had her opiate, and is getting to sleep. I have not much material of which to make letters, sitting all day in a dark room in almost total silence. Your father is reading about Hans Christian Andersen; you must read the article in the *Living Age*, No. 1,631; it is ever so funny.
>
> I had such a queer dream last night. I dreamed that Maggie plagued us so that your father went to New York and brought back *two* cooks. I said I only wanted one. 'Oh, but these are so rare,' he said; 'come out and see them.' So he led me into the kitchen, and there sat at the table, eating dinner very solemnly, two *ostriches!* Now what that dream was made of I cannot imagine. Now I must go to bed, pretty tired. When you are lonely and blue, think how we all love you. Good-night.[5]

Writing her letters and books was fitted around the needs of her family and not the other way round. Elizabeth's views on motherhood and child-rearing are explained in *The Home at Greylock*: firm boundaries, but lots of love and lots of fun. Above all, she wanted her own children to know the love of God, and she believed that the most effective way to teach such spiritual truths to one's own children was to live out vital Christianity in an exemplary, attractive, and winsome way.

ELIZABETH AS A WRITER

When Elizabeth began to write books for children she found that in doing so her mind was gently diverted away from the grief she had suffered over the loss of her two infants. It was also a way of ministering to others when her health was too poor to do much else. Later, when supporting her husband in his pastoral ministry, she frequently found herself visiting women who were suffering from illness, bereavements, or family problems. It was in an attempt to bring pastoral help to such women that Elizabeth began to write books addressed to adults.

The appeal of her writings lay in the way in which her own life experiences equipped her to empathize with others. As a child she had suffered the loss of her dearly loved father. Her frequent health problems and chronic insomnia gave Elizabeth a tender sensitivity to the feelings of those who were ill. The grief she endured when Eddy and Bessie died united her in a special bond with other mothers who had lost infants. The collapse of her husband's health and his resignation from the pastorate meant that she knew what it was to be uncertain about the future. The illness and premature death of so many of her relatives and friends made her keenly aware of those around her who were also passing through bereavement.

The writings of Elizabeth Prentiss are still popular today because of the way they show women that faithfulness in simple everyday tasks has eternal significance. Elizabeth lived at a time when Christians divided fiercely over the question of holiness and how it can be achieved. While she denied that 'sinless perfection' can be attained in this life, she did insist that the quest for holiness was one in which every Christian must be engaged. Her friend Eliza Warner wrote:

> Believing in Christ was to her not so much a duty as the
> deepest joy of her life, heightening all other joys, and she

was not satisfied until her friends shared with her in this experience. She believed it to be attainable by all, founded on a complete submitting of the human to the Divine will in all things, great and small.[6]

This was what drove Elizabeth to write so prolifically. She wanted to bring the joy and comfort of the love of Christ into the lives of others.

In particular, Elizabeth Prentiss wrote for women, showing them that surrender to the will of God can provide strength for mundane tasks and grace for the various challenges within family relationships.

Undoubtedly, *Stepping Heavenward* was the most successful of her books. Of all her novels, this is the most lifelike account of her own spiritual experience. Katy is a believable heroine, simply because she exhibits so many of Elizabeth's own weaknesses; to the reader her life has a true ring about it because it so honestly portrays Elizabeth's own struggles.

ELIZABETH AND THE 'CULT OF TRUE WOMANHOOD'

One historian has outlined how 'the cult of true womanhood' in nineteenth-century America promoted the four virtues of *piety, purity, submissiveness, and domesticity*.[7] In many ways Elizabeth Prentiss's life and writings exemplify this thesis.

All her writings communicate love for God, or *piety*. Her own testimony was one of a personal knowledge of Christ. 'There is certainly enough in our Saviour, if we only open our eyes that we may see it, to solve every doubt and satisfy every longing of the heart; and He is willing to give it in full measure.'[8] 'If a glimpse of our Saviour here on earth can be so refreshing, so delightful, what will it be in heaven?'[9] 'A soul that has known what it is to live to Christ can be happy only in Him.'[10] 'You will never be really happy until Christ becomes your dearest and most intimate friend.'[11]

Her life was characterized by an ongoing quest for more holiness. Elizabeth never thought she had 'arrived' and her writings reflect her great concern to overcome personal sin. She was always concerned about the state of her own heart; she did not worry about what others thought of Elizabeth Prentiss, but about what God thought of her. This desire for single-minded integrity is reflected in this seemingly trivial incident, recalled by a friend:

> She was honest, truthful, *genuine* to the highest degree. It may have sometimes led her into seeming lack of courtesy, but even this was a failing which 'leaned to virtue's side'. I chanced to know of her once calling with a friend on a country neighbour, and finding the good housewife busy over a rag-carpet. Mrs Prentiss, who had never chanced to see one of these bits o' rural manufacture in its elementary processes, was full of questions and interest, thereby quite evidently pleasing the unassuming artist in assorted rags and home-made dyes. When the visitors were safely outside the door, Mrs Prentiss' friend turned to her with the exclamation, 'What tact you have! She really thought you were interested in her work!' The quick blood sprang into Mrs Prentiss' face, and she turned upon her friend a look of amazement and rebuke. 'Tact!' she said, 'I despise such tact! – do you think *I would look or act a lie?*'[12]

Thus, *purity* was one of her constant themes, in the broadest sense of wanting to please God. But her writings for women were also concerned to encourage the female virtues of modesty and chastity, that is, 'purity' in the narrower sense.

Submission to the will of God is a third identifiable theme, and this was no abstract theory. Her letters and journals show that she submitted to God's will in the illness and death of her children, in her own critical illness, and in her husband's physical breakdown. 'Let us take our lot in life just as it comes, courageously, patiently and faithfully, never wondering at anything the Master does.'[13] She had absolute confidence in the sovereignty of God; nothing happens 'by mistake':

> Lay down this principle as a law, – God does nothing arbitrary. If he takes away your health for instance, it is because He has some reason for doing so; and this is true of everything you value; and if you have real faith in Him, you will not insist on knowing this reason. If you find in the course of everyday events, that your self-con-secration was not perfect, – that is, that your will revolts at His will, – do not be discouraged, but fly to your Saviour, and stay in His presence till you obtain the spirit in which He cried in His hour of anguish, 'Father, if Thou be willing, remove this cup from me; nevertheless, not my will, but Thine be done.'[14]

Elizabeth believed that submission should be seen within the structure and relationships of the family; she accepted that George was 'head' of the family, and her 'marriage manual', *Aunt Jane's Hero,* and many of her other writings, enjoined the virtue of submission for young wives. Her own life showed that such submission was not mindless or passive. It is also clear that her husband respected her as a fully equal partner. He was so very proud of her achievements and took great delight in receiving compliments on her behalf and conveying them to her.

Elizabeth's life and writings also demonstrate the ideal of *domesticity*. She was a gifted homemaker and took great delight in being creative in decorating, cooking, gardening, and giving hospitality. Her books promote the notion that being a homemaker is a calling in itself, to be respected, and to be taken seriously, even if it was unpaid and often unappreciated.

Many feminists have reacted violently against the notion that a woman can find satisfaction in homemaking and family life. They have advocated leaving the domestic sphere altogether. But another strand of feminism has acknowledged gender distinctions, recognizing that, for many women, marriage and children are central to the experience of womanhood, and that, as a consequence, they have chosen to spend a significant proportion of their time in the home. In their view, homemaking ought to be more highly valued than it so often is.

Elizabeth Prentiss' writings, especially her trilogy of novels for women (*Stepping Heavenward; Aunt Jane's Hero,* and *The Home at Greylock*) emphasized each of these themes (piety, purity, submission, domesticity). The biblical basis of these virtues is implicitly assumed, rather than explicitly developed.[15]

Some critics have argued that such literature idealized the very qualities that kept women weak and powerless. But Elizabeth Prentiss, and other proponents of 'true womanhood', would have maintained that female influence was in fact the stronger for not competing with men in the marketplace, the office or the law court. The 'separate spheres' idea differentiated between male strength (suited to the competition and cut-and-thrust of the workplace) and female strength (suited to the different but equally draining demands of the sickroom, the nursery, and the home). The man's role was to provide for his family, to protect them from need. The woman's role was to nurture and care for her family.[16] The expectation of nineteenth-century society was that the role of the wife and mother focused primarily on the home, and not in the seeking of outside recognition. Far from challenging that expectation, Elizabeth Prentiss lived it out and encouraged other women to accept it. Her novels reinforced this ideal of the female role as the self-sacrificial wife, mother, and homemaker.

But if the 'two-spheres' teaching accorded dignity to homemaking, it also tended to divide roles in a decidedly rigid way. Women were given charge of the home and given responsibility for the spiritual well-being of the family in a way that sometimes undercut the spiritual responsibility of the husband and father.[17] In earlier Puritan thinking the husband was also spiritual 'head' of the home. By contrast, during the nineteenth century it became commonplace to regard the woman as the prime spiritual influence within the family. Even if the father still led daily devotions, the chief moral and spiritual guardian was understood to be the mother who was often described as the 'angel of the home'. In practice the mother took over the leading of daily devotions in many families.

To some extent, no doubt, this reflected the reality that, generally speaking, there were more women than men in the church,[18] sometimes outnumbering them by two-to-one. The British writer Frances Trollope gave a lively account of her impressions of American life in 1832, making the comment that she had not seen another country where 'religion had so strong a hold upon the women or a slighter hold upon the men'.[19] But in emphasizing this female propensity for piety, it could be argued that the churches actually deterred many men from getting actively involved. 'The churches were releasing men from the responsibility of being religious leaders. They were turning religion and morality into the domain of women – something soft and comforting, not bracing and demanding.'[20]

Of course this is not a development that Prentiss would have deliberately endorsed. She offered pastoral advice to the many Christian wives of unbelieving husbands on how to best influence their families for good. Her books aimed to help such women win their men over to a more godly way of life; however, the 'two-spheres' teaching tended to put spiritual and family matters so firmly in the 'feminine' box that the man's spiritual responsibility was often diminished.[21] It sat uneasily with the biblical teaching that the father should not only take primary responsibility for the spiritual well-being of his family, but also play an active part in the training of his children (*Eph.* 5:23; 6:4).

The other major flaw in the 'two-spheres' teaching was that it offered no practical help for women who needed to support themselves. Single or widowed women often found themselves dependent on family charity, and if that was not available, they frequently found themselves in desperate need. Moreover, women without children of their own, were rarely able to use their gifts outside the home. Throughout the period of Elizabeth's life (1818–78) opportunities for women in further education and professional employment were very limited. It was only towards the end of the nineteenth century that significant changes in these areas began to take place. The idealization of 'true womanhood', which Prentiss advocated through her novels, reinforced the idea that the woman's place is ever and only in the home.

There are some indications of the cruel situation suffered by single women without family wealth in Prentiss's novels. There is dignity in work, and where necessary, a single woman or widow should take paid employment, however menial or degrading, if she was unable to teach. Elizabeth herself worked as a teacher until she was twenty-seven. However, she does not seem to advocate that women should seek out other opportunities to support themselves. It seems instead that she confined herself to offering advice on how to work within the social constraints of the day and was not aware of any need of a campaign for change.[22]

THE FEMINIZATION OF AMERICAN CULTURE?

Elizabeth Prentiss is named in Ann Douglas's seminal work *The Feminization of American Culture* as one of the female writers who exemplified the move to a more sentimental approach to religion. Douglas argues that the nineteenth century saw a shift in American theology and culture.[23] At the beginning of the century the rigorous Calvinism of the old school still held sway. As a result of Adam's original transgression, mankind was born into a state of sin and misery; only by God's sovereign grace was a distinction made between the saved (foreordained to eternal salvation) and the lost (who would suffer the just punishment of their sins eternally). By the end of the nineteenth century, those old orthodoxies had largely been replaced by a more liberal creed. Indeed, many churches had become universalistic in doctrine, holding out the prospect that all will be saved in the end.

Even those churches that did not go all the way down that route became Arminian in emphasis, stressing that each individual had within them the power or free will to choose to be saved. And of those churches that did not become Arminian, many placed less of an emphasis on doctrines such as total depravity and eternal punishment. In particular, a more sentimental view of children developed; little was heard about innate depravity. Most assumed that in the tragic case of an infant death, the child went straight to heaven. The appallingly high rate of infant mortality led to an outpouring of 'consolation' literature, much of it of a highly speculative and sentimental nature.

Douglas argues that the growing influence of female writers (many of them daughters and wives of clergymen) played a significant part in this process, and she names thirty key women writers, including Elizabeth Prentiss.[24]

It is accepted that the nineteenth century did witness the feminization of American culture, at least in some degree. Certainly some of Elizabeth Prentiss' published writings and private letters reflect the sentimentality of the culture of her day. She was, after all, a child of her time. But in none of her writings is there a trace of Universalism, still less Unitarianism. Indeed, she intensely disliked any such 'watering down' of the Christian gospel and was willing to stand up for what she believed to be the basic (if unpopular) truths of the Bible.

It is clear that Elizabeth Prentiss' writings reflected the cultural assumptions of the nineteenth century. Nevertheless, she communicates exalted truth about God in a real, down-to-earth style, which is grounded in the practicalities of day-to-day experience. Her understanding of the love of God, her grasp of the sovereignty of God in times of pain and suffering, her conviction that the Christian is 'stepping heavenward' in each passing day – these are big truths that can still inspire men and women today. In particular, those passing through suffering still find comfort in Elizabeth Prentiss' confidence, drawn from Scripture, that God works out all things for the good of his people (*Rom.* 8:28). Casting an eye back over her own bereavements, Elizabeth often said that she would not dare change a thing:

> Let sorrow do its work, send grief or pain;
> Sweet are Thy messengers, sweet their refrain,
> When they can sing with me,
> More love, O Christ, to Thee,
> More love to Thee, more love to Thee!

ENDNOTES TO CHAPTER I

[1] George Lewis Prentiss, *More Love to Thee: The Life and Letters of Elizabeth Prentiss,* (New York: A. D. F. Randolph & Co., 1882; repr. Amityville, New York: Calvary Press, 1993) p. 10.

[2] Thomas Baker, *N. Nathaniel Parker Willis and the Trials of Literary Fame* (New York, Oxford: Oxford University Press, 1999), p. 16. Compare this extract from the *Life of Dr Payson*:

Commercial calamities, arising from war, fell at this time with peculiar weight upon the inhabitants of Portland. The distresses of the times are the subject of frequent allusion by Mr Payson, in his diary. The stagnation of business, the failures among the principal merchants, the hundreds of citizens and seamen thrown out of employment, and left destitute of the means of subsistence, and the sufferings of the poor, called forth largely his sympathy. To him the town seemed threatened with universal bankruptcy; and, whether with good reason or not, he considered the means of his own temporal support as cut off. But the tranquillity of his mind was never more uniform, than at this calamitous season; and the object of his supreme desire and efforts, was to turn the distresses of the people to their spiritual advantage, rightly judging, that 'the walls of Jerusalem might be built in troublesome times.' A picture of these distresses, as they appeared to him at the time, is drawn in a letter to his parents, dated Portland, 28 Dec. 1807. After describing their calamities, he adds, 'I have scarcely a hope of receiving more than enough to pay my board, if I should stay till next spring; and Mr K. will want all his salary to support himself, as he fears that all his property is swallowed up in the general destruction. These failures have brought to light many instances of dishonesty among those in whose integrity unbounded confidence was placed. And now, all confidence is lost, no man will trust his neighbour, but every one takes even his brother 'by the throat, saying, Pay me that thou owest.' But I cannot describe, and I doubt whether you can conceive of the distress we are in.

And now you will, perhaps, be griven [sic] at this sudden blast of all my fine prospects, and cry, 'Poor Edward!' But you never had more reason to rejoice on my behalf, and to cry, 'Rich Edward!' than

now; for, blessed be God, my portion does not stand on such totter-
ing foundations, as to be shaken by these commotions. My dear
parents, my dear sister, do not feel one emotion of sorrow on my account, but rather join with me in blessing God, that he keeps me
quiet, resigned, and even happy, in the midst of these troubles. I do
not pretend not to feel them, however. All my worldly hopes are,
apparently, destroyed; and many of those who are now ready to be
turned into the streets, are the dearest friends I have here; not to
mention the distress of the poor, who will, in human probability,
soon be in a starving condition. In these circumstances it is impossible not to feel.

ANON., *Life of the Rev. Edward Payson, D.D.* (London: Religious
Tract Society, abridged from the American edition, n.d.), pp. 45–6.

[3] She married Edward Payson on 8 May 1811. The following year, her
father (along with many other merchants) lost his considerable wealth as
a result of the trade embargo which resulted from the war with Britain
(America was at war with Britain between 1812 and 1815).

[4] Quoted in Prentiss, *Life and Letters*, p. 19.　[5] Ibid, pp. 16–17.

[6] Iain H. Murray, *Revival and Revivalism* (Edinburgh: Banner of Truth,
1994), pp. 212–3.

[7] Prentiss, *Life and Letters*, p. 5.

[8] *Life of the Rev. Edward Payson, D.D.*, p. 127.

[9] Prentiss, *Life and Letters*, p. 69 n.

[10] Ibid., pp. 8-9.　[11] Ibid., p. 515.

ENDNOTES TO CHAPTER 2

[1] Louisa Payson Hopkins, *The Pastor's Daughter* (1835; repr. Birming-
ham, Alabama: Solid Ground Christian Books, 2004).

[2] The Willis family were: Lucy (b. 1804); Nathaniel (1806); Louisa
(1807); Julia (1809); Sara (1811); Mary (1813); Edward (1816); Richard
(1819) and Ellen (1821). Louisa Payson, born in 1812, was thus closest in
age to Louisa, Julia, Sara and Mary. Elizabeth Payson, born in 1818, was
closest in age to Ellen.

[3] Dr Asa Cummings wrote the *Life of Edward Payson*. He also compiled
the three-volume set of Dr Payson's sermons.

[4] Prentiss, *Life and Letters,* p. 12.

[5] *The Works of John Owen*, vol. 6 (repr. London: Banner of Truth, 1967).

[6] *The Works of John Flavel,* vol. 1 (repr. London: Banner of Truth, 1968).

[7] Prentiss, *Life and Letters*, pp. 24–5.

[8] Ibid., p. 25, n 1.   [9] Ibid., p. 29.   [10] Ibid., p. 45.

[11] Philip Doddridge (1702–51) was a dissenting (Independent/Congregational) minister in England. He played a key role in the training of dissenting ministers, and wrote some well-loved hymns, including 'O happy day that fixed my choice'. But he is best known as the author of *The Rise and Progress of Religion in the Soul* (1745). This religious classic, translated into many languages, was instrumental in the conversion of William Wilberforce among others. The early chapters deal with sin, and the inability of the sinner to save himself.

[12] Prentiss, *Life and Letters*, pp. 31–2.

[13] Ibid., p. 32. This account of her experience was written in a letter to her cousin, George Shipman, see note 14.

[14] George Elias Shipman was born in New York in 1820. His father and Elizabeth's mother were siblings; Elizabeth's mother was instrumental in her brother's conversion. George became a doctor, and later a leading homeopath. He had a large practice in Chicago, and, in 1848 founded the *Northwestern Journal of Homeopathy*. In 1871 he and his wife felt led to begin an orphanage in Chicago, run along the lines of George Muller's orphanages in England (i.e., run on 'faith', trusting in God alone for funds, and never asking for money). In 1874 he opened a new building costing over $40,000. Over the first 13 years, 4,978 children were cared for.

[15] Prentiss, *Life and Letters,* p. 35.

[16] Ibid., p. 440: 'I also believe in, because I have experienced it, and find my experience in the Word of God, a work of the Spirit subsequent to conversion . . . A great many years ago, disgusted with my spiritual life, I was led into new relations to Christ to which I could give no name, for I never had heard of such an experience.'

ENDNOTES TO CHAPTER 3

[1] In Elizabeth Prentiss' later book, *Urbane and His Friends*, she explained her reasoning in offering help to other young people who were trying to balance the demands of the Great Commission (Christ's command to evangelize all nations) with the needs of elderly parents. Helvia confides to an older Christian woman (Claudia) her desire to volunteer for the mission field. Claudia bluntly tells Helvia that it would be wrong to leave her elderly widowed father. Her first duty is to him. Care provided 'for hire' is never the same as care given by a loving relative. After his death, she would be free, if she still wished, to volunteer for foreign service.

Claudia tells Helvia that there are plenty of 'heathen' at home to evangelize, and Helvia eventually finds her vocation as a Christian wife and mother. Elizabeth Prentiss, *Urbane and His Friends* (repr. Ithaca, MI: A. B. Publishing, 1999), pp. 257–67.

[2] Prentiss, *Life and Letters*, p. 36.

[3] Ibid., p. 51.

[4] Ibid., p. 77.

[5] Ibid., pp. 55-56.

[6] Ibid., p. 50.

[7] Elizabeth's description of her symptoms sounds as if she may have suffered some kind of mercury poisoning: children in the early nineteenth century were routinely prescribed 'blue pills' (containing mercury) for a range of illnesses. These had a range of unpleasant side effects, and the nervous system was often adversely affected: 'I am all the time so nervous that life would be unsupportable if I had not the comfort of comforts to rejoice in. I often think that mother would not trust me to carry the dishes to the closet, if she knew how strong an effort I have to make to avoid dashing them all to pieces. When I am at the head of the stairs I can hardly help throwing myself down, and I believe that it is just such a state as this which induces the suicide to put an end to his existence. It was never so bad with me before. Do you know anything of such a feeling as this? Tonight, for instance, my head began to feel all at once as if it were enlarging till at last it seemed to fill the room, and I thought it large enough to carry away the house. Then every object of which I thought enlarged in proportion. When this goes off the sense of contraction is equally singular. My head felt about the size of a pin's head; our church and everybody in it appeared about the bigness of a cup etc. These strange sensations terminate invariably with one still more singular and particularly pleasant – I cannot describe it – it is a sense of smoothness and a little of dizziness. If you never had such feelings this will all be nonsense to you, but if you have and can explain them to me, why I shall be indeed thankful. I have been subject to them ever since I can remember. I never met with a physician yet who seemed to know what is the matter with me, or to care a fig whether I got well or not. All they do is roll up their eyes and shake their heads and say "Oh!"' (Prentiss, *Life and Letters*, pp. 65-66). See chapter 8 for further comment on Elizabeth's health.

[8] Prentiss, *Life and Letters*, pp. 70–1.

[9] Ibid., p. 70.

[10] John Wesley, *Letters*, vol. 8, p. 190. See Iain H. Murray, *Wesley and Men who Followed* (Edinburgh: Banner of Truth, 2003), pp. 46–7.

[11] Charles White, article on Phoebe Palmer, *Christian History & Biography Magazine*, Issue 82, Spring 2004, vol. xxiii.

[12] Prentiss, *Life and Letters*, p. 74.

ENDNOTES TO CHAPTER 4

[1] Prentiss, *Life and Letters*, p. 54.

[2] Prentiss, George Lewis, *The Bright Side of Life: Glimpses of It through Fourscore Years, a Family History,* 2 volumes. (Privately Published: Ansbury Park, New Jersey, 1901), vol. 1, p. 364.

[3] Prentiss, *Family History*, vol. 1, p. 356.

[4] George M. Marsden, *The Evangelical Mind and the New School Presbyterian Experience* (New Haven and London: Yale University Press, 1970), p. 169.

[5] Prentiss, *Family History*, vol. 1, p. 106.

[6] Prentiss, *Life and Letters*, p. 84.

[7] Ibid., pp. 88–9.

[8] Prentiss, *Family History,* vol. 1, p. 357.

[9] Ibid., p.361.

[10] Ibid., p.365.

[11] Ibid., p. 361.

[12] Prentiss, *Life and Letters,* p. 98.

[13] Prentiss, *Family History,* vol. 1, p. 365.

[14] Ibid., p. 395.

[15] Ibid., p. 404.

[16] Generally in New England at the time, middle class families depended on domestic 'help' which was increasingly difficult to get as better wages were offered in factories.

[17] Prentiss, *Life and Letters*, pp. 100-101.

[18] Prentiss, *Family History*, vol. 1, p. 362.

ENDNOTES TO CHAPTER 5

[1] Prentiss, *Life and Letters,* p. 102.

[2] Ibid., p. 103, note 1.   [3] Ibid., pp. 109–10.

[4] Jeannie, George, Seargent, and Una.

[5] Prentiss, *Life and Letters*, p. 122.

[6] At this time there was a more or less reciprocal arrangement between the New-School Presbyterian congregations and the Congregational churches.

[7] Prentiss, *Life and Letters*, p. 128. [8] Ibid., p. 129.

[9] Hugh Brogan, *The Penguin History of the United States* (London: Longman, 1985, repr. London: Penguin, 1990), p. 407.

[10] Prentiss, *Life and Letters*, p. 149.

[11] While both branches of the Presbyterian Church were evangelical, the designation 'Old School' was given to those distinctly Calvinistic, while 'New School' men were sympathetic to the moderating influences of New England theology. According to a 'Plan of Union' in 1801, New England Congregational ministers could be called to Presbyterian pulpits – a decision revoked by the Old School majority in the General Assembly of 1837. Although re-union occurred in 1869, differences were to remain.

[12] Seargent's youngest child, Annie's cousin.

[13] Medicine at that time followed the ancient belief that the humours (or fluids) in the body had to be balanced out. The methods used were drastic and painful, including 'blistering'. Plasters soaked in various substances were applied. These caused blisters to appear, either as a counter-irritant or to draw out bodily fluid.

[14] Prentiss, *Family History*, vol. 2, pp. 32–3.

[15] Elizabeth Prentiss, *How Sorrow Was Changed into Sympathy: Words of Cheer for Mothers Bereft of Little Children.* (London: Hodder & Stoughton, 1884).

[16] Prentiss, *Life and Letters*, pp. 131-2.

[17] Prentiss, *Sorrow Changed into Sympathy,* p. 107. [18] Ibid., p. 108.

[19] Prentiss, *Life and Letters*, pp. 136–7.

ENDNOTES TO CHAPTER 6

[1] Prentiss, *Sorrow Changed into Sympathy*, p. 126.

[2] Elizabeth Prentiss, 'God's Way', *Golden Hours* (1873; repr. Vestavia Hills, Alabama: Solid Ground Christian Books, 2001), pp. 85–6.

[3] Prentiss, *Golden Hours*, pp. 88–9.

[4] While its publication did help the family finances, the lack of copyright rules meant that Susan Warner made far less money from it than its success warranted. The only novel to sell more copies was Harriet Beecher Stowe's *Uncle Tom's Cabin. The Wide, Wide World* was originally published under a pseudonym (Elizabeth Wetherell). The novel can be read on-line at http://digital.library.upenn.edu/wo.../wide/wide/html

[5] Prentiss, *Life and Letters,* p. 140.

⁶ Ibid., p. 141. There is a discrepancy here with the dates of published works on p. 568, where 1856 is cited as the publication date for *The Flower of the Family.*

⁷ Ibid., p. 141.   ⁸ Ibid., pp. 141–2.

⁹ Prentiss, *Sorrow Changed into Sympathy*, p. 133.

¹⁰ Ibid., p. 136.

¹¹ Prentiss, *Family History*, vol. 2, p. 37.

¹² Prentiss, *Sorrow Changed into Sympathy,* pp. 137–8.

¹³ George's Memoir, *The Bright Side of Life, A Family History,* was written to his daughter Minnie.

¹⁴ Prentiss, *Family History,* vol. 2, p. 37.

¹⁵ Elizabeth Prentiss, *Stepping Heavenward* (1869; repr. Amityville, New York: Calvary Press, 1992), p. 248.

¹⁶ Prentiss, *Life and Letters,* pp. 153–4.   ¹⁷ Ibid., pp. 156–7.

¹⁸ Prentiss, *Family History,* vol. 2, p. 57.

¹⁹ *The Revival,* January 1859, quoted in Marsden, *The Evangelical Mind and the New School Presbyterian Experience,* p. 182.

²⁰ Prentiss, *Family History,* vol. 1, p. 58.

ENDNOTES TO CHAPTER 7

¹ George expressed something of this romantic viewpoint when he wrote of Elizabeth: 'During these years [in Europe] she [Elizabeth] was first initiated into full communion with Nature.' Prentiss, *Life and Letters,* p. 160.

² Prentiss, *Family History, vol. 2,* pp. 74–5.

³ Ibid., p. 74.

⁴ Ibid., p. 80.

⁵ Prentiss, *Life and Letters,* pp. 177–8.

⁶ Prentiss, *Family History, vol. 2,* p. 97.

⁷ Prentiss, *Life and Letters,* p. 185–6.

⁸ Prentiss, *Family History, vol. 2,* p.97.

⁹ Ibid., p. 98.

¹⁰ Prentiss, *Life and Letters,* p. 189.

ENDNOTES TO CHAPTER 8

¹ The attitudes held by George and Elizabeth were typical of the response of New-School Presbyterians. 'From the outset of the war New-

School Presbyterians were united in maintaining that it was the duty of Christians to help preserve the federal government.' The New-School General Assembly pledged support for President Lincoln. Ministers commonly drew parallels between ancient Israel and modern America in their sermons. In an address at Dartmouth College, George argued that the Confederate rebellion against the Federal Government was a rebellion against God himself. 'The Union is all in all, the very ark of the covenant, to us and our children.' 'Stand up! Stand up for Jesus, Ye soldiers of the Cross!', written by New-School Presbyterian George Duffield, Jr., became 'one of the most popular hymns sung by the Union armies during the Civil War'.

The cause of Christ and the cause of Union were virtually identical in the minds of many in the north. See Marsden, *The Evangelical Mind and the New School Presbyterian Experience*, p. 200.

[2] Prentiss, *Life and Letters,* p. 206.

[3] Louisa Payson Hopkins' published works included: *The Pastor's Daughter*, *Lessons on the Book of Proverbs*, *The Young Christian Encouraged*, *Henry Langdon*, *The Guiding Star*, *The Silent Comforter; A Companion for the Sick-Room*.

[4] Prentiss, *Life and Letters*, p. 207.

[5] The second great battle at Bull Run (or Second Manassas) was fought from 29 to 30 August 1862. General Lee led brilliantly to inflict a heavy defeat on the Union side, which suffered 14,462 casualties out of about 63,000 men.

[6] Prentiss, *Life and Letters*, pp. 208–9.

[7] Elizabeth Prentiss, *Avis Benson: or Mine and Thine, with Other Sketches* (London: James Nisbet, 1880), p. 151.

[8] Prentiss, *Life and Letters*, pp. 210–211.

[9] Ibid., p. 212.

[10] This was the bloodiest battle of the war. The Confederates suffered losses of more than 28,000 men out of a total of 77,000. The Union lost more than 25,000 out of a total of 93,500.

[11] This is the first line of a hymn by Johann Kaspar Lavater. Elizabeth Prentiss included a translation of this hymn in *Golden Hours*. 'He must increase, but I must decrease.' This line reads 'O Jesus Christ, dwell Thou in me.' Elizabeth Prentiss, *Golden Hours: Heart-Hymns of the Christian Life*. (repr. Vestavia Hills, Alabama: Solid Ground Christian Books, 2001) pp. 76–7.

[12] Prentiss, *Life and Letters*, pp. 214–5.

Endnotes

¹³ Elizabeth Prentiss, *Aunt Jane's Hero* (1871; repr. Amityville, New York: Calvary Press, 1999), p. 60.

¹⁴ A total of 2,200,000 men had enlisted on the Union (Northern) side, and 800,000 on the Confederate (Southern) side. Their average age was twenty-five. More than 21 per cent of these had lost their lives. Total deaths were 360,222 (Union); 258,000 (Confederate). Total wounded were 275,175 (Union); 383,000 (Confederate).

¹⁵ Prentiss, *Life and Letters,* p. 225.

¹⁶ I am indebted for information in this section to Joan Hedrick, *Harriet Beecher Stowe* (Oxford: Oxford University Press, 1994), pp. 173–85.

¹⁷ Roy Porter comments: 'Hydropathic establishments continued to have a following amongst those with faith in the healing powers of nature, cold water and physiological puritanism: no pain, no gain.' *The Greatest Benefit to Mankind: A Medical History of Humanity from Antiquity to the Present* (London: HarperCollins 1997), p. 393.

ENDNOTES TO CHAPTER 9

¹ Marsden, *The Evangelical Mind,* p. 211.
² Prentiss, *Life and Letters*, p. 235.
³ Ibid., p. 182.
⁴ Ibid., p. 236.
⁵ Ibid., p.243.
⁶ The poem was *Griselda*; it was published in 1876.
⁷ Prentiss, *Life and Letters*, p. 251.

ENDNOTES TO CHAPTER 10

¹ Prentiss, *Life and Letters,* p. 253.
² Catherine Beecher, sister of Harriet Beecher Stowe, travelled extensively through America researching the health of women. She found that the majority of wives and mothers suffered poor health, and many were invalids. 'A perfectly healthy woman, especially a perfectly healthy mother, is so infrequent in some of the wealthier classes, that those who are so may be regarded as the exceptions, and not as the general rule.' Catherine Beecher, *Treatise on Domestic Economy* (1841; repr. New York: Source Book Press, 1970), p. 20.
³ Prentiss, *Stepping Heavenward*, p. 246.
⁴ Ibid., p. 255.   ⁵ Ibid., pp. 257–8.

[6] Ibid., pp. 230–1. [7] Ibid., pp. 270–1.

[8] Miho Yamaguchi, 'Elizabeth Prentiss' Faith in Suffering and Perplexity about the Wesleyan and the Higher Life Doctrines', *Literature and Theology,* 2004, 18, no.4, pp. 415–26.

[9] In the nineteenth century, Evangelical believers were divided on the subject of holiness. Some believed that a Christian could reach sinless perfection in this life; others that there is always indwelling sin. Some believed that 'entire sanctification' is a unique and instantaneous experience; others that sanctification is a life-long process. During the 1830s, the revivalist Charles G. Finney and the President of Oberlin College, Asa Mahan, both began to teach that human beings could fulfil God's command to 'be perfect'. The teaching that entire sanctification is possible in this life began to spread among New-School Presbyterians, as well as in other denominations. In 1858, W. E. Boardman published *The Higher Christian Life.* The stress on the necessity of perfectionism put massive pressure on tender consciences. 'Poor M– has gone crazy on *Holiness by Faith*', wrote Elizabeth, 'and will probably have to go to an asylum.'

[10] See further discussion on pp. 167–9.

[11] See her husband's comments on this, Prentiss, *Life and Letters*, pp. 433–4. Also further discussion on pp. 167–9.

[12] Prentiss, *Life and Letters*, p. 244.

[13] Ibid., p. 461.

[14] He had qualified as a doctor, branched very successfully into homeopathy, and now, with his wife, ran a large orphanage in Chicago. See also note 14 on p. 219.

ENDNOTES TO CHAPTER 11

[1] Prentiss, *Life and Letters*, pp. 296–8.

[2] Ibid., p. 301. The quotation is an allusion to Schiller's *Wallenstein*.

[3] As we saw earlier, hydropathy, or water treatment, was very popular at this time. See above, pp. 125–7.

[4] Ibid., pp. 344–5.   [5] Ibid., p. 345, note 1.

[6] Ibid., pp. 307–8.   [7] Ibid., pp. 346–55.

[8] Ibid., p. 319.

[9] Elizabeth Prentiss, Letter to George Prentiss, 25 March 1872. Included in 1999 reprint of *Urbane and His Friends,* pp. 302–5.

[10] Madame Guyon (1648–1717) was a French mystical writer.

[11] Elizabeth Prentiss, Letter to George Prentiss, 23 May 1872. Included

in 1999 reprint of *Urbane and His Friends*, pp. 306–8.

[12] Prentiss, *Life and Letters*, p. 293.

[13] The turning point in Madame Guyon's spiritual search came when a monk told her that her difficulties came because she was looking for God outside herself: she should look within. 'Accustom yourself to seek God in your heart, and you will find him there.' She looked 'within' for God and truth. Guyon used the text 'the kingdom of God is within you' (*Luke* 17:21) to teach that God is within each person. But Jesus was not teaching that God was 'within' each of the Pharisees he was addressing. He was saying that because he, the King was among them, so the kingdom was among them too.

[14] Prentiss, *Life and Letters,* p. 378.

[15] Ibid., p. 479.

[16] Elizabeth Prentiss, Letter to George Prentiss, 25 March 1872. Included in 1999 reprint of *Urbane and His Friends,* p. 303.

[17] Elizabeth Prentiss, Letter to Mrs A.B.H., 27 April 1877. Included in 1999 reprint of *Urbane and His Friends*, pp. 313–4.

[18] Prentiss, *Life and Letters*, p.377.

[19] Ibid., p. 383.   [20] Ibid., pp. 378– 9.

[21] Elizabeth Prentiss, *Aunt Jane's Hero* (repr. Amityville, New York: Calvary Press, 1999).

[22] Ibid., p. 39.

[23] Ibid., pp. 122-3; 160–1, provide examples of Maggie taking the initiative spiritually.

[24] Further discussion on this point is in the conclusion.

[25] Prentiss, *Life and Letters*, p. 394.

[26] Ibid., p. 387.   [27] Ibid., p. 390.

[28] Ibid., p. 263.   [29] Ibid., p. 313.

[30] Ibid., pp. 409–10.

ENDNOTES TO CHAPTER 12

[1] Elizabeth Prentiss, *Golden Hours: Heart-Hymns of the Christian Life.* (repr.Vestavia Hills, Alabama: Solid Ground Christian Books, 2001), p. ii.

[2] Ibid.

[3] Ibid., p. i.

[4] Ibid., p. 4. 'Thanksgiving' is clearly Trinitarian.

[5] 'Go and tell Jesus', ibid., p. 66.

[6] 'Life's Promises', ibid., p. 16.

[7] 'Choose', *Golden Hours,* p. 18.

[8] Elizabeth Prentiss, *Urbane and His Friends* (1874; repr. Ithaca, Michigan: A. B. Publishing, 1999).

[9] Ibid., p. 274.

[10] Ibid., p. 202.

[11] Ibid., p. 111.

[12] Ibid., p. 219.

[13] Ibid., p. 220.

[14] Prentiss, *Family History, vol. 2,* pp. 260-261.

[15] Elizabeth Prentiss, Letter to Mrs C. H. L., Dorset, 13 July 1874. included in 1999 reprint of *Urbane and His Friends*, p. 313.

[16] Prentiss, *Life and Letters*, pp. 444–5.

[17] Ibid., pp. 445–6.

[18] Prentiss, *Family History, vol. 2,* p. 537.

[19] Prentiss, *Life and Letters,* pp. 414–5.

[20] Ibid., p. 449.

[21] Ibid., p. 458.

[22] Elizabeth Prentiss, *The Home at Greylock* (1876; repr. Amityville, New York: Calvary Press, 1999).

[23] Prentiss, *Life and Letters,* p. 449.

[24] 'You ask about my book; it is a sort of story; had to be to get read.' Ibid., p. 455.

[25] Prentiss, *Greylock*, p. 166.

[26] Ibid., pp. 89–93.

[27] Ibid., p. 81.

[28] Ibid., p. 63.

[29] While some of the characters, especially Margaret, are well drawn, the plot is very thin. The various mechanisms by which the issues of parenting are raised (for example the visit of Mrs Grey to the Thayer family) are somewhat clumsy. The structure is lopsided, in that chapters 19 to 21 are taken up with a short story written by one of Mrs Grey's daughters: a story which bears no relation to the rest of the plot but which serves as a useful peg on which to hang more principles of child-rearing. The ferry disaster at the end of the book kills off Mrs Grey rather too neatly. The sickness and untimely death of the most lovable and attractive of Mrs Grey's granddaughters seems contrived, fulfilling all the stereotypes of the Victorian 'death of children' scenes. The book seems to have been written in a hurry, in that there are internal inconsistencies: at the begin-

ning Mrs Grey is said to be the mother of seven children; in fact we only ever hear about five of them.

³⁰ Prentiss, *Life and Letters*, p. 483.

³¹ Ibid., p. 520.

³² Ibid., pp. 411–2.

ENDNOTES TO EPILOGUE

¹ Prentiss, *Family History, vol. 2*, p. 429

² Ibid., p. 75.

³ This was precipitated when Charles Augustus Briggs (1841–1913), delivered an address on 'The Authority of Scripture' on his induction to the Chair of Biblical Studies in 1891. In this address he attacked the doctrine of the verbal inspiration and inerrancy of Scripture. The General Assembly vetoed his appointment, and declared him guilty of heresy. The Board of Union Theological Seminary refused to accept this judgment, retained Briggs, and rescinded the Assembly's power of veto. George supported the Seminary in this decision. Briggs was an advocate of 'higher critical' views, and editor, with F. Brown and F. S. Driver of *A Hebrew and English Lexicon of the Old Testament* (1906) popularly known as *Brown, Driver and Briggs*. He was also one of the original editors of the *International Critical Commentary Series*. With hindsight one can clearly see the disastrous effects the accommodation of such higher-critical views brought upon the church. At the time, however, there were a number of good and godly people who did not see the danger.

⁴ Prentiss, *Family History, vol. 2*, p. 437.

⁵ Ibid., p. 590.

ENDNOTES TO CONCLUSION

¹ Prentiss, *Life and Letters*, p. 311.

² Ibid., p. 418.

³ Ibid., p. 420.

⁴ Ibid., p.436.

⁵ Ibid., p. 445.

⁶ Ibid., pp. 285.

⁷ Barbara Welter, *Dimity Convictions: The American Woman in the Nineteenth Century* (Athens, Ohio: Ohio University Press, 1976).

8 Elizabeth Prentiss, *Thoughts concerning the King* (Boston: Randolph, 1890), p. 9.

9 Ibid., p. 9.   10 Ibid., p. 11.   11 Ibid., p. 52.

12 Prentiss, *Life and Letters,* pp. 358–9.

13 Prentiss, *Thoughts,* p. 31.   14 Ibid., pp. 38–9.

15 She rarely refers directly to the biblical texts which directly encourage women to pursue piety (*1 Pet.* 3:1-6); purity (*Titus* 2:5); submission (*1 Pet.* 3:1-6; *Eph.* 5:22-33; *Col.* 3:18; *Titus* 2:5) and domesticity (*Prov.* 31; *Titus* 2:5; *1 Tim.* 5:9-10). Perhaps this is because within her context such texts were well-known, even over-used.

16 For example, Elizabeth Prentiss' novels all emphasize the role that many nineteenth-century women played in nursing the sick. Hospitals were only used as a last resort: they were breeding grounds for infection; it was much preferred to nurse the sick at home. Female relatives often travelled long distances to be with ill family members; or else invited them into their own homes. Thus large numbers of women had to gain some proficiency in nursing. Many received instruction in nursing from their own mothers, but books, such as Catherine Beecher's popular *Treatise on Domestic Economy* (repr. New York: Source Book Press, 1970), which included chapters on nursing the sick, were also used. While Prentiss' novels conveyed practical hints on how to make invalids comfortable, they also provided a forceful argument for society to prize this high calling. In her day, nursing, social work, and the care of the elderly, were not yet professionalized. Prentiss, and others besides her, highlighted the vital role played by women in this area. Where would the sick, the elderly, the needy be without them?

17 There is a helpful discussion of this trend in Nancy Pearcey, *Total Truth: Liberating Christianity from Its Cultural Captivity* (Wheaton, Illinois: Crossway, 2004), Chapter 12, pp. 325–48.

18 For instance, Timothy Dwight gave church membership statistics for New England in the early nineteenth century: women significantly outnumbered men. *Travels in New England,* 4 vols. 1821–2.

19 Quoted in Pearcey, *Total Truth,* p. 334.   20 Ibid., p. 335.

21 See discussion of *Aunt Jane's Hero* in Chapter 11, pp. 178–80. *Stepping Heavenward, Aunt Jane's Hero,* and *The Home at Greylock* are essentially portraits of female piety. The women outstrip the men in terms of godliness, prayerfulness, submission to the will of God and understanding of others.

In a telling scene at the end of *The Home at Greylock,* members of the family gather, awaiting news of the fate of Mrs Grey, who has disappeared after a ferry disaster. Eventually her body is brought in. Her son-in-law, an ordained minister, suggests that they should pray. He breaks down, as does her son. It is Belle who rises to the occasion: 'Then a woman's gentle, calm tones were heard; gentle and calm, but strong and victorious; they almost saw the gates of heaven opened, and the triumphant entrance of a glad and glorified spirit into the presence of Christ' (p. 517).

Equally telling is the closing chapter. Mrs Grey is dead. She was the one who had exerted 'immense power' over the whole family. Now, 'the strong character of the mother lived still. In every one of the homes this was done, that was left undone, to please her.' Interestingly also, it is the destiny of the women of the family which is highlighted. Belle inherits her piety, Laura inherits her writing ability, Gabrielle inherits her gifts at homemaking, and Margaret becomes the 'true woman' that Mrs Grey had been. The men are not even mentioned (pp. 336–8).

Prentiss also advocates the role of mother as 'ruling' the house. In *The Home at Greylock,* Belle, the godliest of Mrs Grey's daughters, writes: 'As to Cyril [her clergyman husband], you know his doctrine – that it is the mother who should rule the house, and beyond setting them a perfectly beautiful example and frolicking with them, he will do nothing for them.' (p. 192).

[22] In this regard one could contrast her with another nineteenth-century minister's wife. Josephine Butler married an Anglican clergyman and lecturer. Her only daughter died in a tragic accident, and Josephine turned her energies outwards. When her husband began working in inner-city Liverpool, she found a ministry among desperately poor women who had fallen into prostitution and were dying of disease. At first, she brought them into her own home to die, and then founded a shelter which could provide refuge for many more. She then became aware that the lack of education and employment opportunities for women was a factor in their turning to prostitution, especially when there was no other way of providing food for their children. Her work with prostitutes led her, logically, to support the expansion of education and employment for women. They had to be provided with alternative employment. Butler's philanthropic ministries inevitably led her to challenge the injustices of society at that time. Prentiss did not go down this route.

Or, one could contrast her with another British minister's wife, Elizabeth Gaskell. Like Prentiss, Gaskell first turned to writing as a means of coping with the grief of losing a child. Her husband was a minister in inner-city Manchester, and Elizabeth saw first hand the appalling working conditions in the factories and the degradation of the slums. Her passionate indignation led her to write powerful novels such as *Mary Barton* and *North and South* which contained searing indictments of that era's social injustice. For example, her description in *Mary Barton* of a factory girl dying of lung disease brought on by the foul air in her factory is unforgettable. Her novels formed as powerful a polemic against the abuse of the British labour force as *Uncle Tom's Cabin* did against the abuse of slaves. But Prentiss, while undeniably moved to compassion and action on a personal level by individual cases of poverty, did not challenge the structural causes behind that poverty.

[23] Ann Douglas, *The Feminization of American Culture* (New York: Alfred A. Knopf, 1977; repr. London: Papermac, 1996).

[24] Douglas argues that Edward Payson represented the classic Reformed type of orthodox Christianity (and 'magnified the religious importance of prayer'). His daughter Elizabeth carried his teaching further, making 'this devotional and undogmatic exercise [i.e. prayer] the absolute centre of Christian life' (Douglas, *Feminization,* p. 87).

Douglas sees *Stepping Heavenward* as a 'prayer manual', but, in all fairness, it should also be noted that Prentiss' other works (such as *Urbane and his Friends*) do emphasize Bible study as well. Taking Prentiss's works as a whole, the stress is certainly more on individual piety than on church life, and one can see some truth in Douglas's thesis that female writers tended to individualize and sentimentalize piety.

Raised in a conservative, Calvinistic home, Prentiss never openly questioned her spiritual heritage, in the way that her contemporary Harriet Beecher Stowe did. She maintained the evangelical worldview, that mankind is divided between the saved and the lost, and that individual salvation is imperative, and is based on a personal faith-relationship with Christ. Eternal punishment is only indirectly taught in her writings, although she does insist that it is a fearful thing to die without a personal knowledge of Christ (cf. Prentiss, *Stepping Heavenward*, pp. 60; 180).

During the nineteenth century, the ideas of Higher Criticism gained ground in a number of American seminaries and Elizabeth's husband George, although fundamentally orthodox himself, became increasingly sympathetic to such ideas.

Suggestions for Further Reading

FOR THOSE WHO WISH to explore Elizabeth Prentiss' life and writings further, several of her works are currently in print. Calvary Press of Amityville, New York, have reprinted *Stepping Heavenward* (1992), *The Little Preacher* (1993), *Aunt Jane's Hero* (1999), and *The Home at Greylock* (1999), as well as *More Love to Thee: The Life and Letters of Elizabeth Prentiss* by George Prentiss (1994). A. B. Publishing of Ithaca, Michigan, have reprinted *Little Susy Stories* (three books in one; 1999), *The Flower of the Family* (1999), and *Urbane and His Friends* (1999). Finally, Solid Ground Christian Books of Vestavia Hills, Alabama, have reprinted *Golden Hours: Heart-Hymns of the Christian Life* (2001). *Stepping Heavenward* and *The Life and Letters of Elizabeth Prentiss* are also both freely available to read or download from the Project Gutenberg website: www.gutenberg.org, as are several of the books listed below.

Select Bibliography

ANON., *Life of the Rev. Edward Payson,* abridged from the American edition; London: Religious Tract Society, n.d.

BAKER, THOMAS N., *Nathaniel Parker Willis and the Trials of Literary Fame*, New York/Oxford: Oxford University Press, 1999.

BEECHER, CATHERINE, *Treatise on Domestic Economy,* New York: Source Book Press, 1970.

BROGAN, HUGH, *The Penguin History of the United States*, London: Penguin, 1985.

DE TOCQUEVILLE, ALEXIS, *Democracy in America,* many editions.

DOUGLAS, ANN, *The Feminization of American Culture*, London: Papermac, 1977.

FENELON, FRANÇOIS, *Spiritual Counsels,* various editions.

GUYON, MME JEANNE-MARIE, *Autobiography,* various editions.

HANDY, ROBERT T. A., *A History of Union Theological Seminary in New York,* New York: Columbia University Press, 1987.

HART, D. G. & NOLL, MARK A.(EDS.) *Dictionary of the Presbyterian and Reformed Tradition in America,* Downers Grove, IL: IVP, 1999.

HEDRICK, JOAN D., *Harriet Beecher Stowe,* Oxford: The University Press, 1994.

HOPKINS, LOUISA PAYSON, *The Pastor's Daughter,* 1835; repr. Vestavia Hills, AL: Solid Ground Christian Books, 1994.

MACDONALD, JOHN, *Great Battles of the American Civil War,* London: Angus Books, 1988.

MARSDEN, GEORGE M., *The Evangelical Mind and the New School Presbyterian Experience,* New Haven/London: Yale University Press, 1970.

MURRAY, IAIN H., *Revival and Revivalism,* Edinburgh: Banner of Truth, 1994.

PAYSON, EDWARD, *Complete Works,* 3 volumes, 1859; repr. Vestavia Hills, AL: Solid Ground Christian Books, 2004.

— *Legacy of a Legend: Spiritual Treasure from the Heart of Edward Payson,* Vestavia Hills, AL: Solid Ground Christian Books, 2000.

PEARCEY, NANCY, *Total Truth: Liberating Christianity from Its Cultural Captivity,* Wheaton, IL: Crossway, 2004.

PORTER, ROY, *The Greatest Benefit to Mankind: A Medical History of Humanity from Antiquity to the Present,* London: HarperCollins, 1997

PRENTISS, ELIZABETH, *Aunt Jane's Hero,* 1871; repr. Amityville, NY: Calvary Press, 1999.

— *Avis Benson; or, Mine and Thine, with other Sketches,* 1879; repr. London: James Nisbet, 1880.

— *The Flower of the Family,* 1854; repr. Ithaca, MI: A.B. Publishing, 1999.

— *Follow Me, and Other Stories,* repr. Racine, WI: Whitman Publishing Co., 1932.

Bibliography

— *Gentleman Jim,* 1878; repr. London: Nelson, 1885.

— *Golden Hours: Heart-Hymns of the Christian Life,* 1873; repr. Vestavia Hills, AL: Solid Ground Christian Books, 2001.

— *Griselda* (translated from German for the YWCA), 1876.

— *The Home at Greylock,* 1876; repr. Amityville, New York: Calvary Press, 1999.

— *How Sorrow Was Changed into Sympathy: Words of Cheer for Mothers Bereft of Little Children,* London: Hodder & Stoughton, 1884.

—*Little Lou's Sayings and Doings,* London: James Nisbet, 1868.

— *The Little Preacher,* 1869; repr. Amityville, New York: Calvary Press, 1993.

— *Little Susy Stories.,* 1856; repr. Ithaca, MI: A. B. Publishing, 1999.

— *Old Brown Pitcher,* National Temperance Society, 1869

— *Pemaquid: A Story of Old Times in New England,* New York: A. D. F. Randolph, 1877.

— *Stepping Heavenward,* 1869; repr. Amityville, New York: Calvary Press, 1993 (distributed in the UK by Evangelical Press).

— *The Story of the Percys,* New York: A. D. F. Randolph, 1870.

— *The Story Lizzy Told,* 1870; repr. London: Hodder & Stoughton, 1877.

— *Thoughts concerning the King,* New York: A. D. F. Randolph, 1890.

— *Urbané and His Friends.* 1874; repr. Ithaca, MI: A.B. Publishing, 1999.

PRENTISS, GEORGE LEWIS, *The Bright Side of Life: Glimpses of It through Fourscore Years, a Family History,* 2 vols., privately published, Ansbury Park, New Jersey, 1901.

— *Memoir of Seargent S. Prentiss,* 1855.

— *More Love to Thee: The Life and Letters of Elizabeth Prentiss,* 1882; repr. Amityville, New York: Calvary Press, 1993 (distributed in the UK by Evangelical Press).

ELIZABETH PRENTISS

THOMAS À KEMPIS, *The Imitation of Christ,* various editions.

WARNER, SUSAN, *The Wide, Wide World,* 1850. The novel can be read on-line at http://digital.library.upenn.edu/wo.../wide/wide/html.

WALKER, NANCY A., *Fanny Fern,* New York: Twayne Publishers, 1993.

WARREN, JOYCE W., *Fanny Fern: An Independent Woman,* Piscataway, NJ: Rutgers University Press, 1994.

BARBARA WELTER, *Dimity Convictions: The American Woman in the Nineteenth Century,* Athens, OH: Ohio University Press, 1976.

ARTICLES:

YAMAGUCHI, MIHO, 'Elizabeth Prentiss' Faith in Suffering and Perplexity about the Wesleyan and the Higher Life Doctrines: On *Stepping Heavenward*', *Literature and Theology,* Oxford University Press, 2004, 18(4): 415–26.

INDEX

American Chapel, Paris, 108–11
American Civil War, 114–23,
  214–5
Appomattox Court House, 123
Arminian emphases, 215
Aunt Jane's Hero, 123, 172–4, 191,
  211–2, 225, 227, 230
Avis Benson, 224

Baptism in the Spirit, 182–3
Barnum's Museum, New York, 68
Beecher, Catherine, 225, 230
Beecher, Lyman, 15
Bonaparte, Napoleon, 98–9
Boston, Mass., 13
Brattleboro Spa, 127
Bright Side of Life, The, 221, 223
Briggs, C. A., 229
Bull Run, Battle of, 117, 224
Butler, Benjamin F., 102–3
Butler, Josephine, 231

Centennial Exhibition, 190–1
Château-d'Oex, 99–102
Chicago Advance, The, 143
Chicago fire of 1871, 171–2
Chicago Seminary, 160–1, 169–71
Christian at Work, The, 193
Church membership statistics
  (New England), 230

Church of the Covenant, New
  York, 124–5, 134, 171, 176,
  195
Collegiate Reformed Church,
  New York, 189
Condit, Jonathan, 22, 65–6
Crystal Palace, London, 112
Crystal Palace, New York, 82
Cummings, Asa, 218
Cunard, Samuel, 97

Dartmouth College, 224
Dickens, Charles, 17
Dimity Convictions (Welter), 229
Doddridge, Philip, 23, 219
Dorset, Vermont, 133–5, 138, 140,
  152–4, 160–3, 177, 179, 184–7,
  190, 195, 198, 201–2
Douglas, Ann, 214–5, 232
Duffield, George, Jr., 95, 224
Dwight, Timothy, 230

Eliot, John, 2
European tourism, 97
Evangelical Mind, The (Marsden),
  221, 223–4

Feminism, xiii–xiv, 212
*Feminization of American Culture,
  The* (Douglas), 214–6, 232

Index

Index

Tyler, Bennet, 15

—◦⟨⟨⊙⟩⟩◦—